The Decline and Fall
of the
Catholic Church
in America

David Carlin

The Decline and Fall
of the
Catholic Church
in America

SOPHIA INSTITUTE PRESS®
Manchester, New Hampshire

Sophia Institute Press®
Box 5284, Manchester, NH 03108
1-800-888-9344
www.sophiainstitute.com

Library of Congress Cataloging-in-Publication Data

Carlin, David (David R.)
    The decline and fall of the Catholic Church in
America / David Carlin.
        p. cm.
    Includes bibliographical references.
    ISBN 978-1-622821-69-3 (ppbk)
    1. Catholic Church — United States. I. Title.
BX1406.3 .C37 2003
282'.73 — dc22   2003015660

Contents

Part III: Evolution of a National Religion

Part IV: The Deeper Problem of Catholic Identity

Part V: The Search for a National Moral Consensus

Preface

The Great Catholic Sex Scandal of 2002 — a twofold scandal that involved priests molesting minors and bishops covering up for many of the molesters — was in more ways than one merely the tip of the iceberg.

In one way, it corroborates the suspicion that many people have had for a long time — namely, that homosexuality is rife in the American Catholic priesthood. If this is true, it is a deeper and even graver problem than the tremendous problem of criminal sex abuse. For a Catholic Church led by a priesthood that is twenty or thirty percent (or more) homosexual is simply not going to work.

But there is a still deeper problem, of which the widespread homosexuality, the molestation, and the cover-ups are merely symptoms. The root problem is that the Catholic Church in the United States has largely ceased to be Catholic. A few decades back, it quietly hung its Catholicism in the closet and put on an attractive new garment, that of *generic Christianity* or *Christianity-in-general*. The new garment is more "modern," more "American," and more lightweight, suitable for the hustle and bustle of the contemporary world. (Of course, the old garment was not destroyed; it was only hidden away. This means it can be taken out and donned on certain ceremonial occasions, and it can be dusted off and held up to rebuff someone who asserts — as I do — that the Church in America has largely abandoned its Catholicism.)

This book is an attempt to explore and analyze this deeper problem.

In some ways, I confess, I personally find "generic Christianity" an attractive ideal. After all, it is very tolerant, and tolerance is a great and important American virtue, and I myself am a thorough-going American. So how could I not find the ideal attractive? Besides, I have spent many years of my life as a politician, and politics in America is not an especially ideological sport. For the most part, the American political animal is a thoroughly practical animal, not troubling to explore and debate the doctrinal underpinnings of action. Christianity-in-general, which abstains from splitting doctrinal hairs, is just the kind of religion that would appeal to the nondoctrinal political mind.

But I am not only an American and not only a politician. I am also a Catholic with an interest in history and sociology. As such, I have become convinced that generic Christianity (or, as it may also be called, "liberal Christianity"), attractive though it may be in the short run, is, in the long run, fatal for any church that embraces it. Once any church begins shedding its unfashionable dogmas, it finds itself unable to stop; it has set foot on a slippery slope. First this dogma will go, then that one, and then another, until finally the church has no dogma left — only a gentle wish: "Can't we all just be nice to one another?"

Long before reaching that zero-point, most people will come to realize that there is no reason to belong to this church rather than that church; indeed, there is no real point in belonging to any church at all. For American Catholics to embrace generic Christianity, then, is to embrace gradual institutional suicide.

One may ask, "What's wrong with everybody being nice to everybody else? If generic Christianity terminates in such a fine attitude, isn't that a consummation devoutly to be wished?"

Maybe. But the trouble is, everybody will not end up being nice to one another. The churches that remain open on Sunday mornings will preach niceness to their few remaining members, but in the meantime, the religious vacuum in society will have created a moral vacuum, and who knows what monsters will rush in to fill those vacuums? The nineteenth-century decline of religion in Europe, especially among European intellectuals, was followed in the twentieth century by Communism and Nazism. The decline in American religion that began in the 1960s was soon followed by the widespread practice of abortion, which has been taking place at the rate of more than one million per year for the last thirty years.

Although, as I have already revealed, I am not an impartial observer of developments in American Catholicism, I have honestly tried to write this book — well, the first twenty-six chapters of the book, after which I become frankly partisan — as though I *were* an impartial observer. I have tried to write a piece of pure sociology, the kind of thing that could have been written by someone completely indifferent to Catholicism. It is not, however, a piece of empirical sociology; that is to say, I have done no original research, nor uncovered any facts that are not commonly known to anyone familiar with the Church in the United States.

Rather, it is an essay in sociological interpretation. I have taken certain "common knowledge" facts about American Catholicism and about the United States as a whole, and I have tried to link them together in a coherent pattern that explains what has happened to American Catholicism in the last forty years. After arriving at some very pessimistic conclusions about the future of the American Church, I have added a few more chapters in which I look — perhaps not very successfully — for grounds for hope and optimism.

The Decline and Fall
of the
Catholic Church
in America

Introduction

Bad Sermons

Why are Catholic sermons so bad? That is, why are Catholic Sunday homilies typically so dull, boring, uninspiring, soporific, and so on? More particularly, why are they so much worse than the average Evangelical Protestant sermon?

The perennial reason has to do with the nature of the Catholic religion. In a Catholic Mass, the essential function of the priest is sacramental. And in Catholicism, the sacrament of the Eucharist, like all of the seven great sacraments, is not simply a *symbol* that represents grace; it is also a *means* of effecting grace. In Evangelical Protestantism, by contrast, the sermon is the means of grace. The task of the minister is to touch the hearts of his listeners, to lead them to conversion. The Catholic priest who does not deliver a good sermon is a disappointment; but the Protestant minister who does not deliver a good sermon is a failure.

Certainly, there have been splendid preachers and orators in the history — even recent history — of the Catholic Church. But the fact remains: the sermon is the centerpiece of an Evangelical service, whereas, in a Catholic Mass, it is secondary to the consecration and distribution of the Sacrament. Not surprisingly, then, most Protestant ministers take sermons more seriously than do Catholic priests: they think about them harder, research them more diligently, and spend more time writing and rehearsing them.

The Decline and Fall of the Catholic Church in America

In short, Catholic sermons tend to be inferior to Protestant sermons because they can afford to be.

The telling *Boston Globe* survey

But I think there is another, more contemporary reason that Catholic sermons — in America, in particular — are dull and boring. To illustrate this reason, we cannot do much better than to look at a survey of Boston Catholics commissioned by the *Boston Globe* — the newspaper that in 2002 published hundreds of articles exposing priestly sex abuse in the Archdiocese of Boston and the ineptitude, if not culpability, of Church authorities in handling reports of this abuse. The results of the survey, conducted May 4-6, 2003 through telephone interviews of four hundred self-identified Catholics living in the Archdiocese of Boston, were published in the Sunday *Globe* of May 11, 2003.

The survey gives a striking picture of a Catholic Church made up of members who are not very Catholic in their beliefs and religious practices.

Indeed, to judge from this survey, the Catholic Church in Boston seems rather like a political party, most of whose members tend to vote (when they *do* vote) for the opposition party! A political party like this would not have a very bright future. And neither, I suggest, does the Catholic Church in Boston — or in the United States as a whole.

For example, according to the survey, only 35 percent of Boston Catholics say they attend Mass at least once a week. This contrasts with the more than 70 percent of American Catholics who used to attend Mass on any given Sunday in the 1950s. It also contrasts with what may well be the actual number of Sunday Mass-goers in Boston. "The last archdiocesan census," reports the *Globe*, "taken in October [2002], found fewer than 300,000 of 2.1 million Catholics in church on Sunday, making actual weekly attendance less than 15 percent." Which number is more likely to be correct, the number from the *Globe* poll or the number counted by the archdiocese? My guess is that the census count is closer to the truth; parish pastors have little motive to undercount those in their pews, whereas the interviewed Catholics would have overestimated, if anything, their churchgoing frequency. Either number, of course, represents a great drop from the Sunday Mass attendance during what may be called the "golden days" of American Catholicism.

The de-Catholicization of Boston Catholics is perhaps even more evident in their responses to questions having to do with the moral teachings of the Catholic Church. When asked, "Do you agree or disagree with the Church's position on abortion?" only 32.1 percent said they agree, while 62.6 percent disagreed (and 5.3 percent either did not know or refused to answer). On contraception, 19.1 percent agreed with the Church; 75.2 percent disagreed. On homosexuality, 24.5 percent agreed with the Church; 61.4 percent disagreed.

On questions related to the priesthood, Boston Catholics once again showed that they were very much out of step with the leadership of the Church. When asked, "Would you support or oppose the ordination of women as priests?" 79.5 percent said they support this idea, while only 16.9 percent oppose. On allowing priests to marry, 86.3 percent support; only 10.8 percent oppose. On prohibiting homosexual men from becoming priests, 58.8 percent oppose such a prohibition; only 34.6 percent support it. Consistent with these opinions, 39 percent of those surveyed said they would support an American Catholic Church independent of the Vatican.

The interviewees were also asked this question: "Which of the following would be most likely to bring you closer to the Church personally?" It was a multiple-choice question, and the answer most frequently chosen (by 52.8 percent) was "modernizing Church attitudes on social issues." Now, the meaning of this response is somewhat vague, but when people speak of modernizing Catholic

Church attitudes on "social issues," they are very probably not suggesting that the Church should adopt "modern" attitudes toward race relations or economic policy or war; no, they are more likely to be thinking of contraception, premarital sex, unmarried cohabitation, remarriage after divorce, abortion, or homosexuality, and perhaps euthanasia as well. These are the "social issues," on which the Catholic Church is notoriously unmodern, even anti-modern.

In other words, the message to the pope and the bishops from Boston Catholics (the vast majority of whom, remember, are at best infrequent churchgoers and who disagree with a number of important and ancient moral teachings of the Church) is this: "Get in step with the modern world, and we'll become churchgoing (and money-contributing) Catholics once again."

Of course, there are problems with this message. One is that the "modern world" they are telling the pope and bishops to get in step with is largely characterized by a culture that is non-Christian, even anti-Christian: a culture of secularism and moral liberalism, atheistic or agnostic in its metaphysical premises, and strongly bent on repudiating traditional Christian morality. Another problem is that "modernizing" the Church on social issues will not really win these people back, at least not in the long run, but it *will* tend to drive away Catholics of the traditional or orthodox kind, who will look elsewhere (probably to Evangelical Protestant churches) for old-fashioned Christianity.

Indeed, the modernizing experiment has already been tried in many of the larger Protestant churches, beginning more than two hundred years ago in Germany, in England, and in the United States. The results of the experiment have long since come in, and they are conclusive: the more a religion turns "modern" or "liberal," the more it declines. At first, modernization may produce a burst of moral energy (it did this in a very striking way in the Unitarian Church in the decades preceding the Civil War), but after a generation or two, as old doctrines and traditions disintegrate, as the religion drifts (or races) further and further away from traditional Christianity, the loyalty and enthusiasm of its members wane, and the church goes into numerical decline.

The facts are telling: as the population of America has grown, the population of the liberal churches has declined; and not just as a percentage of the population, but in absolute numbers as well. This is a decline that can, of course, be observed in an old liberal religion like Unitarianism, but also in churches that first turned in a liberal direction in the twentieth century, such churches as the Congregational, the Episcopal, the Presbyterian, the United Methodist, and the Evangelical Lutheran Church of America — in short, all the "mainline" Protestant churches.

There is absolutely no reason to believe that the Catholic Church in the United States would not experience the same decline if it, too, were similarly to modernize or liberalize. In fact — as this book is intended to show — it *has* dabbled with religious modernization, and it has paid the predictable price: it has gone into decline. And unless it reverses its process of liberalization, it will, I contend, decline even more, finally falling into irrelevancy.

Catholicism has devolved into "generic Christianity"

Let us return to the problem of boring sermons. The second reason for them, the contemporary reason, is this: the religion preached from the typical Catholic pulpit is no longer Catholicism, but generic Christianity. Catholic homilists do not like to preach on specifically Catholic themes — themes that differentiate Catholicism from other Christian denominations. Thus, one rarely hears a Catholic priest sermonize about such moral themes as abortion, homosexuality, euthanasia, and contraception; or about such doctrinal themes as the divinity of Christ, the apostolic character of the Church, or the infallibility of the pope.

Such themes are controversial among Americans who call themselves Christian. Many Christians do not consider abortion and homosexuality to be sinful; some approve of euthanasia; and the vast majority approve of contraception. While all Christians admire Jesus Christ, not all of them agree with the traditional orthodox belief that he is both divine and human, a God-man. The idea that the Church is apostolic is meaningless to many American Christians, perhaps to most. Instead, they think of the Church as a man-made institution, free to change its practices whenever it sees fit. And, of course, the notion that the pope is infallible is nonsense to everyone except Catholics, and there are many Catholics who consider it nonsense as well.[1]

Instead, most Catholic priests prefer to preach on themes that are noncontroversial and acceptable to all Christians, including the most "modern" and "liberal." They affirm the existence of God; they tell us that Jesus was an excellent person, a model of human goodness; they remind us that we should be kind to our neighbors and that we should forgive those who have offended us; and so on. These are themes that belong to generic Christianity, or Christianity-in-general.

This is the Faith — the very boring Faith — that has been proclaimed from the typical Catholic pulpit for the last thirty years.

Protestant churches were the first to accommodate secularism

The term *generic Christianity* may call to mind a book written by the great Anglican apologist C. S. Lewis about sixty years ago, *Mere Christianity*. In it, Lewis meant to explain and defend the

---

[1] Some would, of course, say that "Christians" who disagree with orthodox and ancient Christian teachings, whether doctrinal or moral, are not really Christians at all; they are heretics or apostates. This may be true, theologically speaking, but for purposes of the present sociological discussion, I am, somewhat arbitrarily, counting as Christian anybody who identifies himself as a Christian.

beliefs held in common by *all* Christian denominations, whether Anglican, Catholic, Baptist, Methodist, Presbyterian, Congregationalist, or Greek Orthodox. It was indeed a book about generic Christianity, or Christianity-in-general; more exactly, it was about generic Christianity *as it was in the days when the book was written.*

A lot of moral and doctrinal water has gone under the bridge since then, both in Britain and in America. Among the Christian denominations of both countries sixty years ago, there was a "thick" consensus on Christian doctrine; that is, they agreed on many things, and they disagreed on only a few. But today this has changed radically. Now the consensus is "thin." The denominations agree on far fewer things than they did of old, and they disagree on far more. On a great many moral issues, there is no longer a Christianity-wide consensus. Nor is there any longer a consensus on many articles of the Nicene Creed. In liberal or mainline Protestant denominations, it is not especially unusual for a theologian, a minister, or even a bishop[2] to express his doubts about the Trinity, the Virgin Birth, the divinity of Christ, and the Resurrection. In Lewis's day, "mere" Christianity was a big thing; today it is a much smaller thing.

Liberal Christianity has been present in the United States for at least two hundred years, dating back to the early nineteenth century, when that paradigm of liberal Protestantism, Unitarianism, first surfaced in many of the pulpits and congregations of eastern Massachusetts. Early Unitarianism may be justly described as a synthesis (or rather, an attempted synthesis) of two rather incompatible things, Christianity and Deism.

Deism was the earliest modern form of secularism; and by *secularism*, I mean a moral and intellectual movement intended to discredit Christianity and ultimately to ruin it. The typical Unitarian

[2] See almost any of the writings of the former Episcopal Bishop of Newark, New Jersey, John Shelby Spong.

was someone who had been reared as a Protestant and thus had a strong emotional attachment to Christianity, while believing there was much to be said of the Enlightenment/Deistic critique of Christianity. So he split the difference between the two. He gave up the Trinity and the divinity of Christ; he gave up Original Sin and the atonement; but he retained his strong devotion to Jesus (still a great man, although no longer God), and he continued to hold that the Bible was the revealed word of God — although a revelation that henceforth had to be interpreted in a more enlightened and rational way than had hitherto been the case. Above all, he was a moralist: morality, not doctrine, was the essence of his religion.

The synthesis did not hold, for Unitarianism had set its foot on the slippery slope of increasing liberalism, a slope that, if followed all the way to the bottom, results in the complete eradication of Christianity. The first generation, that of William Ellery Channing and Andrews Norton, was succeeded by the far more liberal and far less doctrinal generation of Ralph Waldo Emerson and Theodore Parker; and that second generation was succeeded by more liberal generations still, until Unitarianism, by being so liberal and broad-minded as to sympathize with all kinds of religion and many kinds of irreligion, ceased to be a recognizably Christian denomination altogether.[3]

No other Protestant denomination became quite as liberal as Unitarianism; which is to say, none moved as rapidly and as thoroughly away from orthodox or traditional Christianity in the direction of a more "modernized" Christianity. Yet over the past two hundred years, many denominations have attempted, although perhaps in a less radical way, to do what the early Unitarians did: to blend elements of secularism with Christianity.

This happened during two main periods. One was the post–Civil War era, at the end of the nineteenth and beginning of the

[3] See the website of today's Unitarian-Universalist Association.

twentieth centuries. At this time, secularism's two great intellectual weapons against Christianity were Darwin's theory of evolution and (the largely German) Higher Criticism of the Bible. Liberal Protestants accepted the Darwinian theory while contending that it did not necessarily carry the atheistic implications that many of its adherents (Thomas Henry Huxley, for example) claimed for it. And they responded to Higher Criticism by contending that the beliefs which it undermined (e.g., supernatural miracles and the plenary inspiration of Scripture) were not *essential*; you could drop such doctrines and still retain the essence of Christianity.

This liberal compromise with the secularist critique of Christianity led, in the United States, to the great split in the early twentieth century between Protestant liberals or "modernists" and Protestant "fundamentalists." The fundamentalists were horrified by the liberal accommodation of secularism, and they rejected liberal Christianity as nothing less than a betrayal of the Faith. Liberals, as viewed by fundamentalists, were in many ways worse enemies of Christianity than were outright secularists. For at least the secularists made no secret of their enmity, while liberals — in an act of deception or self-deception — pretended to be Christians. In fact, from the fundamentalist point of view, liberalism was a Trojan Horse; or to change the metaphor, liberals were a fifth column, destroying Christianity from within.

The climactic moment in the struggle between modernists and fundamentalists took place in 1926 in Dayton, Tennessee, at the Scopes trial, the so-called "Monkey Trial." The fundamentalists won the legal battle in the courtroom, but were trounced in the nationwide court of public opinion. Fundamentalist Protestantism looked foolish; modernist Protestantism looked commonsensical.

The other compromise between liberal Protestant Christianity and secularism took place in the last third of the twentieth century. The earlier great accommodation had been doctrinal; this time it was moral. A great moral revolution took place in the United States (and not only the United States) in the 1960s and '70s, and much of this revolution — a secularist revolution — consisted in rejecting the traditional sexual morality of Christianity. Premarital sex now became widely acceptable; so did unmarried cohabitation; so did relatively easy divorce and remarriage; so did homosexuality; and so did abortion — all of this representing a "new morality" that was completely unacceptable from the point of view of traditional Christianity.

Liberal Protestantism accommodated this new secularist morality. It discovered, nearly twenty centuries after the founding of the religion, that, when properly understood, Christianity really had no objection to any of these former sins and vices, provided, of course, they were done in a "loving" and "responsible" manner. Christianity, after all, is a religion of love, which means, we were now told, that love trumps all the old sexual taboos. There is only one moral absolute, said Joseph Fletcher, one of the earliest and most influential liberal theologians who attempted to effect a synthesis between Christianity and the new morality, and that absolute is that we must act in the spirit of love.[4] This new liberal Christianity — a synthesis of doctrinally modernist Christianity with the new moral liberalism — soon went from novel to normal in most mainline Protestant denominations.

What is more (and more to the point, for the purposes of this book), this kind of liberal Christianity became influential among the liberal Catholics who emerged in the United States in the immediate aftermath of the Second Vatican Council (which ended in 1965). Catholic doctrinal liberalism had been pretty effectively squelched early in the twentieth century by Pope Pius X when he issued the encyclical letter *Pascendi Dominici Gregis* (1907), which severely denounced "modernism," another name for doctrinal

---

[4] See Fletcher's *Situation Ethics* (Westminster, 1966).

liberalism. Yet modernism did not completely disappear from the Catholic world.

Partly it lived on in a kind of underground existence among a few theologians who whispered their semi-heretical views rather than shouting them from the rooftops. Mostly, however, it lived on as no more than an aspiration: a relatively inarticulate hope among many Catholics, both lay and clerical, that the Church would someday renounce many of its old-fashioned ways and take a modern turn. In the 1930s and '40s and '50s, many of these "aspirational" modernists expressed their sentiments by supporting political liberalism — opposing, for instance, Franco's rebellion and rule in Spain. This permitted them, while not challenging the doctrinal Magisterium of the Church, to differ on an important policy question from the great majority of Catholic bishops, including American bishops, and even from two popes, Pius XI and Pius XII.

American Catholicism sets foot
on the slippery slope of tolerance

Back to the generic Christianity preached by most American Catholic priests nowadays. Why are they preaching this small thing, this anemic and undersized Christianity-in-general? Why, instead, are they not preaching "old-time religion" — the Faith that was delivered to the Church by the Apostles? Have our Catholic priests secretly become heretics and apostates? Are they covert theological liberals and modernists? Have they abandoned the Catholic religion in favor of generic Christianity — rather the way, around 1800, many of the Congregational preachers of Boston and its vicinity quietly abandoned old-fashioned, high-doctrine Calvinism and drifted into newfangled, low-doctrine Unitarianism?

Perhaps this is true of *some* Catholic priests. Maybe some have decided that orthodox Catholicism is passé and that the religion of the present and future will have to be a very "thin" and very noncontroversial generic Christianity. But I doubt this is true of most priests. The explanation instead, I submit, is that, no matter what their own personal orthodoxy, they fear that many of the Catholics in the pews are not very orthodox. They feel that there are many more or less generic Christians in the congregation, borderline Catholics who would be offended by specifically Catholic sermons; people who might even be offended by a single mention of contraception or abortion or homosexuality. And if these laypersons were offended, they might cease to attend church; they might break off their affiliation with the parish community; they might not bother to rear their children as Catholics.

These are dire potential consequences. The priest who runs such a risk puts a heavy burden on his conscience. Why not instead remain noncontroversial? Better to preach that God loves us all (to which may be added the pop-psychology clarification, "He loves us just the way we are") and that our brother Jesus is an excellent moral example for all of us? And if this bores people to death, well, at least it does not drive those borderline Catholics out of the Church. Maybe someday things will settle down; maybe the secular hostility to orthodox Christianity will fade away; and maybe then everybody in the pews will be prepared to digest stronger doctrinal and moral meat. But it probably will not happen, the priest says to himself, in my time. My job is not so much to feed the sheep nutritious food as to keep them from running away. In the meantime, I will feed them a little third-rate clover. This will keep them alive until a better day arrives.

Are priests justified in their fear that preaching undiluted Catholicism might drive people away from the Church? To a limited degree, yes. It is bound to happen that some people will walk away when they hear traditional Catholic teachings stressed from the pulpit, especially moral teachings that contradict the prevailing morality of the day — or when those teachings indict them in their own lifestyles. But not many will walk away; for most of those likely to exit on account of a reiteration of ancient and unfashionable Christian teachings have already taken their walks, some years ago.

Of the still-remaining Catholics likely to be offended by such teachings, many will not be found sitting in the pews on Sunday mornings anyway; for generic Christians are far less likely than strictly orthodox Catholics to be faithful attendees at Sunday Mass. The orthodox never fail to go to Mass, except for very serious reasons, while the generic Christian feels that Mass-going, while a very nice thing, is not strictly necessary. And of the generic Christians who are in the pews on Sunday, most would not be seriously offended by an emphasis on Catholic doctrine. After all, it is a Catholic Church, is it not? So what complaint do I have if I hear an occasional Catholic sermon, even if I do not approve of it? And some may even approve of it.

Even allowing for all these subtractions, it is almost certainly true that a vast number of American Catholics — that is, people who identify themselves as Catholic — are not so much Catholic in their doctrinal and moral beliefs as they are generic Christians. Why is this? Because generic Christianity is the dominant religion in the United States today, and Catholics (except for recent immigrants from Latin America) are fully Americanized. If one is fully American, is it surprising that one would embrace the dominant American religion?

The Christian religions of the United States can be divided into three main branches. One of them is Catholicism: I mean official Catholicism, Catholicism in the dogmatic and old-fashioned sense of the word. A second is conservative Protestantism: the Protestantism of the fundamentalist, Evangelical, and Pentecostal churches, along with that of the ambiguously Protestant, quasi-Christian religions of Mormonism and the Jehovah's Witnesses. And a third is generic or liberal Christianity: a division that includes many Catholics, as well as many Protestants who are members of the mainline denominations and many nondenominational people who are "spiritual but not religious." Of the three, this last is today the dominant religion in the United States.

It is dominant because it accords with the dominant value complex in America today: the liberty/tolerance complex. Americans have, of course, always been great believers in personal liberty, but never have they given it so high a rank as in the last thirty or forty years. And the necessary corollary of personal liberty, it goes without saying, is tolerance. For how can I be free to say what I like and do what I like unless my neighbors are willing to tolerate my personal preferences? Freedom without tolerance is empty; indeed, it is a contradiction in terms. Thus, tolerance — tolerance of all kinds: racial, ethnic, moral, religious, intellectual, artistic — has become during the last few decades the supreme virtue in the United States, while intolerance has become the most deplorable sin. If a contemporary American had to recite the law and the prophets while standing on one leg, he would say, "Practice tolerance."

Generic Christianity, which is nothing if it is not tolerant, fits in very nicely with all this. If you share the liberty/tolerance value complex and you happen to be religiously inclined, generic Christianity will be just your cup of tea. Further, if you share this value complex, yet are *not* religiously inclined — if you are a secularist — you will find generic Christianity the least objectionable form of Christianity. If you are a believer in the primacy of tolerance, orthodox Catholicism and conservative Protestantism will never do, for they are both doctrinally intolerant. That is to say, they both insist that they have the correct answers when it comes to questions of religious doctrine and morality. They insist that they are right and other people wrong. For a historically Christian nation that has elevated tolerance to the level of the paramount virtue, generic Christianity is just the right religion.

The Church in America becomes "Protestantized"

Historians and sociologists agree that immigrant groups are usually rapidly "Americanized" not long after arriving in the United States, a process largely complete within two or three generations. They absorb American culture; they learn the English language; they come to believe in our political, economic, and educational values; they learn to play our games and eat our food (and we, in turn, learn to eat their food). There is, however, one great exception to this process of assimilation: religion.

If religious assimilation had followed the pattern of linguistic assimilation, we would all now be Protestant, just as we all now speak English; for Protestantism was the original American religion, the religion of more than 95 percent of the population at time of the Republic's founding. Yet this did not happen. Catholic immigrant groups (Irish, Italians, Polish, French-Canadians, et cetera) remained Catholic after arriving in the United States, and Jewish groups (German Jews and Jews from the Russian Empire) remained Jewish.

Yet, in a way, Catholics *did* become Protestant. That is, they turned their religion into a kind of Protestantized Catholicism.[5]

An essential element of Protestantism has always been the principle of *private judgment*: that is, in the last analysis, the individual Christian will have to decide for himself what to believe. The Bible is, of course, the ultimate guide for the traditional Protestant, but the Bible does not read itself; it needs to be read and interpreted by the individual believer, for there is no pope or bishop who can render an authoritative interpretation. In the end, it comes down to the individual believer. In more recent times and among more liberal Protestants, the principle of private

---

[5] And the Jews turned Judaism into a kind of Protestantized Judaism: witness Conservative and Reform Judaism, the dominant forms of Judaism in America, in contrast to traditional Judaism, i.e., orthodox or rabbinical Judaism.

judgment has been extended, so that now one is no longer limited to making judgments in accordance with the Bible; now one can make judgments *on* the Bible and can dismiss certain biblical beliefs and commandments if these fail to suit one's scientific or ethical principles, or both.

For instance, it seems pretty clear that the Bible, in both the Old and the New Testaments, takes an extremely negative view of homosexual activity; yet if one has arrived at an approving or tolerant view of homosexuality, one simply dismisses the biblical condemnations — often by citing some "higher" or "more fundamental" biblical principle (e.g., the Golden Rule) that trumps any specific positive commandment or proscription, or perhaps by citing a Scripture scholar who casts doubt on the meaning or authenticity of the condemnations. Armed with this technique of *post facto* justification, one can remain a sort of Christian, even after having adopted the moral fashions of the contemporary world.

The United States being a historically Protestant country, it is not surprising that private judgment in religion is a deeply rooted American value. Nowadays this right to private judgment applies not only to judgments within a given religion, but to judgments made when comparing religions. That is to say, it is understood that I am morally free to choose whichever religion I like, whether Protestant or Catholic or Jewish or Muslim or Hindu or Buddhist or New Age or no religion at all. The only religious authority I am bound to recognize is the authority of my own conscience, of my own private judgment.

Now, this American ideal of private judgment is completely incompatible with a key principle of Catholicism, which holds that the Catholic Church is God's great repository of religious truth on earth, and that popes and bishops and their authorized agents are the ordinary teachers of that divinely revealed truth. Religious truth is not something I discover by means of a private quest; it is something I discover by listening to the voice of the

Church. Could anything be more opposed to the theory of private judgment?

Yet American Catholics are American as well as Catholic. Thus, it is nearly impossible for an American Catholic to reject the principle of private judgment, nearly impossible for him to say, "Yes, I realize that my non-Catholic neighbors think for themselves when it comes to religion — but not me. I follow the thinking of my pope and bishop, for they are better informed as to the content of divine revelation than I am."

But by the 1960s, Catholics in this country who sprang from the old European immigrant groups (as opposed to the newer Latino groups) had become thoroughly Americanized; and so, with exceptions here and there, they embraced the American ideal of private judgment in religion. What emerged is something that has been called "cafeteria Catholicism," a pick-and-choose religion that allowed people to claim a Catholic identity and to retain membership in the Catholic Church while at the same time rejecting the Catholic rules and doctrines they disagreed with. The most notorious example of this phenomenon was the widespread rejection of the Catholic teaching that artificial contraception is sinful: a rejection that came to a head in the immediate aftermath of Pope Paul VI's 1968 encyclical letter *Humanae Vitae*.

This rejection did not consist merely in widespread violations of the no-contraception rule. (After all, Catholics, being sinners, had violated many a moral rule over the centuries, yet had commonly done so without rejecting the rule. While agreeing with the Church that it is wrong to lie, cheat, steal, and so forth, they nonetheless proceeded to lie, cheat, steal, and so forth.) After 1968, many American Catholic married couples, probably most of them, not only broke the rule, but fundamentally *rejected* it. They thought the pope had made a mistake. They held that contraception was not sinful in all cases; that it was morally permissible in many cases; and even that it was morally mandatory in some cases.

The Decline and Fall of the Catholic Church in America

The contraception issue was the best-known example of cafeteria Catholicism, but it was far from the only example. Premarital sex, including unmarried cohabitation, was another. Over the past three or four decades, many young Catholics have come to reject the Church's teaching that such conduct is sinful — and in many cases, their parents and grandparents have agreed with them, even though parents and grandparents may have observed the rule in their own day.

Still another example is abortion. American Catholics have been far less ready to approve abortion than to approve contraception or premarital sex, but many of them — exercising their American right of private judgment — have felt that the Church has gone too far in its total condemnation of abortion. They are convinced that there are hard cases in which abortion is morally permissible as the "lesser of two evils." Even more are convinced that the Church is mistaken when it attempts to persuade legislatures and courts to erect substantial legal barriers to abortion.

Cafeteria, or private-judgment, Catholicism is not limited to moral questions. For instance, American Catholics have largely abandoned the sacrament of Penance (called "Reconciliation" since Vatican II), no longer believing, it seems, that confession to a priest is a necessary element in getting one's sins forgiven. Here is a very striking instance of the "Protestantization" of American Catholicism. Catholics have adopted the traditional Protestant idea that confession is unnecessary, since God can directly forgive the repentant sinner without using the priest as intermediary.

If Catholics (with the exception of relatively new immigrants) have become thoroughly Americanized, and if generic Christianity is the dominant American religion, then it should come as no surprise that millions of American Catholics have, in effect, abandoned orthodox Catholicism and adopted generic Christianity. This is the American way. It should also come as no surprise that many priests, when delivering their Sunday homilies, avoid giving offense to these generic-Christians-masked-as-Catholics by avoiding specifically Catholic themes.

This brings us to the central question posed by this book: Can Catholicism survive in a society in which most "Catholics" are really not Catholic, but, rather, generic Christians, and in which Catholic bishops and priests, either through timidity or policy or conviction, are reluctant to press upon their people a specifically Catholic form of Christianity? Or to put the question in a slightly different form: Can Catholicism survive in an American culture dominated by a partnership between secularism and religious liberalism? Or is it doomed to decline and fall?

Part I

The Great Transformation

Chapter 1

The End of the
Immutable Fortress Church

No one will deny that American Catholicism experienced a great transformation beginning in the mid-to-late 1960s. The old religion, still familiar to American Catholics in the early '60s, had undergone a dramatic change in less than ten years — a change that involved, among other things, a dramatic decline in Sunday church attendance, a precipitous drop in the number of religious vocations; thousands of priests and tens of thousands of nuns renouncing their vows; the closing of many Catholic elementary and secondary schools and the progressive secularization of Catholic colleges and universities; and a decline in respect for episcopal authority.[6] Today we live in the aftermath of that change.

Three social factors converged by historical accident to produce the "perfect storm" that would effect this great transformation: first, Vatican II; second, the end of the Catholic "ghetto" in the United States; and third, the great American cultural revolution of the late 1960s and early '70s. Any one of these factors operating all by itself would have had a significant impact on American Catholicism. But the convergence of all three at a single historical

---

[6] See Appendix 1 for more changes and statistics.

moment made the impact far more than merely significant. It was explosive.

In this first part of the book, I will examine all three of these developments.

The Second Vatican Council

Vatican II and its immediate aftermath had a great transform-ing effect on American Catholicism (and, of course, on Catholi-cism in the rest of the world), not so much because of particular changes introduced by the council, but by virtue of the fact that any changes were made at all. Consider for a moment a few of the authorized changes that took place in American Catholicism in the years just following the council. Most of these changes were not directly mandated by the council itself. Rather, they were cor-ollaries of council mandates; they followed in an almost logical manner from changes directly mandated by the council. Hence, they can be counted as part of the changes introduced by the council.

- The Mass celebrated in English, not in Latin.
- The priest turning to face the people.
- Replacing old hymns sung at Mass with new hymns of a contemporary style.
- The practice of congregational singing at Mass.
- The "kiss" (or rather, the handshake) of peace at Mass.
- Three Scripture readings at Sunday Mass (four, counting the psalm), instead of two.
- The removal of the altar rail in most churches.
- At Communion, reception of the Host in the hand.
- The end of mandatory meatless Fridays outside of Lent.
- Religious sisters abandoning their old-fashioned habits for more modern ones (or for no religious habit at all).
- The disappearance of the *Index of Prohibited Books*.

- The disappearance of the Legion of Decency and its movie ratings.
- Greater tolerance of "mixed marriages" between Catholics and non-Catholics.
- A new stress on ecumenism, including interfaith "dialogue" and even joint prayer services.
- The establishment of parish councils of laypersons to advise the pastor.
- The re-establishment of the permanent diaconate.

Now, someone taking a long view of Church history might contemplate these changes as they were in the process of being made and conclude that they were relatively minor, mere ripples on the surface of an otherwise placid pond. After all, in the many changes listed here, nothing essential to Catholicism was altered: no changes in dogma, no changes in Church polity, no changes in fundamental moral principles. Liturgical changes were the biggest of the alterations, but even here the changes did not touch essentials. The Mass, despite a number of incidental modifications, remained substantially what it had always been.

But Catholics — at least American Catholics, the subset of all Catholics with which we are concerned — ended up with something that resembled a tidal wave more than it did ripples on a pond. Perhaps ordinary Catholics did not take a sufficiently long view of Church history. Whatever the reason, they could not help feeling that their religion had undergone a radical change. At an intellectual level, they understood that this was the same Church, the same religion they had belonged to all their lives. But at the level of imagination, it no longer looked or felt the same. And although, in principle, intellect is more authoritative than imagination, in practice, imagination is often far more powerful.

Catholics had long been in the habit of thinking of their Church as immutable. And this immutability was, to their minds, not a merely incidental feature of the Church, but an essential feature. Should the Church cease to be immutable, it would cease to be the Church.

Then, all of a sudden, it changed. The theologically trained Catholic could distinguish between the essential (and unchangeable) features of the religion and its incidental (and therefore changeable) features. But vast numbers of Catholics with little or no theological training were bewildered by the changes. A Catholic Church that changes seemed to be a contradiction in terms.

The Church was not always immutable

To the ordinary pre–Vatican II Catholic, the Church seemed to remain exactly the same year after year, century after century: the same doctrine, the same ritual, the same morality, the same polity. Nothing in the Apostles' Creed or the creeds of Nicea and Chalcedon had been dropped or repudiated. The form of the Mass was, it seemed, never-changing. The theological virtues of faith, hope, and charity were, as they had always been, demanded of Catholics; and so was compliance with the ever-valid Ten Commandments (with particular emphasis on the Sixth Commandment, the one that prohibits, not only adultery, but, according to the traditional Catholic reading of this commandment, all forms of unchastity). The Bishop of Rome was, as he had apparently always been from the time of the Apostles, the supreme ruler of the Church, Vicar of Christ on Earth.

The historian, of course, understood that the reality did not fully correspond to the image. To one who took a sufficiently long view of things, it was clear that the Church had always been a somewhat changing, evolving institution. Let us glance at some of these changes.

• Over the centuries new doctrines had emerged, declared by ecumenical councils and popes. Now, the Church holds that "new" doctrines — doctrines such as the Immaculate Conception (1854), the infallibility of the Pope (1870), and the Assumption of the Blessed Virgin Mary (1950) — are not really new at all. They were present in revelation from the beginning, either explicitly or implicitly. If they were not declared to be Church dogma until some much later date, this is either because there was no pressing need to declare them earlier or because it took time for the Church to develop the theological and philosophical vocabulary needed to define them. To a non-Catholic (or an anti-Catholic) this line of argument may seem to be little more than a convenient theological fiction. To a Catholic, it is the idea of the development of doctrine.[7] Nonetheless, even if only organic, developmental changes, they were, to all outward appearances, changes.

• The form of the Mass itself had been changed frequently over the centuries, not to mention lesser devotions, of which new forms had continually arisen in the course of history, while old forms had continually died out. The essence of the Mass as eucharistic sacrifice and feast seems to have been fixed in apostolic times, but the incidentals had changed throughout history, depending on time and place. The sixteenth-century Council of Trent had introduced a form of the Mass that remained stable and universal in the Latin Rite for four centuries, until it was replaced by the new form of the Mass that emerged out of Vatican II. This degree of stability was the exception, not the rule.

• The Church's rules of conduct fell into three broad categories: natural law, divine positive law, and ecclesiastical positive law. The last of these comprised rules enacted by Church authorities (e.g., the ban on eating meat on Fridays). Hence, there was no

---

[7] The best-known defense of this idea is given by John Henry Newman in his work *An Essay on the Development of Doctrine*, which he wrote in the months just before his entry into the Catholic Church, in 1845.

theoretical objection to changing these rules, and in the course of Church history, such rules had frequently been enacted and re-pealed. By contrast, the rules of natural law and divine positive law were considered unchangeable.

• As for Church government, there had been a steady aug-mentation of papal power over the centuries. In the early centu-ries, Catholicism had been a fairly decentralized religion, local bishops being largely autonomous, although in some sense, the primacy of the Roman bishop was recognized from very early on. The most common display of centralized power in the early Church was an occasional ecumenical council, which sat for no more than a few weeks or a few months before final adjournment. By the late nineteenth century, all this had changed radically: the Catholic religion had become highly centralized, the pope a kind of abso-lute monarch, and bishops little more than branch managers of the pope's local churches. In the early Church, bishops had often been elected by the clergy and laity of the local diocese; in the middle ages and early modern times, they had in many cases been in effect appointed by local secular rulers; yet by the end of the nineteenth century, the pope appointed them all.

The Church's perceived immutability lent it legitimacy

In reality, then, Catholicism was not all that unchangeable; or rather, only a few absolutely essential elements of it were un-changeable. But to other than careful students of history, pre–Vatican II Catholicism certainly *looked* immutable.

One of the reasons for this appearance, of course, was that the Church deliberately cultivated an image of immutability. Hu-manly speaking, the legitimacy of the Church in the eyes of its members depended on the conviction that the Church of the twentieth century was the very same Church that had been instituted by Jesus Christ in the first century. Otherwise, what authority could it claim?

Of Max Weber's two kinds of non-charismatic legitimacy, traditional and rational,[8] the authority of the Church is of the former kind. Rational authority is future-oriented: an institution claiming this kind of authority (e.g., a modern government or business corporation) has to produce satisfactory results; if it does not, it will be rejected.

By contrast, traditional authority is past-oriented: an institution claiming this kind of authority has to persuade its members that it retains the essence it possessed at its beginning. It may be possible to accomplish this feat of persuasion without making a claim of immutability; a claim of unbroken continuity will be sufficient. We say that John Smith, a fifty-five-year-old man, is identical with the John Smith who was a baby fifty-five years ago, even though the two do not look much like one another; in this case, we are making a continuity claim without making an immutability claim. Yet the task of asserting traditional legitimacy is much easier if the immutability claim can be made as well, for, in that case, there is no question that the institution has been faithful to its origins.

Further, if, as Catholic philosophers and theologians had always held, God is immutable, then it is altogether fit and proper that God's Church should also be immutable. For insofar as the Church is mutable, it is not a perfect reflection of God; and insofar as it is not a perfect reflection of God, questions can be raised about its legitimacy.

It is far from surprising, then, that the pre–Vatican II Church deliberately cultivated an image of immutability.

---

[8] Weber, "Politics as a Vocation," in *From Max Weber*, H. H. Gerth and C. Wright Mills, eds. (New York, Oxford University Press, 1958), 78-79.

The Decline and Fall of the Catholic Church in America

After Trent, the Church built a fortress around itself

Yet another reason for the appearance of immutability is that, in truth, the Catholic religion was at least relatively immutable — at all events, since the time of the Council of Trent.

The greatest shock in the history of Christendom was the outbreak of the Protestant Reformation in the years around 1520. Almost overnight, all of Scandinavia and northern Germany were lost to Rome. Geneva, Zurich, and much of Switzerland soon followed. In time, so did the section of the Low Countries north of the Rhine delta. So did portions of Eastern Europe. Scotland and England were lost. France was seriously threatened. Rome, it seemed, was in real danger of being completely overthrown. Catholicism was threatened with utter dissolution.

One of the great hymns of the Reformation was Martin Luther's "A Mighty Fortress Is Our God." In its reaction to the Reformation, Catholicism might well have taken the title of this hymn for its own slogan — for that is what the Church became; it turned itself, metaphorically speaking, into a mighty ecclesiastical fortress. Eventually it recognized that the chances of regaining most of the lost provinces were slim, but it was absolutely determined to hold on to what remained: France, Spain, Portugal, Italy, southern Germany, Poland, Ireland, and (an area of great new gains) Latin America. This siege mentality prevailed in the Counter-Reformation Church — a mentality that placed primary importance on survival.

Construction of the anti-Protestant fortress did not happen immediately. Indeed, for a few decades, no one seemed quite sure how to proceed. But by the middle of the sixteenth century, the work was underway, and by the end of the great Council of Trent (1545-1564), the entire scheme of defense had been clearly outlined; it was just a matter of filling in the details.

In the course of history, many a fortified city has fallen because disloyal insiders opened the gates to the enemy. One of the most vital things that needs to be done during a siege, therefore, is to make sure there is no disloyalty inside the walls, no fifth column. For this you need educators and police: educators to enhance the loyalty of those inclined to loyalty in the first place; police to root out those actually or potentially disloyal. On the police side, the Church instituted the Roman Inquisition, to investigate and prosecute heresy; it also instituted the *Index of Prohibited Books*, to stop the flow of ideas that might stimulate disloyalty.

On the educator side, a massive effort of instruction was begun. It was now expected that every diocese would operate its own seminary to ensure a well-instructed priesthood — a priesthood that could readily spot the difference between orthodoxy and heresy. Schools and colleges were opened for the purposes of educating Catholic laymen, especially boys and young men who were royal, noble, or rich — those who, when they became adults, were likely to exercise a disproportionate share of social, political, and cultural influence. For the better instruction of rank-and-file Catholics, a new catechism was published, more plentiful and more effective sermons were preached, and more stress was placed on the sacrament of Confession.

But it is not enough to have a program for police and education work. You have to have the personnel to staff such programs. This personnel was largely provided through the creation of new priestly societies, whose members were characterized by great zeal, learning, eloquence, and, above all, loyalty to Rome. The most important and influential of all these new religious communities was, of course, the Society of Jesus — the Jesuits — founded by Ignatius Loyola in 1534.

A besieged city also needs a strong central authority. In Republican Rome, during times of great crisis, a dictator was appointed, and virtually all authority in the state was temporarily vested in his hands. When Julius Caesar became sole ruler of Rome, the legal basis for his rule was a vote declaring him to be perpetual dictator. Increasingly the papacy became a kind of perpetual dictatorship in the Church — that is, an absolute monarchy. The theory for this absolutism had been laid down long ago, in the middle ages, and the full translation of theory into practice would not be achieved until the papacy of Pius IX in the nineteenth century (it was during his reign that the doctrine of papal infallibility was finally defined); but the critical shift from a largely theoretical absolutism to a practical absolutism took place during the Counter-Reformation.

Most important, if a fortress intends to sustain a long siege, those inside the walls have to keep their spirits up; and for this to happen, they have to remain convinced that what they are fighting for is indeed worth fighting for. In physical warfare, it is often enough to persuade people that their enemies are monsters and that defeat will cost them their property, their freedom, and their lives. But in the kind of "warfare" that was going on between the old religion and the new, Catholics had to be convinced that Catholicism was right and Protestantism wrong. So the differences between them had to be magnified; a bright line of division had to be drawn between Catholicism and Protestantism.

The Tridentine Church defines
itself in opposition to Protestantism

And how was this to be done? Easy enough: it was just a matter of taking every aspect of Catholicism that Protestants found objectionable and, so far from toning it down, glorying in it. Do Protestants object to "worship" of the Virgin and the saints? Let us venerate them more wholeheartedly than ever. Do they object to the doctrine of transubstantiation? Then let us emphasize it; let us even develop a ritual in which we adore the consecrated Host. Do Protestants think it absurd for religious services to be conducted in anything other than the vernacular? Then let us keep on saying the Mass in a dead language, Latin. Do Protestants of the puritanical sort object to ornate churches? Let's make Catholic churches even more ornate. Baroque church architecture is a manifesto in stone and painting of the popular Catholicism of the Counter-Reformation. It was a way of proclaiming that there is an unbridgeable gap between the two religions. In the presence of these new church buildings or (what was often the case) redesigned old church buildings, even the dullest person could understand that Catholicism had no intention of yielding one inch to Protestantism.

In short, Catholicism defined itself negatively as being anti-Protestant. True, it was "anti-" a lot of other things as well. It was anti-Jewish, anti-Muslim, anti-Greek, anti-atheist. But although Jews, Muslims, and Greeks had been enemies in the past, and although atheists were to be enemies in the future, none of them was a particularly dangerous enemy at the moment. But Protestantism was. The Church had to emphasize, indeed overemphasize, how it differed from Protestantism.

This anti-Protestant self-definition of Catholicism was easier to put in place due to the fact that Protestantism, in turn, defined itself as anti-Catholic. Even during the lifetime of Luther, Protestantism, as a result of its principle of private judgment, had begun proliferating into numerous churches and sects, a proliferation that would continue for centuries (and continues to this day in the United States, the happy hunting ground of sectarian Protestantism, where new sects crop up on a nearly daily basis). It was hard to say what all Protestants had in common — except for this: they were not papists. Nor was this merely a *pro forma* notation of their religious affiliation. Their anti-Romanism was passionate. They did not merely disagree with Rome and the popes. They held the papal church to be the "scarlet woman" of the book of Revelation, the "whore of Babylon." The pope was "the anti-Christ." In the face of such animosity and contempt, it was the easiest thing in the world for Catholicism to think of itself as anti-Protestant.

The Decline and Fall of the Catholic Church in America

Catholicism's anti-Protestant identity persisted for four hundred years, right down to the time of Vatican II. During this long era, almost everything about Catholicism — its beliefs, its sacraments, its government, its architecture, its literature, its popular devotions — was meant to proclaim, "We are not Protestant; we reject Protestantism." This proclamation was made every time a Catholic wore a religious medal, said the Rosary, went to Confession, abstained from meat on Fridays, and so forth.

So although, on the eve of Vatican II, it was not true that the Catholic Church had actually been immutable during its entire history, at least this much was true: it had been *nearly* immutable since Trent and the Counter-Reformation — that is, since the moment when fortress Catholicism decided to define itself as, above all, anti-Protestant. Thus, the changes introduced by and after Vatican II, regardless of their content or merit, shattered the Catholic image of immutability; and by shattering the image, the changes did much to undermine Catholic legitimacy, which had been largely tied to the image of an immutable Church.

Chapter 2

The Construction of the
American Catholic Ghetto

At the beginning of the previous chapter, I said there were three factors which, converging about thirty or thirty-five years ago, created a "perfect storm" that had a catastrophic impact on Catholicism in the United States: Vatican II, the end of the Catholic "ghetto," and the American cultural revolution of the 1960s and '70s. We have looked at the first of these factors; in this chapter, we will review the second.

To understand the formation of the Catholic ghetto, a useful distinction can be made between two kinds of religion: closed and open.

By a closed religion, I have in mind a religion like that of the Amish or the Hasidic Jews. This kind of religion goes to great lengths to erect a wall of separation between itself and the outside world. Its members typically wear a distinctive garb and pursue a lifestyle strikingly different from that of others. Except for commercial relations with outsiders, the members pretty much stick to themselves, residing close to one another in residential enclaves. They socialize inside the group, dine inside the group, and, above all, marry inside the group. Their children avoid public schools, attending instead schools run by the religious community; and they usually avoid higher education altogether. They avoid cultural contacts with the outside world; so you will not find them at the theater, at concerts, or at movies; and they are not very likely to own TV sets.

By an open religion, I mean just the opposite: a religion that has no wall of separation between itself and the outside world. It is open to all sorts of contacts with the outside world: commercial, social, educational, and cultural. Its members are allowed to intermarry with members of other groups. So open to the outside world is a religion of this type that it would hardly make sense for them to speak of an "outside" world at all.

The "ghetto" is actually a quasi-ghetto

But purely open and purely closed religions are found at opposite ends of a spectrum. Between these extremes are found all kinds of mixed religions, semi-open and semi-closed.

Prior to the 1960s, Catholicism in the United States was a semi-closed religion. This is what people mean when they say that the Catholics of that day lived in a "Catholic ghetto." Of course, the word *ghetto* was a great exaggeration, for pre-1960s Catholicism was certainly not anywhere near as closed as the religion of the Amish or the Hasidim; both of these groups may quite accurately be said to live in a religious ghetto. If we picture a spectrum running from purely open religions at the left-hand extreme to purely closed religions at the right, pre-1960s American Catholicism would be a little to the right of the midpoint. In other words, if Catholicism was a semi-closed religion, it was just barely such; its closed elements were mixed with a lot of open elements.

And yet, even if only barely so, it was still more closed than open. This was an inheritance from the nineteenth and early twentieth centuries, when American Catholicism was largely a religion of immigrants and their children: a non-Protestant (or rather, anti-Protestant) religion trying to survive in Protestant America. It was not until survival seemed assured, until Catholics had become thoroughly Americanized and had acquired a social status roughly equal to that of their Protestant fellow citizens, that American Catholicism could afford to throw down its ghetto walls and become a truly open religion.

Consider some of the "closed" features that characterized American Catholicism from the early nineteenth century until the early 1960s.

• *Schools.* The ideal was that Catholics should avoid public schools and be educated in Catholic schools instead. Of course, there were never enough Catholic schools to take care of all Catholic kids. Yet the ideal was far from an empty formula. A vast Catholic educational system was erected: elementary schools, secondary schools, colleges, even a few universities. Next to the system of public education, it was America's largest school system. Tens of millions of young Catholics passed through the system, having a Catholic identity emphatically impressed upon them during the most impressionable years of their lives, while at the same time being kept relatively isolated from the great Protestant world that surrounded them.

• *Code of conduct.* There was a distinctive Catholic code of conduct. While most of this Catholic code conformed to the general American code (which was really a Protestant code), Catholics added further, often more rigorous elements, that distinguished them from most of their Protestant neighbors. (They were also less rigorous on certain points, e.g., drinking and gambling; this laxness also helped distinguish them from the outer world.) Let's look at some of these.

• There was the meatless-Friday rule, along with Lenten rules for fast and abstinence.

• There was the strict requirement that Mass must be attended on Sundays. Good Protestants, of course, went to church on Sundays, too, but they did not really *have* to go. If it was inconvenient for them — if, let us say, the weather was bad, or if they were planning a family picnic, or if they had just experienced an especially late and tiresome Saturday night — then skipping church now and then was acceptable; God would understand; just do not make a habit of it. But Catholics were required to go to church on Sunday on pain of mortal sin. That is, if you skipped Mass for less than a very grave reason — say, because of a serious illness or disability, or because you were in jail — you stood in danger of being punished for your omission by an eternity in Hell.

• Catholicism taught an especially strict sexual ethic. This is not to say that Protestantism taught a lax sexual ethic, for it did not. Yet in general, Protestants were not so thoroughly convinced as were Catholics of the extreme wickedness of sexual impropriety. Here again, the Catholic doctrine of mortal sin played a major role in raising the stakes. Fornication could land you in Hell for eternity; so indeed could touching your girlfriend's breasts; in fact, even thinking about this illicit touch, if you dwelled on and took carnal pleasure in the thought, could land you in Hell.

• A special case of this sexual rigor was found in the Catholic prohibition of artificial contraception. In the nineteenth and early twentieth centuries, Protestants found the notion of contraception as shocking as Catholics did. The "Comstock laws" prohibiting the sale and use of contraceptives, after all, were not put on the books by Catholics but, at least in the main, by late nineteenth-century Protestants. By the 1950s, however, American Protestantism had long since abandoned its opposition to contraception. In fact, it had made a 180-degree turn.

This turn began with the Church of England's Lambeth Conference[9] of 1930, which adopted a "conservative" pro-contraception position: conservative in the sense that it did not give blanket approval to the use of contraception, but approved it only in "hard cases" (and, of course, only for married couples). This Anglican endorsement broke down an ancient Christian barrier, and it was followed in the next generation or so by a generalized Protestant approval of contraception. In 1931, the Federal Council of Churches[10] adopted a similar "conservative" endorsement of contraception. By 1961, contraception had become so normalized in Protestant churches that the National Council of Churches endorsed a "liberal" policy on contraception; that is, it said that contraception is morally permissible for Christian married couples, provided only that there be mutual consent of husband and wife.

Most Protestants would by this late date — the early 1960s — say that responsible parenthood requires married couples to make prudent use of contraception. Continued opposition to contraception clearly distinguished Catholicism from the outer world of American society and culture.

• Catholics and Protestants agreed that movies should be sexually inoffensive. It was largely through Catholic efforts, however, that Hollywood adopted a code spelling out

---

[9] The Lambeth Conference is a periodic "ecumenical council" of the Anglican Communion, taking its name from Lambeth Palace, the London residence of the Archbishop of Canterbury. Since 1948, the conference has been held every ten years; prior to that, it was held at irregular intervals beginning in the mid-nineteenth century.

[10] A federation of non-fundamentalist, or "mainline," Protestant churches that later renamed itself the National Council of Churches of Christ.

just what was and what was not acceptable. Yet this code did not go quite far enough, from a Catholic point of view; so it was supplemented, inside the walls of the "ghetto," by the Legion of Decency. The Legion was a creation of the Catholic bishops. It rated movies, stigmatizing those that, despite the Hollywood code, remained offensive from a Catholic point of view. These ratings were routinely published in Catholic diocesan newspapers, and once a year, Catholics were asked to stand up at a Sunday Mass and pledge that they would stay away from movies condemned by the Legion of Decency. The fact that it was a very un-Protestant name simply added to its charm; it was one more way of differentiating Catholics from Protestants.

• Perhaps the clearest moral differentiation between Catholics and Protestants had to do with divorce. Protestants, of course, were not exactly keen on divorce. Until sometime in the 1960s, American society still attached a stigma to the divorced person, but this stigma was growing increasingly faint with the passage of decades.

Traditionally there had been two great differences in the Catholic and Protestant theories of Christian marriage. For one thing, marriage was a sacrament in the Catholic Church, but not in the Protestant churches, which typically recognized only two sacraments, Baptism and Communion. For another, from the time of the Reformation, Protestantism had accepted, at least in principle, the moral acceptability of divorce in cases where adultery had been committed. This was based on the Protestant interpretation of Matthew 19:9: "And I say to you: whoever divorces his wife, except for unchastity, and marries another, commits adultery."

In practice, however, during most of the centuries since the Reformation, divorce and remarriage had been almost as hard to come by in Protestant countries as in Catholic countries. This situation changed in the United States beginning in the post–Civil War period. The law came to recognize new causes for divorce, not just adultery. The divorce rate began to creep upward. For a time, to be sure, it was still low, but it moved steadily in an upward direction, until, by the middle of the twentieth century, it was relatively common. Yet it still was not nearly as common as it would become by the early 1970s, when the American social taboo on divorce vanished completely.[11]

An illustration of the shift may be found in the cases of Adlai Stevenson and Ronald Reagan. Stevenson (the Democratic candidate for president in 1952 and 1956) was a divorced man. And although his divorce was not granted for any fault that he was guilty of, and although he had not remarried, still there was something just a bit shocking in the fact that, for the first time in American history, a divorced man was a major party candidate for president. No doubt he still would have lost to Eisenhower even if he had been happily married; but his divorce certainly did not help. Contrast the Stevenson case with that of Ronald Reagan, elected president in 1980 and 1984, more than a decade after the cultural revolution of the 1960s had removed the divorce stigma. Reagan was divorced and remarried, yet no one held this against him, not even the religious and

[11] In 1955 the American divorce rate was 2.3 divorces per 1,000 population. In 1960, it was 2.2, and in 1965, it was 2.5. By 1970, however, when what I have called the "cultural revolution" was in full tide, it had jumped to 3.5. By 1975, it had jumped again, to 4.8, and by 1979, it hit an all-time high of 5.3, nearly two and a half times higher than it had been a quarter-century earlier. (These figures are from the U.S. Census Bureau, *The 2001 Statistical Abstract of the United States*, 59.)

social conservatives who supported him in such immense numbers.

By the early 1960s, despite the greatly increased acceptance of divorce among Protestants, American Catholicism was still a holdout; it was still insisting that marriage was a lifetime thing, regardless of any unanticipated disappointments that might crop up after the wedding. In a really bad domestic situation, separation — even civil divorce — might be permitted. But the Church still taught that true divorce was an impossibility: the bonds of marriage, once licitly established, could not be broken until death.[12]

• *Mixed marriages.* Another way of keeping Catholicism relatively closed was the ban on marriages between Catholics and non-Catholics, the non-Catholic usually being, of course, Protestant. This was severely frowned upon, not only by the Church's priestly leadership, but by rank-and-file Catholics as well. Parents fretted over the possibility that their kids might marry outside the Church. This concern was quite natural. After all, God would forgive Protestants for not being Catholic, since they did not know any better. But a Catholic who walked out of the Church was a different story. Thus, parents inquired anxiously as to whether their child's latest girlfriend or boyfriend was Catholic. They sent their kids to Catholic schools, and they had them join Catholic organizations (such as the CYO), thus enhancing chances that an intra-Catholic romantic life would develop.

But love is blind, or at all events, young people are frequently perverse, acting in such ways as to maximize alarm in mothers and

---

[12] The practice of granting annulments — official declarations that a true marriage had never existed in the first place — exploded in the 1970s, helping to make *de facto* divorce and remarriage almost as common among Catholics as among non-Catholics today.

fathers. Despite the best efforts of priests and parents, young Catholics from time to time fell in love with young Protestants and resolved to marry them. That is when Plan B came into effect. If you could not keep them from marrying a Protestant, the next best thing was to get the couple to marry inside the Catholic Church. But this could not be an ordinary marriage, like one between two Catholics. For one thing, the Protestant partner had to promise to allow any children resulting from the marriage to be raised Catholic. For another, there could be no full-blown wedding ceremony. The rite could not take place in the parish church, in front of a large crowd of invited guests. It would have to take place somewhere else, usually in the rectory, with only a handful of witnesses. This secrecy and lukewarm blessing was a way of showing that the Church did not really approve of this kind of thing, even though it might grudgingly permit it.

The seriousness with which a religion enforces the taboo on intermarriage with outsiders is the most important indicator of how "closed" the religion is. In a certain sense, all the other measures intended to keep the religion closed are ordered to this ultimate measure, the prevention of mixed marriages; for a religion that is highly tolerant of intermarriage with outsiders will not be able to thrive in the long run; indeed, it may not even be able to survive. Where do most religions recruit their new generations of believers? From the children of the current generation. But if those of the current generation marry outsiders, their children will be far less available for recruitment, since the children of mixed marriages are likely to have either divided religious loyalties or no religious loyalties at all. Keep this up long enough, and the religion will wither away.

Look at America's Jews today. Forty years ago, it was almost unthinkable for a Jew — regardless of whether he was Orthodox, Conservative, Reform, or even nonreligious — to marry a non-Jew. Today more than half of America's Jews marry non-Jews. The result is a shrinking Jewish population, a trend which, if it continues, could cause something like the disappearance of American Judaism.

• *Peculiar lifestyles*. Earlier I said that among the characteristics of a closed religion is a peculiar lifestyle, often including peculiar habits of dress. This is clearly the case with religious groups such as the Amish and the Hasidim. But this did not seem to apply to pre-1960s American Catholics. They dressed like other Americans. Their lifestyle, although it may have exhibited a small number of peculiarities, such as meatless Fridays, was essentially the same as everyone else's. They married, they had children, they worked at ordinary jobs, they owned or at least aspired to own their own houses — just like Protestant Americans.

Nonetheless, Catholics *were* peculiar — but in a vicarious way. The Catholics *par excellence* of the era were not the lay rank and file, but, rather, the religious elite, the Catholic clerical class (including under this heading, not only priests, but nuns, monks, friars, and brothers); and this clerical class lived very peculiar lives indeed. They wore unusual clothing (the clothing of the women religious being especially unusual). They lived lives vowed to celibacy and chastity, neither marrying nor having children nor engaging in any kind of sexual relations. Those who were members of religious orders (this included all nuns and brothers and many priests) took further vows of poverty and obedience. In short, they renounced the three things Americans were most devoted to: family, money, and personal freedom.

These were very peculiar people indeed (at least when measured by common American standards), yet the rest of the Catholic population honored them as ideal Catholics; and American non-Catholics understood that this was the view of ordinary Catholics. This honor and recognition was in keeping with traditional Catholic teaching, which held that the religious "state" was higher than the lay state. This was not to say that every cleric was morally superior to every layperson; not at all. But it was to say that the life of Christian perfection was more readily achievable in the clerical state than in the lay state, due to the latter's innumerable cares and anxieties having to do with jobs, property, spouse, children, and the temptations of everyday worldly life.

In holding the clerical elite in high honor, ordinary lay Catholics were vicariously identifying with the elite's peculiar way of living, including its way of dressing. They were saying to the outside world, "Let these priests, nuns, and the others represent all the rest of us. Judge us by them. They are the best of us. They are what we would all wish to be like if we were not poor sinners, suffering from weakness of will and shortage of grace."

This was a fitting compromise for a religion that was not fully closed, but only semi-closed. In a fully closed religion, *all* members of the faith will live a peculiar lifestyle. In a semi-closed religion, it is enough that some members live a peculiar lifestyle, provided those peculiar few are regarded not as deviants but as ideal symbols of the whole religious community.

How the quasi-ghetto was created and sustained

So there we have some of the features that made American Catholicism a semi-closed religion up until the 1960s.

But this state of affairs could not continue indefinitely. If Catholicism had been a sectarian religion, like the Jehovah's Witnesses, it could have continued, for the natural tendency of a sectarian religion is to withdraw from society, to shield itself from the prevailing culture. But Catholicism is the very opposite of a sectarian religion; it is, to use the terminology of the sociologists, a churchly religion. That is to say, its natural tendency is not to withdraw from the world and its culture, but to mix freely, to engage the world in a cultural dialectic — influencing the world's culture and being influenced by it in return.

The Decline and Fall of the Catholic Church in America

The semi-closed character of American Catholicism prior to the 1960s was an abnormal state of affairs, the result of an abnormal historical situation. In the countries of Europe where American Catholic immigrants originated, Catholicism was, by a wide margin, the majority religion, and it had been so from time out of mind. In the United States, by contrast, Protestantism was the majority religion, and it had been so from the time of the first English settlements in the early seventeenth century. Moreover, in the nineteenth century, although the United States was already, religiously speaking, a fairly tolerant land, the old Protestant contempt for Catholicism had not yet disappeared; it was still a living thing. Indeed, it was the glue that bound the otherwise diverse Protestant sects and denominations into a loose collective whole. In such a setting, it would have been organizational suicide for American Catholicism to adopt an "open-door policy" to the culture of the surrounding world.

Yet even in this setting, such a policy might nonetheless have been adopted by default, had it not been for a number of factors working in the other direction.

For one thing, Protestants were not all that eager to welcome the Catholic newcomers into full membership in American society. This was partly due to the old anti-Catholic religious bias. It was also partly due to ethnic bias: many of the new Catholics, after all, came from non-English-speaking countries, such as Italy and Poland; while the English-speaking ones came from Ireland, and American Protestants, like their English cousins, had long disdained Irish Catholics as much for their Irishness as for their Catholicism. It was due, further, to the relatively low socioeconomic status that the immigrants and their children continued to occupy long after arriving in the United States.

These three factors — religion, ethnicity, and socioeconomic status — were not carefully differentiated in the minds of most Protestants. They were lumped together; they created a global impression, each factor reinforcing the other two. And this global impression was anything but favorable; it did not inspire Protestants with a burning desire to throw open the doors of respectable American society and welcome the newcomers into the parlor. This made it all the easier for the Catholic clerical leadership to begin building the walls of a Catholic ghetto. It is easier to segregate your people in when the surrounding world wants to segregate them out.

For another, Catholicism in the nineteenth century was still very much in the Trent era; it was still dominated by the anti-Protestant siege mentality it had adopted three centuries earlier. Had the United States been dominated, not by Protestants, but by Greek Orthodox Christians, the story might have been different, for Catholics were not prepared to regard Greeks as especially menacing. But Protestantism was dangerous. Indeed, it was the great danger; every Catholic knew that. Above all, the Catholic clergy knew that.

Again, most of the early Catholic immigrants and most of their clergy came from Ireland, where, during the last couple of centuries, Catholics had acquired a vast amount of experience at holding their own group together in the face of hostile Protestant domination. In Ireland, Catholics were the majority, but Protestants the ruling class. In the eighteenth century, the heyday of the "penal laws," Catholics were virtually propertyless and were totally devoid of political power; and their propertyless condition continued well into the nineteenth century, even when their political powerlessness began to abate. As an inevitable result, there was no eighteenth-century social class — no Catholic gentry or bourgeoisie — that could supply effective leadership to Catholics; the Catholic community had been decapitated.

At least this was true on the secular side, on the side of the Catholic laity. There remained, however, a clerical leadership. Many obstacles, it is true, had been thrown in the way of the activity and even the existence of the Catholic clergy (for instance, no seminary was permitted in Ireland until Maynooth opened in the early nineteenth century). Yet priests continued to function during this difficult century, and the Catholic Irish — impoverished, illiterate, debased — maintained their solidarity by grouping themselves under this clerical leadership. As a result, the Irish priesthood learned how to be more than mere priests; they learned how to be leaders of the community. All this, of course, was a terrific preparation for the arrival of Catholicism in a Protestant-dominated United States.

A final factor: the manpower — and equally important, the womanpower — was soon on hand to establish a semi-closed American Catholic community. It could not be done without an ample supply of priests and nuns, and the priests and nuns were available. As the European immigrants came to America, priests and nuns followed. They created a sense of community purpose; they mobilized the laity; they built churches, schools, colleges, and hospitals; they created a Catholic press. And the result of it all was that American Catholicism became, at least to a notable degree, a world within a world, an *imperium in imperio*; and this great creation was still intact. Indeed, it was flourishing more than ever as the United States moved into the 1960s.

Chapter 3

Dismantling the Ghetto in the 1960s

In the 1960s, everything changed, and the walls of the Catholic ghetto came tumbling down. There were two main causes of this development: at home, the full Americanization of American Catholics; and in Rome, Vatican II.

At long last, Catholics become real Americans

The Catholic people of the United States were no longer what they had once been. They were no longer immigrants or the children of immigrants. They were no longer poor and badly educated. In short, they were no longer marginal Americans. Instead, they were now three or four generations away from Europe and Quebec; they had done their fair share of patriotic fighting and dying in World War II; they had become middle class; they had moved to the suburbs; they were sending their kids to college. In short, except for their religion, they were just like everyone else; they had become fully Americanized.

And their religion itself was no longer a barrier to full membership in American society. Protestant America had lost most of its old anti-Catholic prejudice. It was ready to accept Catholics as full members of American society. By way of doing this, the unofficial religion of the United States had gradually been changed from Protestantism to that three-faith hybrid, Judeo-Christianity.

The Decline and Fall of the Catholic Church in America

Catholicism was no longer an alien faith; it had become a "normal" American religion, just as entitled as, say, Presbyterianism or Lutheranism to wrap itself in the American flag. This helps explain why John Kennedy, the first (and, to date, the only) Catholic elected to the White House, could win so many Protestant votes in the election of 1960 — not a majority of the Protestant votes, to be sure, but enough of a substantial minority to give him the victory. And those Protestants who voted against him mostly did so because he was a Democrat, not because he was a Catholic. The Kennedy victory could not have happened thirty or forty years earlier; indeed, it did not happen in 1928 when an earlier Catholic, Al Smith, ran for president.

American Catholics prove their patriotic worth

This process of Americanizing Catholicism had been going on since early in the nineteenth century, but it became a sure thing during World War II and in the early years of the Cold War.

During World War II, it was important, for obvious reasons, for the United States to have a high degree of national solidarity. All groups — regardless of race, religion, national origin, sex, or social class — were expected to contribute to the war effort. Most important, of course, they had to serve in the military. But almost equally important, they had to contribute on the home front. As workers, they had to produce the goods the soldiers and sailors needed to fight the war: guns, bullets, jeeps, tanks, airplanes, ships, uniforms, and, of course, food. As consumers, they had to be willing to sacrifice so that the military might be well supplied: they had to do without new automobiles and new houses, and their weekly meat consumption had to be rationed. And as investors and money-makers, they had to put up with price controls on a wide variety of goods and services. As thrifty savers, they had to buy war bonds. Given the universal need for help in the war effort, the nation could not afford to treat group X or group Y as second-class Americans. The time for group insults had ended. It was essential to persuade all groups that they now counted as true Americans, that they were full-fledged members of the American team, a team that, we hoped, would soon be victorious.

American blacks, to be sure, were still not treated as first-class Americans, even though they were expected to make the same contributions to the war effort as everybody else, and even though they rose to the level of this expectation. Yet even blacks were elevated closer to first-class status during the war. Although the segregation regime remained in place, even in the military itself, the idea that blacks were true Americans — not simply an alien people living in our midst in order to hew wood and draw water — made great progress during the war years.

But if even blacks made progress toward full American status during the war, Catholics, who, of course, began the war with a social rank that was much higher than that of blacks, ended it by having removed almost all their social inferiority. Before the war, many Protestant Americans still had doubts that a Catholic could be a good American and a good citizen of a democracy; for, after all, was not the Catholic's first loyalty to a "foreign prince," the pope of Rome? This old accusation went back at least to the time of Queen Elizabeth I, whose reign began in 1558. And to the charge that Catholics were essentially unpatriotic was added the further charge that they were essentially unsympathetic to political liberty — not surprising, given that they are adherents of an autocratic religion, the pope being seen as a religious tyrant.

Quite naturally, American Protestants inherited this bigoted English Protestant view of Catholics. And as the United States in the decades following the American Revolution became increasingly democratic, the anti-liberty accusation against Catholics was transmuted into an anti-democracy accusation. This accusation, unfortunately, was given some credence by the fact that Catholic voters in the nineteenth and early twentieth centuries often used their votes to support corrupt municipal regimes, e.g., Tammany Hall in New York City. Many of the most notorious political crooks in America were Irish Catholics.

But this old Protestant image of the American Catholic — the image of a person whose patriotism, love of liberty, and attachment to democracy were all doubtful — had been largely erased by the end of World War II. For Catholics had fought as hard, and died as often, as the most American of Protestants in a great patriotic war in defense of liberty and democracy. Who except the most closed-minded of bigots could continue to doubt that Catholics were good Americans?

For those of us living in the early twenty-first century, nearly six decades after the end of World War II, perhaps the easiest way to get a sense of the new inclusiveness, including the new inclusion of Catholics, is to look at war movies from that era. It was virtually mandatory in Hollywood that every military unit should include men with Irish, Italian, Polish, and Jewish names. Even blacks often found themselves included in war movies.

But the final nail was driven into the coffin of the old anti-Catholic prejudice in the early years of the Cold War. Suddenly Soviet Communism was the great enemy of the United States. This was nothing new for Catholics. Soviet Communism had always been recognized as a great enemy by the Vatican. And Rome — unlike the American government, which had allied itself with the Soviet Union during the war years, and whose leader (FDR) imagined that he could have friendly relations with the Soviet leader (Stalin) — had never blown alternately hot and cold about the Soviet Union; Rome always blew cold, very cold.

In the aftermath of World War II, when eastern and central Europe (including Catholic Poland) had been brought under Communist control, when the Church was being openly persecuted in Communist lands (remember Cardinal Mindszenty in Hungary), and when Communists were knocking on the door in

Italy itself, the Vatican developed a still icier view of Communism. Rome's definitive denunciation of Communism was issued in 1937 by Pope Pius XI in his encyclical letter *Divini Redemptoris* ("On Atheistic Communism," to give it its customary English title); and in the '40s and '50s, further warnings and denunciations streamed forth from Pius XII.

In the period from the late '40s through the early '60s, emotionally the most intense period of the Cold War, being a loyal Catholic and being a patriotic American converged at a central point — namely, a strong hostility toward Communism. Catholic Americans yielded to no one in their belief that Communism was colossally wicked and that it was the mission of the United States to save mankind from this world-historical wickedness. After this, what Protestant could doubt that Catholics were thoroughgoing Americans? And what Catholic could any longer doubt it, even if he might hitherto have regarded himself and his coreligionists as outsiders? The anti-Catholic prejudice that became part of the Protestant Anglo-American mind-set when Queen Elizabeth mounted the throne in 1558 had finally vanished almost four hundred years to the day later; and with it vanished the Catholic sense of alienation.

Vatican II liquidates the Tridentine fortress

It was during this same period, the early 1960s, that the second Vatican Council met to bring to a close the long age of Church history that had begun at Trent four centuries earlier. Catholicism had survived the Protestant assault. On a worldwide basis, Catholics greatly outnumbered Protestants, even when one added all the Protestant churches and denominations and sects together. While the Catholic Church remained united under the pope (indeed, it was more united at that moment than it had ever been), Protestantism had fragmented into hundreds — thousands — of divisions and subdivisions. Further, while Protestantism had made no substantial advances in countries that were left Catholic at the end of the era of religious wars (1648, the year of the Treaty of Westphalia, which ended the Thirty Years War in Germany), Catholicism had made significant advances in Protestant countries: in England, in Holland, in parts of Germany, in Hungary, and, above all, in the United States.

In short, the siege was over; Protestantism was no longer a danger; the gates of the fortress could be opened while its walls were left to decay. To be sure, there was more to Vatican II than this, but this was the crucial thing. Historically speaking, the great achievement of the council was the liquidation of the struggle against Protestantism and, no less important, the concomitant dismantling of the fortress mentality that this struggle had imposed upon Catholics. The age of Trent was finished.

The Catholic ghetto is dismantled

Given these two developments — the end of the Tridentine era in Rome, combined with the assimilation of American Catholics and their full acceptance by Protestants — how could the semi-closed nature of American Catholicism be maintained any longer? It now made no sense. This was quickly understood by all, and the process of dismantling the American Catholic ghetto began.

Consider the four distinctive features of traditional American Catholicism outlined in a previous chapter: its separate school system, its distinctive code of conduct, its ban on intermarriage, and its peculiar lifestyle. These all suffered great erosion in the late '60s and early '70s, eventually no longer differentiating Catholics from non-Catholics.

• *Catholic elementary and high schools shrank in size during these years.* Partly this was due to a waning interest on the part of Catholic parents, partly to the great numbers of religious sisters who were abandoning their convents and the very small numbers being recruited to replace them; for nuns had always been a marvelously cheap source of teaching labor in Catholic schools. Fewer nuns meant higher tuition fees, and higher tuition meant fewer students.

Partly, too, it was due to the fact that the leadership of the Church — the bishops — no longer had the intense belief their predecessors had in the value and indispensability of Catholic education. When, beginning in the late 1960s, a Catholic school shrank in size, when its enrollment grew so small that it was no longer viable, hardly anyone in the leadership regarded this as what it truly was, a major cause for alarm. Little serious effort was made to save the faltering schools; instead they were closed or consolidated. The market was allowed to work its will. The Catholic leadership — the bishops — accepted defeat as inevitable, downsizing the once-mighty school system that had been one of the proudest boasts of American Catholicism. No doubt some bishops hoped that, at some future date, God's Providence would retrieve the situation. Others saw little need for a distinctive Catholic school system now that Vatican II had opened the windows of the Church to let the breezes of the modern world blow through. Still others simply felt powerless to help.

In fairness to the bishops, it should be noted that they were in an extraordinarily difficult position beginning in the late 1960s, a position that made it very hard to stand and fight. Nuns were leaving, priests were leaving, and the number of new recruits for convent and priesthood was dropping precipitously. And the laity was of little help: they were attending Sunday Mass in smaller numbers; they were contributing less money; and, above all, they were in open rebellion against long-established Church norms, most notably the ban on contraception.

In higher education, the situation was at first glance very different. Catholic colleges and universities continued to flourish; in fact, they flourished more than ever. They grew in size, their academic quality improved, and they overcame the old reproach of intellectual narrowness and provincialism. But a closer inspection revealed a different situation. The "improvement" of Catholic institutions took the form of redesigning them so that they more closely resembled their secular counterparts. Boards of trustees, which formerly had been dominated by the religious order which staffed the college or university in question, were laicized. The colleges turned co-ed. More people with Ph.D.s were hired, most of them non-clerics, many of them non-Catholics. The percentage of teaching clerics dropped sharply, so that faculties which had a clerical majority only a few years earlier now had a clerical minority, often a very small one. Priests and sisters became a rarity in the classroom, being strategically concentrated instead in administrative and counseling posts.

Formerly, a large number of philosophy and theology courses had been required of undergraduates. In the aftermath of Vatican II, however, the philosophy requirement was lessened, and the philosophy taught in these new courses rarely had a Catholic flavor. Theology changed its name to "religious studies," and it became less distinctively Catholic. In the old, pre-Vatican II days, hardly any Catholic colleges taught courses on the Bible. Bible-reading, after all, was a mark of Protestantism; by a kind of perverse logic, therefore, biblical ignorance became a Catholic trait. This changed after the council, but the typical Scripture course in the redesigned Catholic colleges served less as an introduction to Catholic theology and more as an introduction to modern biblical criticism, which tended to have an anti-orthodox bias.

Catholic colleges and universities managed to survive, but the price they paid for survival was to become strikingly less Catholic than they once had been. This is not to say that they ceased to be Catholic, for they did not. But they began traveling down a road that many older Protestant colleges and universities — Harvard,

Yale, Princeton, Brown, Boston University, Northwestern, Southern Cal, and many others — had traveled in the nineteenth and early twentieth centuries — a road leading to full secularization.[13] Whether the Catholic institutions will fully duplicate the experience of their Protestant predecessors, or whether, instead, they will be able to halt at some point along the way, remains to be seen.

• *The distinctive Catholic code of conduct rapidly dissolved in the late 1960s and early '70s.* For one thing, the Church rule requiring meatless Fridays was made optional (except during Lent) — meaning that, in practice, it was essentially abandoned. Eating meat on Friday was not intrinsically wrong, nor contrary to Divine Law. It was wrong only by virtue of a Church prohibition, an ecclesiastical positive law.

By contrast, the ban on contraception was maintained. But this — as Pope Paul VI explained in his 1968 encyclical *Humanae Vitae* — is a God-made rule, part of natural law; it is not a Church-made rule and therefore is not subject to repeal by the Vatican. This theological point was lost in translation when communicated to ordinary Catholics. By and large, American Catholics no longer believed in the ban; and they certainly did not see it as part of an unwritten moral law or Divine Law. As they saw it, it was little more than a Vatican rule, akin to the no-meat-on-Friday rule. Formerly, in the pre–Vatican II days, married Catholics utilized contraception less often than Protestants, and when they did use it, they usually did so with something of a guilty conscience. Now their rate of contraceptive use caught up with that of Protestants; more important, they practiced contraception with an unbothered conscience.

---

[13] For a fine account of the secularizing of Protestant colleges and universities, see George Marsden's book, *The Soul of the American University: From Establishment to Established Nonbelief* (New York: Oxford University Press, 1994).

Moreover, their rebellion against the contraception ban was now out in the open. When Catholics privately practiced contraception, no one knew but the couple involved.[14] But when they expressed their dissent from the Vatican on this subject, everyone knew. It was now clear that most Catholics took the same view of contraception as did other Americans; hence, just as much as others, they considered the papal teaching on this subject to be anachronistic. Once again, a differentiating mark of Catholics had vanished.

Then there was divorce. Within a couple of years of the ending of Vatican II, the American divorce rate began to climb; more accurately, it began to skyrocket, the result of the libertine cultural revolution of the time, combined with "no-fault" divorce laws that were enacted in every state in the union in the late '60s and early '70s. The divorce rate moved sharply upward throughout the '70s, peaking at an all-time high in 1979; it dropped slightly the next year and then remained pretty much at the same level during the '80s and most of the '90s, dropping off slightly toward the end of the '90s.[15] This was the famous "divorce revolution," wherein divorce became for the first time a thoroughly normal fact of American life and the last remaining elements of stigma were removed from it. I do not suggest that this revolution was in any way, or at least in any significant way, the product of the council or of the collapse of the American Catholic ghetto. But when the divorce revolution occurred, Catholics, newly liberated from their semi-closed-religion status, newly freed to become full participants in the mainstream of American culture, were ready to keep up with the divorce rate of their neighbors. A special abhorrence of divorce ceased to be a distinguishing Catholic characteristic.

---

[14] No one *knew*, but many, of course, *guessed* when the marriage produced a small number of children.

[15] *The 2001 Statistical Abstract of the United States*, 59.

Moreover, the American Church leadership soon adjusted to this new phenomenon. Marriage annulment, hitherto a rare event, became common. By the late 1970s, tens of thousands of annulments were being granted to American Catholics every year, more than three-quarters of the worldwide Catholic total. This allowed Catholics who had been married in the Church and later received a civil divorce to remarry in the Church. Technically speaking, of course, it was not a remarriage, since the annulment was a finding that the first "marriage" had not really been a marriage at all, only an apparent or attempted marriage; some impediment had stood in its way. But the typical marriage tribunal, motivated by a compassionate pastoral concern to help Catholics whose marriages had been shipwrecked in a divorce-prone culture, took a very liberal view of what constituted an impediment. In many cases, annulment was little more than a legal-theological fiction. In practice, it was "Catholic divorce." Another Catholic mark of differentiation had disappeared.

• *Intermarriage became commonplace.* When Catholic immigrants first came to the United States, they tried to enforce an ethnic endogamy rule on their children; that is, they tried to convince their children to choose marriage partners from within their own ethnic group, Irish marrying Irish, Italians marrying Italians, and so forth. With the first generation of American-raised children, this rule was commonly — although not universally — obeyed. But in the second and third generations, it increasingly broke down, as marriage across ethnic lines became common.

At that point, a religious endogamy rule emerged. It had always been present, but in the background; it now came front and center. If young people, responding to the American melting-pot ideal, would not stay within ethnic boundaries, at least they could stay within religious boundaries. If Irish married Italians, that was not so bad, since Italians and Irish were both Catholic; at least they were not marrying Swedish Protestants.[16]

And so it was through the 1950s, and not just among Catholics, but among Protestants and Jews as well. With relatively few exceptions, Catholics married Catholics, Protestants married Protestants, and Jews married Jews. This phenomenon of in-group marriage was especially striking among Jews, 95 percent of whom married other Jews. Thus, it was relatively easy for American Catholicism to enforce its taboo against interreligious marriage, since this taboo was consistent with the general American cultural norm. Catholics willing to marry non-Catholics would find few non-Catholics willing to marry them.

This changed with the cultural revolution of the 1960s; it changed for Americans in general and Catholics in particular. If religious affiliation was dropping in value and individual freedom and choice was rising, as was the case beginning in the mid-1960s, what sense did it make to choose marriage partners on the basis of religious identity? To do so was evidence of an old-fashioned mentality, proof that you were not living up to the level of the age. And if Catholics were to enter into the mainstream of American culture, how could they refuse to go along with the new, highly permissive American intermarriage norm?

And here again, as in the case of divorce, it was not simply a matter of the rank and file rebelling against an old taboo; it was also a matter of the official Church trying to accommodate the rebels. Gone was the wedding ceremony in the rectory, suggesting something shameful about a mixed marriage. Instead, such weddings could now be performed in church, in the full light of day. A non-Catholic cleric representing the non-Catholic partner could even assist the priest in performing the wedding ceremony! Or if

---

[16] For a good account of this, see Will Herberg's book, *Protestant-Catholic-Jew* (New York: Doubleday and Company, 1955).

the couple preferred, they could marry in a non-Catholic setting, and the Catholic priest would assist the non-Catholic cleric. Gone, too, was the old requirement that the non-Catholic partner must promise in writing that the children of the union would be raised Catholic.

• *Catholics began to live like everyone else.* Prior to the '60s, as noted earlier, Catholics, like people of all other closed religions, had a peculiar lifestyle; this peculiar lifestyle was lived, not by rank-and-file Catholics, however, but by those exemplary Catholics: priests, nuns, and brothers. Ordinary lay Catholics lived this lifestyle vicariously, by means of the honor they paid to their celibate and oddly dressed clerical elite.

But this began to change in the immediate post–Vatican II years, partly the result of the cultural revolution going on in the United States, partly the result of the council. When I say "the result of the council," I do not mean that the council mandated all or most of these changes. Far from it. But by making any changes at all in what had been perceived as a virtually immutable religion, the council unleashed a great urge to experiment. A hint from the council that this or that should be changed was almost certain to be taken much further than the council intended.

Vatican II called upon religious orders and communities to re-examine their basic principles to see how best to apply them in the modern world. This re-examination led many societies of religious sisters to get rid of their traditional dress. In its place, they adopted either a very scaled-down religious habit, or they abandoned wearing a habit altogether, dressing instead in clothes that any contemporary middle-class woman would wear. Further, many of them decided to leave their traditional place of residence, the convent. Instead, they set up housekeeping, in twos, threes, and fours, in city apartments. In many cases, they also abandoned their trademark occupations, teaching and nursing, turning instead to various kinds of social work. In sum, they became far less "peculiar" than they had been only a few years earlier.

The council reaffirmed the New Testament idea of the "priesthood of all believers." This was an idea Martin Luther had stressed in the early days of the Reformation. Being a Protestant theme, it was, of course, downplayed during the four centuries following Trent. But now that the age of Trent was ended, it was time once again to talk about the priesthood of all believers; this was tantamount to declaring that the status of the laity was upgraded, since they, too, were priests. The council stressed that all Catholics are called by God to live lives of sanctity, thus repudiating the vulgar superstition that only the clerical elite is truly called to sanctity. At the same time, however, the council preserved the crucial distinction between priests and laity, reaffirming the reality of a second priesthood, the sacramental priesthood, which laypersons do not share. Thus, priests would still outrank the laity, in the sense that they performed a higher ecclesiastical function; but they no longer occupied a higher "state" in life; and, *a fortiori*, neither did religious sisters and brothers.

This closing of the dignity gap between the laity and the clerical class (priests, nuns, and brothers) meant that the clerical class could no longer function as an ideal symbol of the entire Catholic people. The notion that only the clerical elite is truly called to a life of sanctity made this idealization of the clergy possible. Get rid of that notion, and you get rid of the idealization as well. The clergy were no longer a higher breed of Catholic. There was no longer an identifiable group of Catholics that could serve as an ideal symbol for Catholics as a whole.

But if the clerical class no longer counted as the ideal symbol for all Catholics, then the peculiar lifestyle of this class — such of it, at all events, as remained after the post-council fallout — could no longer count as a vicarious lifestyle for all Catholics. It becomes no more than the peculiar lifestyle of a certain group of Catholics.

Hence, American Catholicism loses one more trait of a closed religion.

The vocations crisis explained

This goes a long way, I suggest, toward explaining an astonishing development that took place in the years just after Vatican II: the flight of many priests from the priesthood and of even more nuns from the life of the convent, combined with a precipitous drop in the number of young people deciding to enter the clerical life. Demographers explain migration in terms of two factors: something negative and unattractive about the place the migrants leave, and something positive and attractive about the place they go to. A combination of both is needed to get someone to move. Well, the same mode of explanation can be applied to the flight of priests and nuns. The loss of its symbolic function — the cleric as the ideal Catholic — was the negative factor, greatly diminishing the attractiveness of the clerical life; while the upgrading of the laity in combination with the end of the Tridentine fortress mentality was the positive factor, enhancing the attractiveness of the lay life in the world.

Chapter 4

The American Cultural
Revolution Blindsides the Church

In the preceding three chapters, we have looked at two of the three factors that produced the immense transformation of American Catholicism in the 1960s and '70s: Vatican II's liquidation of the fortress mentality of the Tridentine era and the dismantling of the American Catholic quasi-ghetto. In this very brief chapter, we will look at the remaining factor: the great American cultural revolution, which Catholic leaders had not foreseen, and for which they were not prepared. And in the three chapters immediately following, we will look at three sets of ideas that paved the way for the cultural revolution.

The revolution was characterized
by rebellion against authority

If we are looking for a handy phrase to sum up the American cultural revolution of the '60s and early '70s, we can probably do no better than this: *a generalized rebellion against authority*. Of course, it was more complicated than that; a single phrase can never sum up an era. But all accounts of history involve a simplification of reality, and a simplification is different from a falsification.

From the point of view of the present book, this synoptic phrase — "a generalized rebellion against authority" — has this great advantage: it highlights the problem the Catholic religion was bound to run up against in the atmosphere of such a cultural revolution. Catholicism, like virtually all religions (there are some exceptions, e.g., Unitarianism), is authoritative. Catholicism is more authoritative than most; indeed, in some ways, it is the most authoritative of all authoritative religions. Thus, a generalized rebellion against authority will hurt almost all religions, but it will hit Catholicism especially hard.

Catholicism does not say to its adherents, "Believe what you feel is true; do what you think is best." It is a religion with an elaborate set of dogmas and a complex moral code, and these are binding on its adherents. It says to its members, "You are entitled to a certain amount of freedom in belief and conduct, but the exercise of this freedom is far from absolute; it must take place within the framework of our authorized system of doctrine and morality. Further, if there are any questions as to the content of this doctrine and morality, these questions will ultimately be decided, not by the individual Catholic, but by Church authorities."

Moreover, these authorities are not chosen by a democratic process, but, rather, by a system of co-option; that is, they are chosen from above, not from below. The pope chooses and rules over the bishops, who, in turn, choose and rule over the priests. The only departure from this top-down, undemocratic clerical order comes at the apex of the pyramid, in the case of the election of the pope (by the college of cardinals, comprising mostly bishops). But even this process is far from democratic, because the pope is chosen, not by the Catholic people as a whole, but by the college of cardinals, a kind of ecclesiastical House of Lords, whose members have been appointed by previous popes. In theological theory, of course, if not in sociological practice, this, too, is a top-down election, since the cardinals are not supposed to be choosing whom they will; rather, they are supposed to be discovering whom God wills.

In sum, the polity of the Church is the very opposite of a democracy; it is an absolute monarchy, theoretical sovereignty residing in Jesus Christ, practical sovereignty in the pope. Its nearest analogue in the secular order is not the American constitutional system, but, rather, the constitutional system of Louis XIV of France, who (according to legend) once said, "*L'état, c'est moi.*"

Even in the calmest of times, so authoritative a religion will face enormous troubles in the modern world, which counts personal freedom and democratic government among its most precious and fundamental values. But when times are far from calm, when there is a widespread insurrection against all authority, when authority becomes something of a dirty word — at such a moment, the plight of this kind of religion will be desperate indeed.

The two great protest movements
of the 1960s fed the rebellion

What caused this generalized rebellion against authority to break out in the United States in the mid-1960s?

Obviously there were certain events that provoked it — especially the black civil-rights movement and the anti–Viet Nam War movement. Both protest movements called important authorities into question.

The civil-rights movement questioned the legal authority of states, which had authorized and practiced race discrimination. It questioned the legal authority of the federal government, which had quietly tolerated this state-level discrimination ever since the end of Reconstruction in the late 1870s. And it questioned the moral authority of the nation's political, social, business, and educational leadership, which had done so little to rectify such gross injustices. The system of race discrimination was rotten to the core, and the system of authority that connived in this discrimination must be equally rotten.

The Decline and Fall of the Catholic Church in America

The anti-war movement questioned, above all, the authority of the federal government — its legal authority to compel young men to fight in the war. Hence the symbolic burning of draft cards, the evasion of the draft by many, the refusal by some to respond to their induction notices, the attempts by others to win conscientious-objector status, and the flight of many to Canada and elsewhere. Even more, the movement questioned the *moral* authority of the government. In the eyes of many young people, especially college and university students, a government that prosecuted such a morally indefensible war had lost its moral legitimacy. Thus it did not have to be obeyed.

But it was not just the government that had lost its moral legitimacy. This loss extended to those who supported the government's war policy, either actively (by openly approving the policy) or passively (by failing to oppose it). And who were these supporters? With few exceptions, most of the American elite (or, as it came to be called in those days, "the Establishment") were supporters — elites in politics, in business, in higher education, and in religion. Further, among these active or passive supporters were many non-elite people: namely, the bulk of the older generations.

These two protest movements — anti-racism and anti-war — mutually reinforced one another and thereby mutually undermined the constituted authorities. For those who upheld and tolerated racism were pretty much the same people who supported the war. So they were guilty of two great sins, either one of which alone would be enough to destroy their moral authority. Thus, their authority was destroyed in spades.

All of a sudden, then, the younger generation decided that those in an official position of either legal or moral authority had no real legitimacy. Thus, they did not have to be obeyed; their "wisdom" did not have to be heeded. In many cases, of course, the young might continue to obey from motives of prudence, since those in authority still had the power to pass and flunk, to hire and fire, and to place under arrest. But in the eyes of vast numbers of young people — and those the most vocal, the most active, and the most influential among them — moral legitimacy had shifted from the constituted authorities to the rebels themselves. This was the volatile culture that greeted an unsuspecting and unprepared Church at its most vulnerable moment, the moment it let down its Tridentine guard.

But these protest movements, essential though they were in the generalized rebellion against authority, were far from being the whole story. They did not emerge out of nothingness; they grew up in fertile cultural soil. My concern in the next few chapters is with certain factors that, operating long before the crucial decade of the '60s, made this soil so fertile, so ready to produce the generalized rebellion against authority.

In particular, there are three factors I want to examine in the following chapters: the cultural-relativist school of anthropology; the philosophical theory of ethical emotivism; and the social-psychological study titled *The Authoritarian Personality*.

Part II

Philosophical Undercurrents of the Great Transformation

Chapter 5

Cultural Relativism Seduces a Generation

Franz Boas was the founder of the school of anthropology known as "cultural relativism," but the stars of the school were two of his students, Ruth Benedict and Margaret Mead. Each of the two wrote a book that was read in paperback by hundreds of thousands, maybe even millions, of undergraduates in the two decades following World War II. Benedict's book was *Patterns of Culture*; Mead's, *Coming of Age in Samoa*. One or the other (often both) was required reading in almost every introductory anthropology course (and in many introductory sociology courses as well) taught in America between the late 1940s and the early 1960s.

Cultural relativism combated the "myth of progress"

Cultural relativism was part of a generalized twentieth-century reaction against the evolutionary school that predominated in anthropology during the second half of the nineteenth century. The evolutionists (the most famous of whom was the English philosopher-sociologist Herbert Spencer) held that the human race had made a steady advance from a lower to a higher social and cultural state. Victorians living in an industrial society stood at the high end of the evolutionary scale; primitives living in simple hunting-and-gathering societies stood at the low end; and everyone else — including the ancient Egyptians, the Romans and Greeks, the

Incas and Aztecs, the medieval Europeans — stood somewhere in between the low and high ends. Societies higher in the scale were superior to those lower in the scale: superior in every way — morally, intellectually, technologically, politically, et cetera. Victorian society, however, was not the highest possible product of social evolution, only the highest to date. In future centuries, we may expect human society to get better still, until finally, at some remote future date, a truly ideal society will emerge.

Many twentieth-century anthropologists dissented from this view because they came to disbelieve in the myth of progress, the myth that the condition of the human race grows steadily and inevitably better and better. That myth had a certain plausibility in the century between Waterloo (1815) and August of 1914, since people who lived during that golden era in the industrialized and increasingly liberal-democratic nations of the European world could see things growing visibly better during their own lifetimes. But all of a sudden, the gigantic catastrophe of World War I, soon followed by the rise of totalitarian regimes in Russia, Italy, and Germany, destroyed that plausibility. Anthropologists now looked at the anthropological record with a more jaundiced eye, and they could no longer persuade themselves that what they saw was a uniform movement toward better things. Clearly there were long periods of backsliding, ages of retrogression. Could we honestly say that our postwar world was better than, say, the Roman world at the moment, nearly 1,800 years earlier, when Marcus Aurelius wore the purple?

The cultural-relativist critique of evolutionism cut deeper still, calling into question the very conceivability of progress. For progress to be even a theoretical possibility, we must be able to conceive of a "better" and a "worse" cultural state. But are there such states? Could it be, rather, that every culture is an attempt to adapt to the conditions of life faced by this or that particular society? The Eskimo, for instance, have to adapt to conditions that include few neighbors, low temperatures, a lot of ice and snow, and virtually no fertile land. Americans have a very different set of circumstances to contend with, not just geographical, but political and economic circumstances as well. Is it any wonder that American culture is radically different from Eskimo culture?

Yet who is to say which of the two cultures is better? To date at least, each has been successful — success being measured in terms of survival. Some cultures have been unsuccessful, and proof of their lack of success is that societies with these cultures have disappeared. But the cultures of all surviving societies may be considered equal, since they have all equally accomplished their main purpose, survival. This cultural-relativist line of thinking is borrowed from those evolutionary biologists who reject the notion that some species are "higher" and some "lower." All surviving species, they say, are at the same plane of merit, since all have managed to accomplish their essential task, survival. Biologically speaking, no matter what philosophy and theology have to say about the matter, humans are no "better" or "higher" than cockroaches.

Cultural relativism removed standards
for moral judgment as well as cultural

At first glance, this seems a very odd conclusion. Is it not a matter of plain common sense that American culture — with its science, literature, fine art, democracy, bill of rights, television, indoor plumbing, central air conditioning, skyscrapers, jet planes, computers, and so forth — is superior to cultures having none of these advantages? We may admire primitive cultures for a number of reasons, and we may admit that American society has had and continues to have many imperfections. But when all these concessions have been made, is it not still a plain truth that our culture is superior to theirs?

To make a comparative judgment between two cultures, however, presupposes that there exists some transcultural standard by which we may judge. But — and here we come to the assertion that lies at the heart of cultural relativism — there is no such thing as a transcultural standard of valuation. All standards are culturally specific; all are the creation of this or that society. We Americans quite naturally judge American culture to be superior to, say, Eskimo culture, but in doing so, we are judging by American standards; it is hardly surprising, therefore, that we come to this conclusion. The Eskimo, using standards of judgment provided by Eskimo culture, may well come to an opposite conclusion. All cultural judgments are American judgments, Chinese judgments, Eskimo judgments, et cetera. There are no merely human judgments. To judge another culture by standards provided by our own is to be guilty of the anthropological sin of ethnocentrism.

Now, as a methodological principle of research, there is much to be said for this viewpoint. For it induces the anthropologist to leave his value judgments outside the door when studying an alien culture; and the researcher who is able to approach an alien culture in a value-free way is more likely to understand the function of certain customs than is the researcher who begins with a moral prejudice against those customs. If you deplore cannibalism, for instance, you are less likely to understand the social functions of cannibalism than is your fellow researcher for whom cannibalism is, during the period of research, a morally indifferent matter.

But at least some cultural relativists, especially Ruth Benedict, did not limit the relativist principle to its use as a research orientation. They went much further, offering it as a *moral* principle as well.[17] In a rapidly shrinking world made up of hundreds of cultures, international peace depends on international understanding; and

---

[17] For an example of Benedict's going further, i.e., into moral relativism, see her essay "Anthropology and the Abnormal" in the *Journal of General Psychology*, pp. 59-79 (reprinted in part in *Moral Relativism*, Paul Moser and Thomas Carson, eds. [New York: Oxford University Press, 2001], 80-890.

international understanding is impossible, says the cultural relativist, so long as ethnocentrism prevails — so long, that is, as people insist on using their own culture-specific standards to judge people who live by other standards. If only we would all embrace the cultural-relativist point of view, think what happy results would follow. We would all understand one another and abstain from passing negative judgments on one another. This is the high road to world peace.

Strictly speaking, of course, the relativists should have abstained from proposing *any* moral principles, even mutual tolerance. Instead, they said in essence, "The one absolute rule of morality is that we should never believe there are any absolute rules of morality." In other words, their moral recommendation that we all become cultural relativists self-destructs. In fairness to the cultural relativists, though, it should be noted that theirs is not the first school of thought to fall into this contradiction; it has been common to almost everyone who has taken the trouble to offer a theoretical defense for either limited or wholesale skepticism.[18]

Practically speaking, however, this self-contradiction by the cultural relativists did not matter. It was not the kind of thing that

[18] The skeptics of the ancient world, for instance, taught that we can be certain about nothing; and yet, contradicting themselves, they were certain that we could not be certain. One of the great skeptics of modern times, Montaigne, tried to avoid this trap by expressing his skeptical principle in interrogative, not declarative, terms, adopting as his motto: "What do I know?" But, of course, this was an implied declarative: it meant, "I (and you, too) know nothing." So it did not get Montaigne off the hook. In the nineteenth century, Karl Marx contended that ideologies had no truth-value: they were simply reflex expressions of social structure and class interest. But this critique of ideologies, if valid, would apply to his own ideology and to the critique itself, which was part of that ideology.

would deter any but those having a very strict logical conscience. If you found cultural relativism attractive, you would be sure to find a way of ignoring the contradiction.

Cultural relativism's popularity helps
undermine the American moral code

The books by Benedict and Mead were immensely readable, and they served to "enlighten" vast numbers of undergraduates from the late '40s through the mid-'60s. The books not only told a number of good stories (Benedict's stories from her book *Patterns of Culture* — about the paranoid Dobu, the peaceful Zuni, and the fiercely competitive Kawkiutl — are especially entertaining), but it enabled students to feel more enlightened than the average run of Americans (including their own parents), since the student readers now understood that the American moral code was culture-bound, while their ethnocentric parents and neighbors felt, quite erroneously, that this code had a universal validity.

And not only were they more enlightened as a result of the encounter with these marvelous books; they came to feel, in rather a cheap and easy way, morally superior as well. For ethnocentrism, as the cultural relativists presented it, was not just an intellectual vice. In the modern world — where it leads to intergroup misunderstanding, hostility, racism, persecution, and even warfare — it was a moral vice as well, perhaps the very worst of moral vices. Those who took the gospel of cultural relativism to heart were liberated from this vice. Pity their poor parents and neighbors, who remained ensnared by it.

Still one more conclusion was bound to follow from all this — for our purposes in this chapter, the most important conclusion of all. It was a conclusion cultural relativists did not explicitly call attention to, perhaps because they did not themselves realize it, or perhaps because they would have recoiled from it. But it was an obvious conclusion, one that great numbers of intelligent young people could hardly avoid drawing. It was this: If the American moral code lacks universal validity, then it lacks validity — period. For the validity claims of the American moral code were never merely relativist claims. That is to say, they were never modest claims that said, "This code just happens to be one that our American ancestors made up; we do not say it should apply to anyone else; but we like it, and we propose to live according to it."

No, the American claims were universal claims. Americans said, "We believe our moral code derives from a universal source — either God or reason or human nature — and hence, has universal application. It is not for Americans only, but for all mankind. We accept this code, not because it is *our* code, but because it is the universally *true* code." Thus, to deny (as the cultural relativists urged us to do) that the American moral code has universal validity is to deny it has validity at all.

This will make little difference to a professional anthropologist or a seasoned man of the world, both of whom believe it is perfectly proper for locals to obey the local moral code, no matter what it may happen to be: vegetarianism in some places, cannibalism in others; when in Rome, do as the Romans do. But a young person with just a smattering of anthropological learning and scant worldly sophistication might well reason that the rules of morality were man-made, therefore not necessarily right. What authority would arbitrary rules made by others have over him? None at all, he might conclude.

The widespread popularity of cultural relativism, therefore, was a first step in preparing the ground for the generalized rebellion against authority that took place in the late 1960s. For it taught — by implication, an implication hard to miss — that the prevailing American moral code had no legitimate authority.

Chapter 6

Ethical Emotivism
Creates a Novel Morality

Of course, it does not follow from the conclusion of the foregoing chapter that the young person in question would proceed to live without any moral code, since doing so is nearly a psychological impossibility. Every sane person will subscribe to some form of moral or ethical code.

But what code would it be, and where would it come from? There are three possible sources: either some transcendental source (God, or Absolute Reason), or society, or oneself. We have just ruled out a transcendental source, since the American moral code, as cultural relativism has taught us, is not the creation of God or Absolute Reason. We have also ruled out society, since, although society does create moral codes, it has no authority to impose them on us. That leaves oneself as the only candidate. Each individual, then, must be the author of his own moral code.

This does not mean you have to create your code from scratch. No, you can accept the code society proposes. But this code gets its authority over the individual, not because society has proposed it, but because the individual has accepted it. Society's moral rules can be thought of as so many moral hypotheses; it is up to the individual to decide which of these hypotheses is valid for him or her. The seat of moral authority has been transferred: it is not in God (or any other transcendental source), not in society, but in the individual.

Ethical emotivism offers custom-tailored moral codes

It so happened that this highly individualistic notion of morality tallied rather nicely with a philosophical theory of ethics that first gained currency in the English-speaking world with A. J. Ayer's highly readable book *Language, Truth, and Logic* (London: Victor Gollancz, 1936), a popularization of the philosophy of the Vienna Circle.[19] The philosophy was known as Logical Positivism, and its theory of morality was called emotivism.

The Logical Positivists held something they called the "Verification Principle," according to which statements are "meaningful" only if they can, at least in principle, be verified or falsified by some sense experience; if this could not be done, the statements were "meaningless." Thus, a typical statement made by a scientist (e.g., that water is composed by volume of two parts hydrogen and one part oxygen) is meaningful, since it can be verified by sense observation. Likewise the statement "Many elephants live in the Antarctic" is meaningful, but false.

By contrast, the characteristic statements made by theologians and metaphysicians (e.g., that God exists or that God does not exist, that the soul does or does not survive the death of the body) are meaningless; for there are no conceivable sense experiences that can either prove or disprove such propositions. Meaningful

[19] The Circle was a group of Viennese mathematicians, scientists, and philosophers who met every week or two, from the mid-1920s to the mid-'30s, to discuss questions in the philosophy of science. The leader of the Circle was Moritz Schlick; other leading members were Rudolph Carnap and Otto Neurath. Loosely connected with the Circle, although not members of it, were Ludwig Wittgenstein and Karl Popper. A good brief account of the Circle can be found in Ben Rogers' *A. J. Ayer* (London: Chatto and Windus, 1999), 82-96.

statements, of course, do not have to be verifiable or falsifiable by the unaided senses; observations made with the help of instruments — e.g., telescopes or microscopes — count as well.

More to the point of our current discussion, all value statements, including ethical statements, are meaningless; for how can they be verified? Goodness and badness, after all, are not properties capable of being sensed; nor are rightness and wrongness such properties. If you say, "Murder is bloody," that is a meaningful statement, since blood is something whose presence or absence can be detected by sense observation. But if you say, "Murder is wrong," that is meaningless, for which of our five senses can detect the presence or absence of wrongness?

What follows, then? Shall we abstain from making moral judgments, now that we have learned, thanks to the good offices of the Logical Positivists, that such judgments are meaningless? Not likely, since humans seem to be incorrigible moralizers. Well, then, if we are not making a "meaningful" statement when making a moral judgment, what are we doing? How much does wrongness weigh; what color is it; what does it smell like; and so on?

To this, Ayer and the Logical Positivists had an answer: When we make a moral judgment, we are simply expressing our feelings. When I make the ethical utterance, "Murder is wrong," all I am really saying is, "I dislike murder." When I say, "It is right to be honest," all I am saying is, "I approve of honesty." Grammatically speaking, moral judgments may look like fact-statements, but they are really just expressions of feeling masquerading as fact-statements. I am simply telling you what my emotional attitude is with regard to murder and honesty. Hence the name of the theory: emotivism.

A few years after Ayer's book appeared, the American philosopher Charles Stevenson presented a more refined version of the theory,[20] a version that attempted to meet some of the more obvious

[20] *Ethics and Language* (New Haven: Yale University Press, 1944).

objections that had been raised. One such objection was this: Surely when we say, "Murder is wrong," we are saying more than "I disapprove of murder." We are doing more than merely informing our listener about our feelings. Yes, agreed Stevenson; we are doing much more. We are attempting to *persuade*, that is, we are attempting to induce similar feelings in others. In Stevenson's translation, "Murder is wrong" means "I disapprove of murder; do thou likewise."

But for all this refinement, Stevenson's theory of ethics is essentially the same as Ayer's. Both deny the objectivity of moral law. Both deny that its authority is based on a transcendental source. Both even deny that it is based on the will or collective preferences of society, thereby rejecting the explanation favored by cultural relativists. Both affirm, rather, that it is based on the preference of the individual. And if two or more individuals happen to subscribe to the same rules of morality, this is because they happen to have the same moral preferences.

It is probable that neither Ayer nor Stevenson had as much direct impact on undergraduates as did Benedict and Mead, since the typical college student finds it easier and more pleasant to read accounts of exotic cultures than to read dry and complex philosophical arguments. But the direct impact was far from negligible; evidence of which is the fact that both books were reprinted many times during the era we are concerned with, the twenty years following World War II. (My own copy of Ayer's book shows that the second edition, which first appeared in 1946, had been printed fourteen times by 1960. "In the U.S., where [*Language, Truth and Logic*] was published by Dover, it sold 300,000 copies in the thirty years after the war," i.e., between 1945 and 1975.[21] My 1967 copy of Stevenson's book is the eleventh printing.) But if the direct impact was less, the indirect impact more than made up the difference.

---

[21] Rogers, *A. J. Ayer*, 217.

One could easily learn, from professors and from other students, the theory of emotivism.

By the early 1960s, young college-educated Americans understood that there were respectable thinkers in the world who asserted that moral values are ultimately nothing more than personal preferences. And this view seemed eminently plausible to many of the young, since it corroborated a conclusion they had already drawn from the teachings of the cultural relativists — namely, that since conventional morality is a thing made by fallible men, it has no binding authority over the individual, and hence, the individual is his or her own seat of moral authority.

Up until the 1960s, "emotivism" was an appropriate name for this theory, since it was held that moral values were simply expressions of feeling. But in the 1970s, a slight shift had occurred. It now came to be held among many people, especially young people, that values are based on "choice." This shift was largely the result of the abortion-rights movement. The "right to choose" had proven to be an effective propaganda device for the movement; so why not extend it to all values, not just pro-abortion values? But whether we call it emotivism or "choice-ism" or something else, it comes to essentially the same thing — namely, that the moral rules that guide an individual's life are not given by any transcendental source, are not even given by society, but are simply the preference of the individual.

There is no law: theories of moral autonomy

The traditional name for the theory that there is no moral law is antinomianism (from *anti* and *nomos*, the Greek word for "law"). The word first gained currency during the Reformation, when certain extreme sectarians, taking the Lutheran theory that we are saved by faith, not works, with excessive literalism, concluded that the person of faith is bound by no moral law. It is a word worth reviving today, to designate those who, like the cultural relativists and emotivists (or "choice-ists"), hold that there is no objective moral law.

The other side of the antinomian coin is the theory of moral autonomy — the theory that, since there is no objective moral law, we as individuals are therefore free to create our own moral values.

The concept of autonomy has played an important role in moral philosophy since the days of Immanuel Kant,[22] who distinguished between an autonomous morality (a good thing) and a "heteronomous" morality (a bad thing). A moral code or a set of moral values is heteronomous when it is imposed on the individual by an agency external to the individual: by God, by the church, by the state, by society, et cetera. It is autonomous, on the other hand, when the individual imposes it on himself. At first hearing, this sounds like a sure path to moral anarchy, every individual making up his or her own morality. But Kant was no fan of moral anarchy. When I impose a moral law on myself, he said, this law must come from the highest and best part of myself: not from my emotions, but from my reason. Reason, when it is functioning properly, is the same in all humans. That is why we can all agree in mathematics, and likewise we should all agree in morality. A truly autonomous morality, then, far from leading to moral anarchy, should lead to its opposite: a universal moral code that all humans can, in principle, agree with, regardless of their local cultures.

In America during the last three decades, there has been a popular concept of moral autonomy that, while using Kant's word, omits his universalistic qualifier. That is, the popular idea says we must create our own morality, but it neglects to add that this creation must spring from our faculty of reason, which is the same in all humans. Each of us is morally sovereign, according to the popular theory, and it does not matter whether the edicts of this

---

[22] Kant (1724-1804) was one of the great figures in German philosophy and professor at the University of Koenigsberg.

sovereign issue from its higher reason, its egotistical reason, its emotions, or its sheer arbitrary choices. In other words, the popular theory, taken to its logical conclusion, leads to moral anarchy.

This non-Kantian concept of moral autonomy has migrated from the world of popular discourse into the world of legal theory (or perhaps the migration went the other way around, but in any case, it now inhabits both worlds), and from the world of legal theory into opinions issued by the United States Supreme Court. Take, for example, *Planned Parenthood of Southeastern Pennsylvania v. Casey*, the 1992 decision in which the Court upheld, by a 5-4 vote, the *Roe v. Wade* ruling of 1973 (the famous ruling that made abortion a constitutionally protected right). In *Casey*, Justice Anthony Kennedy, writing for the Court, said, "These matters, involving the most intimate and personal choices a person may make in a lifetime, choices central to personal dignity and *autonomy*, are central to the liberty protected by the Fourteenth Amendment. At the heart of liberty is the right to define one's own concept of existence, of meaning, of the universe, and of the mystery of human life" (emphasis added).

And in a more recent case (2003), *Lawrence et al. v. Texas*, in which the Supreme Court ruled all anti-sodomy laws to be unconstitutional, Justice Anthony Kennedy again, writing for the Court, said, "Liberty presumes an *autonomy* of self that includes freedom of thought, belief, expression, and certain intimate conduct" (emphasis added). And later, just after citing his "mystery" passage in *Casey*, Kennedy says, "In explaining the respect the Constitution demands for the *autonomy* of the person in making these choices, we stated as follows: 'Persons in a homosexual relationship may seek *autonomy* for these purposes, just as heterosexual persons do' " (emphasis added).

The Supreme Court, then, knows how to talk the language of autonomy. But it is not Kantian autonomy it is talking about; it is antinomian autonomy.

Most advocates of the theory hope, of course, that it will not lead to anarchy; they hope that others will choose values not so different from their own values; and they hold (despite an abundance of evidence to the contrary) a tacit theory of human nature that says that humanity is basically benign — which means that, even if anarchy *does* ensue, it will be a benign anarchy. All the same, the practical conclusion of the theory is moral anarchy; and if human nature is not as benign as the proponents of the theory imagine, this moral anarchy may turn out to be very unpleasant.

Chapter 7

The Authoritarian Personality
Legitimizes Suspicion of Authority

So far, we have looked at two theoretical factors that paved the
way for the generalized rebellion against authority of the 1960s:
cultural relativism and ethical emotivism. In this chapter, we will
look at a third such factor, an enormously influential book, *The
Authoritarian Personality*.

Published in 1950, the book was never a bestseller among the
masses. It was too long (nearly a thousand pages), too abstract in
its argument, too technical in its vocabulary, and too laden with
statistical tables to appeal to the common reader. But it was widely
read among the intellectual elite; and it was so widely reported on
in intellectual circles that you did not actually have to hold the
book in your hands to get a pretty good idea of its contents. To a
generation of intellectuals, this book defined the Nazi mentality
in Germany and the "right-wing" mentality in the United States.

Searching for the psychological key to fascism

The research the book was based on was sponsored by the
American Jewish Committee, which, in the aftermath of the Nazi
era and Hitler's genocide of the Jews, wanted to discover the psychological roots of fascism and anti-Semitism. This was not simply
a matter of intellectual curiosity; it was a very practical question as

well. Let us assume that a certain psychological type, common among Germans, contributed significantly to producing the Nazi movement, World War II, and the Holocaust. Is it not possible that this same type could be found outside Germany, even perhaps in the United States? If so, should we not be ready to deal with this type before they mobilize into a tyrannical and homicidal political movement?

The leading figures in the production of *The Authoritarian Personality*, Max Horkheimer and Theodor Adorno, had come to the United States in the early 1930s, Jewish intellectual refugees from Nazi Germany. In Germany, they had been prominent members (Horkheimer had been the Director) of the Institute for Social Research, in Frankfurt. (Members of the institute, who shared a common theoretical orientation, were popularly known as the "Frankfurt School.") This theoretical orientation was a synthesis of Marxism and Freudianism. Marx gave Freud political-historical breadth, while Freud gave Marx psychological depth. In its details, *The Authoritarian Personality* was more psychological than political, more Freud than Marx. But it was a Freud who had been turned into a leftist by his contact with Marx; in other words, the psychology of the book was used to serve a political ideology.

Each of the seven co-authors was responsible for writing one or more of the book's chapters; but the book was not a mere anthology, a collection of loosely related individual studies. It was a cohesive whole, held together by the theoretical framework shared by its authors.

The book dealt with topics such as anti-Semitism, ethnocentrism, political-economic conservatism, fascism, religion, and sex. Psychological tests were developed for measuring attitudes regarding these various topics, and on the basis of these tests, scores were given. By giving you, say, the anti-Semitism test, the researchers claimed that they could say with great precision how anti-Semitic you were. In principle, then, you could be assigned an anti-Semitism score as simply and scientifically as a blood-pressure score; and you could be rank-ordered among the rest of society.

More important, the various tests could be correlated with one another. When this was done, it was discovered that scores in one test often correlated strongly with scores in a second test; for instance, if you scored high in anti-Semitism, you were also likely to score high in ethnocentrism and political-economic conservatism; and if you scored low in one of these, you were likely to score low in the others.

This permitted the authors to develop the comprehensive concept of the "authoritarian personality." Or perhaps we should say, more accurately, that it permitted them to give testable, empirical content to this concept, since the concept had been developed well before they began their study; it was the working hypothesis that lay behind the whole study.[23]

Persons with authoritarian personalities combine a number of traits that the authors of the study considered to be psychopathological. Such persons are anti-Semitic, ethnocentric, sexually repressed, and religiously dogmatic; they have negative attitudes toward women, blacks, homosexuals, and leftists; they favor right-wing political and economic ideologies. If you possess this tangle of mental and moral pathologies, you are a potential fascist. You are ripe for recruitment when a rightist movement with a strong "leader" comes along, promising to keep women, blacks, Jews, foreigners, and other "inferior" types "in their place." The more this

[23] Under the name "authoritarian character," this concept had played a key role in the 1941 social-psychological study of Nazism, *Escape from Freedom* (republished by Avon Books, 1965), authored by Erich Fromm, another Freudian-Marxian who had been connected with the Frankfurt School. Fromm, too, was a Jewish intellectual refugee who had come to the United States from Germany; but he was not one of the co-authors of *The Authoritarian Personality*.

leader demands obedience to authority, even though this may require dispensing with many of the formalities of democracy, the better you like it.

The authors, it should be noted, did not denounce all respect for authority; they denounced only authoritarianism — an exaggerated respect for a particularly vicious kind of authority. But the authors did not stress this distinction between legitimate and illegitimate respect for authority; it was likely to be missed by readers of their study, and it was especially likely to be missed by those who learned its contents, as most did, only secondhand. As the influence of the book spread in the United States, so did the suspicion of anyone who believed in the importance of authority. If you spoke about the social need for authority and for obedience to authority — whether in church, state, school, or elsewhere — you were, in the eyes of those who were psychologically initiated, a suspicious character, possibly mentally unbalanced — a potential fascist.

Aristotle critiques and corrects
The Authoritarian Personality

In his *Nicomachean Ethics*, Aristotle gives a trialistic (or three-cornered) account of virtue and vice. For Aristotle, virtue is a mean between two vicious extremes, one of which carries things too far while the other does not carry them far enough. Thus, for instance, courage is the virtuous mean having to do with fearful things, while foolhardiness is the vice of excess (the foolhardy person having too little fear), and cowardice the vice of deficiency (the coward having too much fear). Aristotelian virtue is like Goldilocks, who wants her porridge to be "just right," neither too hot nor too cold.

By contrast, the authors of *The Authoritarian Personality* offer a dualistic account: having an authoritarian (or potentially fascist) personality is a great vice, while virtue is the opposite of this vice.

The further removed you are from this vice, the more virtuous you are. If the person with an authoritarian personality scores high on ethnocentrism, anti-Semitism, sexual repression, religious dogmatism, et cetera, then the virtuous, non-authoritarian person is one who scores low on all these things, and the lower, the better.

Aristotle (not to mention Goldilocks) would have issued a warning here: as these scores drop to very low levels, there is the danger of falling into another vice, the opposite of the authoritarian one. But the authors of *The Authoritarian Personality* have no such concern. If Aristotle reminds us of Goldilocks, they remind us of the one who said, "A woman can never be too thin or too rich." Our authors seem to believe that a person can never be too far removed from the wickedness of the authoritarian personality.

To assign names to these things, while at the same time looking at them from an Aristotelian point of view, let us say that the authoritarian personality is a vice at one extreme, placing too much value on obedience to authority, too little value on personal freedom; that the anarchical personality is the vice at the other extreme, placing too much value on personal freedom, too little value on obedience to authority; and that the democratic personality (to keep things in a political context) is the happy medium between the two vicious extremes, correctly balancing the values of obedience to authority and personal freedom. The authors of *The Authoritarian Personality* were not aware of the dangers arising from the anarchical personality. Quite the contrary, they seemed to assume that the anarchical personality, since further removed from the authoritarian personality, was an improved version of the democratic personality.

Providing a reason for the
"pathology" of political conservatives

While reflecting on the influence that *The Authoritarian Personality* had on American culture in the 1950s, it is important to examine its influence on the political discourse of the era. During that decade and into the early '60s, nearly all American intellectuals considered themselves political liberals. Conservatism was an emotional force, yes, and it was the battle cry of certain economic interests, but it had very little intellectual respectability. The revival of an intellectually respectable conservatism had barely begun in those days. Russell Kirk's *The Conservative Mind*, which served as a Bible for the nascent conservative intellectual movement, was first published in 1953; and William Buckley's magazine, *National Review*, which did more than any other publication to promote the movement, was first issued in November 1955.

Neither the magazine nor the book, however, created a revolution overnight; they produced their eventually astonishing effects only very gradually. For a long time, they were regarded by the liberal intellectual establishment as little more than cranky aberrations, writings that mimicked serious thought more than engaging in it.

This revived conservatism hit a kind of peak in 1964, when its political hero of the day, Barry Goldwater, became the Republican candidate for president of the United States. Liberal intellectuals (which is to say, nearly all American intellectuals) were not sure whether to be amused or appalled at the Goldwater candidacy. Here was a politician who claimed to stand for a system of ideas. But his ideas were, from a liberal point of view, plainly foolish; and the man himself was obviously quite nonintellectual, not at all a man of ideas. In November, running against President Lyndon Johnson, Goldwater was trounced. Besides his home state, Arizona, he won only a handful of states in the deep South, the region of the country that had been famous since the end of Reconstruction for its lack of both liberalism and intellectualism. The election result seemed a popular ratification of the verdict liberal intellectuals had long since given: that the notion of a conservative system of ideas was something close to a contradiction in terms.

The Authoritarian Personality was very helpful in solving a problem that inevitably arose out of this pro-liberal consensus among intellectuals. Since there appeared to be no rational basis for being a conservative, why, nonetheless, did many nonintellectual Americans remain steadfastly conservative? These conservatives were not the majority, to be sure; not even a very large minority. Still, there were millions of them, probably tens of millions. As a fraction of the American body politic, they were nothing to sneeze at. They were conservative on race relations, labor unions, government regulation of the economy, foreign and military affairs, sex education, et cetera. And as new issues arose, we could safely predict that they would adopt conservative positions on these.

The Authoritarian Personality provided an explanation for the existence of conservatives: they suffer from a psychopathology. They were conservative on race relations because they were ethnocentric. They were conservative on foreign and military affairs because they were xenophobic. Their conservative stance on sex education stemmed from sexual repression. Their attachment to hierarchical order and obedience means they would disapprove of uppity labor unions that were so disobedient as to go on strike. Their dogmatism made them suspicious of independent-minded intellectuals. It went without saying that they would be doctrinaire and authority-bound in their religious beliefs.

And theirs was not just any old psychopathology, but an especially vicious one — one that, in its recent German incarnation, led to dictatorship, concentration camps, worldwide war, and genocide. American conservatives, in other words, were not simply people of goodwill who happened to hold a mistaken set of political beliefs. Rather, they were mentally disturbed; worse still, they were morally perverse, potential fascists. The fact that their numbers were relatively small was no great consolation; after all, for a long time in Germany, the number of Nazi supporters was relatively small, too. It was not until Hitler and the Nazis came to power (despite never having won a majority of votes) that the German people revealed just how authoritarian they truly were. If there were tens of millions of American authoritarians willing to support conservatism even at a time when that ideology appeared to be down and out, who knows how many now-closeted authoritarians would reveal themselves if the day should ever arrive when conservatism came to power?

The Authoritarian Personality provided American liberal intellectuals with all the following: an explanation for why so many conservatives still existed, despite the utter irrationality of conservatism; a right to hold conservatives in contempt as enemies of democracy; and a powerful motive for resisting conservatism and all its pomps and all its works. After all, in resisting conservatism — which was little more than a code name for lunacy and fascism — liberals were fighting for nothing less than the preservation of democracy.

A notable instance of this kind of absurdity took place in 1968, when ABC-TV hired William Buckley and Gore Vidal to perform, respectively, as conservative and liberal commentators at the Democratic National Convention. This was the notorious Chicago convention that produced a memorable street confrontation between antiwar demonstrators and the police of the city, a confrontation that was later described as a "police riot" by the Walker Commission in its postmortem on the event. Angry collisions were not limited, however, to the streets of Chicago. Sparks were bound to fly between the two commentators, and that, no doubt, is precisely what the network had in mind in hiring them.

At one especially heated moment, the sparks turned into a conflagration, with Vidal calling Buckley a "crypto-Nazi" and Buckley retaliating by calling Vidal a "queer." Now, Vidal did not make much of a secret of his homosexuality; still, Buckley's use of such a derogatory label was a serious breach of good manners. From Vidal's liberal-intellectual point of view, however, his own use of the expression "crypto-Nazi" was not unmannerly at all; it was merely scientifically accurate. Buckley was a conservative, was he not? Well, then, it followed (as any student of *The Authoritarian Personality* could tell you) that he must be a crypto-fascist or crypto-Nazi. And if there had been any doubt about this, Buckley dispelled it when he called Vidal a queer — a dead giveaway of Buckley's sexual repression, an essential component of the authoritarian personality.

Stanley Milgram "proves" that
America is repressive and authoritarian

A spin-off, so to speak, from *The Authoritarian Personality* was the famous study done by Yale social psychologist Stanley Milgram. Titled "Obedience to Authority," the study has been favorably reported by a generation of sociology and psychology textbooks.[24]

Milgram was interested in measuring the different reactions to authority on the part of Americans and Germans. He assumed beforehand that Germans, only fifteen years from the end of the Nazi regime, would be far more willing to give blind obedience to authority figures than would Americans. So he devised a clever test, with the idea of first carrying it out in the United States and then later in Germany.

Subjects (Yale students) were recruited for what they were told (falsely) was a study of the effectiveness of punishment in

---

[24] For Milgrim's own reports on his studies, see "Behavioral Study of Obedience," in *Journal of Abnormal and Social Psychology*, 1963:57-76; and "Some Conditions of Obedience and Disobedience to Authority," in *Human Relations*, February 1965. Second-hand accounts of the studies are given in many sociology and psychology textbooks published between the late 1960s and today.

promoting learning. There would be a "teacher" and a "learner." The teacher would supply the learner with certain items of information and later test the learner on what he remembered. The learner — who was situated in such a way that he could be heard by the teacher, but not seen — was hooked up to a set of wires, and whenever he gave the wrong answer to a question, the teacher would punish him by administering an electric shock by means of levers on a control panel. The first shock for the first mistake was very mild; the second for the second mistake somewhat more severe; the third for the third mistake severer still; and so forth.

As the teacher moved from left to right on his control panel, the levers administered progressively graver shocks, and the control panel was labeled in such a way as to indicate that the further one moved to the right, the more high-voltage and powerful the shocks would become. There were three participants in the room as this was done: the teacher, the learner, and the man conducting the experiment (who wore a white lab coat). Subjects were told that the learner and the teacher would be determined by drawing a piece of paper out of a hat.

Of course, both pieces of paper in the hat said "teacher." The learner was in on the game, a confederate of the experimenter. When the learner drew a piece of paper from the hat, it, too, said "teacher," but he reported that it said "learner." And, of course, there were no electric shocks. The learner, as part of the game, simply pretended to be shocked whenever the teacher pulled a lever.

What was really being tested was not the effectiveness of punishment in promoting learning, but how far the subjects (the Yale students) would go in obeying an authority figure — the scientist in the white coat. To Milgram's astonishment, *all* the subjects were willing to go all the way. That is, they were willing to administer even the most severe, high-voltage shocks, and they were willing to do so despite the obvious pain, and even the protests, of the "learners." Some were reluctant to do so, but the scientist in the white coat insisted; he said that the experiment, once begun, had to be carried through to the end; he said the shocks were painful, but not dangerous; he said he would take full responsibility. And so the subjects — every one of them — ended up administering the most severe shocks.

Milgram then altered the experiment, increasing the likelihood, as he thought, that subjects would disobey the authority figure when ordered to give inhumane shocks. He moved the site of the experiment from New Haven to Bridgeport, pretending that it had nothing to do with Yale; for he reasoned that the prestige of Yale University had added weight to the authority of the white-coated scientist. And he removed the screen that separated teacher from learner; now they would be face-to-face; and Milgram reasoned that it is harder to inflict pain on a person you can see than on a person you can only hear. These changes made a difference, but not much of a difference. Some subjects refused to go all the way with the shocks, despite the best efforts of the white-coated scientist; but most continued to go all the way.

Milgram finally gave up on his plan to go to Germany for the second part of the study. His original hypothesis — that Germans would be much more willing than Americans to obey authority figures, even when these figures were ordering the commission of inhumane acts — was now useless. For how could anyone, Germans or anyone else, be more obedient than Americans had shown themselves to be? Milgram concluded that Americans are far more dangerous than he had ever suspected, willing to inflict torture on fellow humans simply because they were ordered to do so by someone in authority. We are lucky that no Hitler has appeared on the American scene, for if he did, he would have no shortage of followers.

But despite the immense popularity of Milgram's study, it proves nothing, because it is based on what logic textbooks call the "fallacy of equivocation." This fallacy arises when one uses a term that has two different meanings, and in the course of the argument shifts, with no one noticing, from one meaning to the other. The word *authority* is one such term. On the one hand, it means "having the right to command, to issue orders." A school principal, a police officer, and a state legislature are examples of this kind of authority. On the other hand, it means "one who is an expert." Examples of this kind of authority are doctors, lawyers, and weathermen; they speak with authority on matters of health, law, and weather.

What kind of authority was the white-coated scientist who presided at Milgram's experiment? Why, the *expertise* kind, of course. Milgram thought he had proven that Americans are ready to obey even inhumane orders from people in positions of command, but in reality all he has shown was that Americans are ready to trust experts. Indeed, American culture teaches us to trust experts: doctors, lawyers, scientists, engineers, et cetera. But it also teaches us to be somewhat *distrustful* of persons in positions of command. Every day the newspaper or TV tells us about a cop or a teacher or a priest or a politician or a corporate executive who abused the trust of those subject to his authority. Rarely does the news tell us of a scientific expert who abused the trust people placed in him by virtue of his expertise. So who can be surprised that Milgram's subjects trusted the white-coated scientist?

What is truly interesting about the Milgram experiment is not its scientific merit, for it has none, but the immense popularity it enjoyed during the period of the cultural revolution of the '60s and '70s. It seemed to confirm the notion, widespread among the young at the time, that America was a repressive society, as well as the parallel notion that one had an ethical right, even an obligation, to rebel against this repression by defying authority. A sensible and unprejudiced person in the year 1968 might have looked around and concluded that the United States was a society that allowed a great deal of personal freedom; so why was there all this talk, he might ask, about rebellion and defiance of authority? Knowing about Milgram's experiment allowed one to answer that it had been scientifically proven, by a Yale scientist no less, that Americans are Nazi-like in their willingness to obey cruel and inhuman commanders. Only by rebelling against authority and disrupting its institutions could we hope to bring real freedom to America.

Milgram's study and its popular reception was a symptom of the mentality of the times. *The Authoritarian Personality* was an important contributing cause of that mentality.

The virtue of rebellion comes into fashion

In conclusion, *The Authoritarian Personality* helped set the stage, during the '50s and early '60s, for the widespread rejection of authority that took place beginning in the mid-1960s. The book had its direct impact on the class of adult intellectuals, many of them college and university professors; but its influence "trickled down" to the younger generation — first to the aspiring intellectuals among them, and then to nearly all young persons, the vast majority of whom had never heard of the book.

The channels by which it trickled down included, of course, college classrooms. But that was far from the only channel, and probably far from the most important. The message was also communicated by Erich Fromm's books (far more readable, hence far more read, than *The Authoritarian Personality*), by the mass media, by churches and schools, by those who gave child-rearing advice to parents, et cetera. By a kind of cultural osmosis, young people absorbed the idea that an eagerness to obey those in authority was at best a suspicious character trait, at worst a very dangerous character defect. The obedient person was a potential fascist; even more so was the person in authority who insisted on being obeyed. Conversely, the rebel, the person who defied those in authority, was a person of fine character, for he had the very opposite of a fascist mentality. It is not surprising, then, that the late 1960s and early '70s were characterized by a widespread glorification of a new set of "three Rs": rebellion, rudeness, and rule-breaking.

Chapter 8

Secularism Emerges as the Dominant American Paradigm

Given the three factors described in the preceding five chapters — Vatican II, the end of the Catholic "ghetto," and the American cultural revolution that began in the mid-1960s — it is plain that Catholics were emerging from the Trent era and becoming full participants in American mainstream culture at precisely the moment when that culture was being revolutionized by a generalized rebellion against authority. The convergence of all three factors was a piece of great historical bad luck for the Catholic Church in the United States. It meant that American Catholicism was bound to undergo a sudden and rapid upheaval.

The first two of those factors were bound to converge, since the liquidation of the Trent era meant that Catholics would inevitably enter the American cultural mainstream. After all, since they were catching up with Protestants in terms of socioeconomic status, there was nothing keeping them out of the mainstream except their Tridentine anti-Protestantism; get rid of the Tridentine fortress mentality, and this last barrier would inevitably collapse.

The convergence of these two factors by themselves would have created a difficult enough experience. A "changeless" religion would have changed, thus damaging its legitimacy in the eyes of many of its members; and Catholics would have been exposed to the full force of a highly Protestantized American culture. Losses would certainly have followed. Many Catholics would have drifted away. The rate of intermarriage would have increased notably. The idea of a relatively non-dogmatic Christianity would have grown more appealing.

But these losses would have been small in comparison with the losses that actually took place. For it was the third converging factor — the general rebellion against authority (in other words, the Great American Cultural Revolution) — that turned a potentially minor squall into the perfect storm. Instead of entering the mainstream of a mainly Protestant American culture, Catholics were now becoming full members of an increasingly secularistic culture; for the cultural revolution of the '60s brought an end to the traditional Protestant hegemony in American cultural life and introduced a new, secularist hegemony.

For more than a century, Catholic leaders had been shielding their people from the influence of an alternative form of Christianity. Just at the moment when the gates were thrown open, when the leaders announced to their people, "The enemy is no longer dangerous, go and mingle," the old enemy, now grown toothless, was replaced with a new enemy.

And this new enemy, secularistic culture, was far from toothless. It was not just anti-Catholic; it was anti-Christian generally; it was even antitheistic. It had no use for the idea of a transcendental order of being; from which it followed that it had no use for the idea of a supernaturally based system of morality. Or perhaps the implication ran the other way around: perhaps the rejection of a morality based on supernaturalism came first and the rejection of a transcendental order of being, second. Either way, each implied the other.

Secularism's antinomian moral theory entailed a rejection of a long list of traditional, religion-based moral rules. Thus, it endorsed — or at any rate, soon would endorse, once it realized the implications of its premises — sexual license, cohabitation, easy divorce, abortion, homosexuality, euthanasia, and suicide. In its satirical mood, it ridiculed the married two-parent family ideal as a quaint "Ozzie and Harriet" notion. In its more philosophical mood, it denounced this family ideal as downright oppressive, oppressive above all to women; it was, to use the favorite analytic term of the more radical branch of the feminist movement, *patriarchal*. The two-parent family was also denounced as racist; since blacks were far more likely than whites to live in single-parent families, treating the married two-parent family as normative obviously had racist consequences, perhaps even racist motivations.

This was the new cultural world Catholics were invited to enter. What followed was catastrophic for the American Church.

Tolerance was secularism's cardinal virtue

This great transformation of American Catholicism meant, among other things, that Catholics had to adopt the mentality of "tolerance" that had long been characteristic of mainline American Protestantism. They adopted it, moreover, at a moment in American cultural history when this mentality was moving into its radical or extreme phase; at a moment, that is to say, when it was turning from an ideal of moderate tolerance into an ideal of virtually absolute tolerance.

Throughout most of its history, remember, the tolerance recommended by the mainline Protestant mentality had been far from absolute. During its first phase, although it tolerated all forms of Protestantism, this mentality had scant tolerance for non-Protestant forms of thought, whether these were religious or nonreligious; in those days, Catholicism was beyond the pale. In a later phase (the first half of the twentieth century), its tolerance became broader; it was now ready to put up with Catholic and Jewish forms of thought as well; but it was still far from prepared to smile upon atheism and agnosticism.

In neither of these phases did it go much beyond doctrinal tolerance to moral tolerance. Rather, it adhered to the traditional Protestant moral code and expected others to adhere to it. There were two notable exceptions to the traditional code, however: an insistence on the strict Puritan Sunday was dropped, since many Protestants wanted Sunday to be a day of sports and recreation; and an insistence on Protestant anti-drinking attitudes was dropped, since Catholics liked to drink and did not believe it to be sinful. These concessions aside, you were expected to be cheerful, honest, industrious, relatively chaste, careful with money, and civic-minded — the chief (and very excellent) virtues of Protestantism.

But the cultural revolution of the '60s and '70s thrust the tolerance mentality into its radical or absolutist phase. For by now, this mentality was no longer an essentially Protestant thing; now it was an essentially secularistic thing. Now all doctrines had to be tolerated, not just religious doctrines, but areligious and antireligious doctrines as well. And now (an even more drastic change) tolerance extended not just to doctrines, but to conduct. Apart from those kinds of conduct which, in an obvious, direct, and tangible way, hurt others or caused social disorder — murder, robbery, rape, et cetera — everything would have to be permitted. To do otherwise would be to commit the great sin of intolerance.

Thus no-fault divorce would have to be permitted; from now on, divorces could be carried out by mutual consent, simply because the two parties had grown tired of the relationship; or they could be effected unilaterally, if only one of the parties wanted out. In short, people were now as free to leave a marriage as they were free to enter one. They were even freer to leave than to enter; for it took the consent of two people to begin a marriage.[25]

---

[25] The nation's first no-fault divorce law was enacted in California in 1969, and in the next ten years, nearly every state in the union followed suit.

The spirit of absolute tolerance also justified other aspects of the sexual revolution (I say "other aspects," for no-fault divorce was itself an aspect of the sexual revolution). Fornication, including casual sex and "one-night stands," had to be permitted. And so did unmarried cohabitation, abortion, homosexuality, and pornography. For to the eye of the person with the absolute-tolerance mentality, these kinds of conduct produced no direct and tangible harm to others; hence, there was no reason for society to prohibit them — by law or by taboo.

American Catholicism fragments
in the aftermath of the cultural revolution

It was this cultural atmosphere, an atmosphere that began to dominate the United States in the late '60s and early '70s, that American Catholics began to breathe as soon as they were released from the confines of the old Catholic ghetto. Over the next decade or two, their varying responses to this atmosphere sorted Catholics into a number of groups.

First, there were those who embraced the new secularistic culture wholeheartedly; these were lost to the Church.

Second, there were those who, while finding the new culture attractive, were yet unwilling to desert the old religion; they hoped to work out a reconciliation between the two, a Catholicism leavened with the broad tolerance characteristic of secularism; these were the liberal or "progressive" Catholics.

Third, there were those repelled by the new culture and equally repelled by the progressives who wanted to introduce elements of it into Catholicism; they increasingly yearned for the good old days before Vatican II; these were the conservative or traditionalist Catholics.

Fourth and finally (and this may be the largest of all the groups), there was a great mass of bewildered Catholics, a mass that included many priests and not a few bishops. They remained committed to Catholicism and retained some nostalgia for the "good old days" before Vatican II. They remained attached to the Church as an institution while no longer being quite sure what that institution stood for. They had a vague feeling that there was something wrong with secularist culture and something odd about those who wanted to introduce elements of that culture into Catholicism; yet they did not feel sufficiently confident in their own beliefs to engage in open resistance to that culture. They were neither progressive Catholics nor traditionalist Catholics. They were wait-and-see Catholics.

These four factions, which had emerged by the late 1960s, can still be found today, and it is still not clear which of them, or which combination of them, will definitively determine the future of American Catholicism. If the first faction prevails, Catholicism will simply wither away. If the second, Catholicism will become a branch of liberal Christianity and, again, it will wither away, only this time more slowly. If the third, American Catholicism will become a kind of curious museum-piece, authentically Catholic yet having little to do with the big world of American society, not affecting it very much, nor being affected by it — a new quasi-ghetto. If the fourth, Catholicism may have a viable future in America, but only if this fourth group abandons its wait-and-see attitude and comes to stand for something definite and something sound. Will this happen? Who knows?[26]

---

[26] More on this in the final chapter of the book.

Part III

Evolution of a National Religion

Chapter 9

America as a Moral
and Religious Community

In the first part of the book, we looked at three great social factors
that transformed American Catholicism about three or four decades ago: Vatican II, the end of the Catholic "ghetto," and the
great American cultural revolution of the 1960s and '70s. In the
second part, we looked at the theoretical underpinnings of the cultural revolution: cultural and moral relativism, ethical emotivism,
and the theory of the authoritarian personality. By the late 1960s,
cultural hegemony was shifting from mainline Protestantism to a
form of secularism that was out to raze the traditional Christian
moral code — especially as it related to sexual matters.

In this part of the book, we will examine the crisis of the national
moral community that arose with the new prominence of secularism. The national moral community had always had a more or less
religious foundation, and this foundation had always been Christian or Judeo-Christian. But the rise of secularism meant that the
community could no longer have a religious basis; its basis would
have to be purely moral. If so, what kind of morality would that be?

The United States is a moral community
In saying that the United States, since its foundation, has been
a "moral community," I have in mind a contrast between a moral

community on the one hand and a "utilitarian association" on the other. The latter is typically a commercial relationship, such as that between the seller and the buyer of a loaf of bread. The association benefits both parties: the buyer gets bread; the seller gets a dollar. Yet neither party is fundamentally motivated by a desire to benefit the other. The fundamental desire is to benefit oneself. To the degree that a wish to benefit the other exists, it is strictly subordinate to the basic goal — namely, benefitting oneself. In other words, the defining characteristics of the utilitarian association is egoism, as opposed to altruism.

A second characteristic of a utilitarian association is its high degree of specificity. The buyer is interested in his partner only as a potential seller of bread; and the seller is interested in his partner only a potential buyer of bread. Neither cares about the other's race, religion, sex, ethnicity, occupation, political loyalties, or favorite NBA team; nor does either care about how the other leads his life, whether the other is good or bad, wise or foolish. To the degree either one does care about any of these things, the relationship becomes less than — or rather, something other than — purely utilitarian.

Moral communities, by contrast, are altruistic and general. Think of a normal family as a typical example. Members of a moral community are altruistic in that they are genuinely concerned about the well-being of other members of the community and feel a sense of responsibility for them. The members of a moral community do not, of course, have to mimic Mother Teresa. But they have to be at least somewhat altruistic; they cannot operate on the purely egoistic basis that characterizes utilitarian associations. Further, this concern for the well-being of others is a very general concern — a concern for their physical, financial, intellectual, and moral well-being. It is a concern that they be well-off generally and over the long run, a concern that they lead worthwhile lives.

In saying that the United States is a moral community, I have no intention of denying that it is also a utilitarian association. It is both, as is any normal nation, and in concrete practice, the two are deeply intermingled with one another. It might be argued, however, that in recent times, the equilibrium between the two has been lost, and that the balance has tipped in the utilitarian direction. If so, this explains a number of contemporary phenomena: why Americans have become more egoistic; why we seem to be less concerned with helping our less fortunate fellow citizens; why we are, on the whole, relatively untroubled by the poor moral character of politicians or celebrities. Nonetheless, these trends have not yet destroyed the national moral community; the United States is still a long way from being a purely utilitarian association.

The clearest illustration of this in recent years was the national reaction to the terrorist attacks of September 11, 2001. Americans did not react to these attacks by saying, "What a pity; this is bad for the economy." No, there was, at least for a few months, a tremendous upsurge of national solidarity. Everywhere flags were flying: from front porches, from automobile antennas, from the lapels of suit jackets. Among Americans, there was a spontaneous sense that we were all together in this, that the attacks that killed a few thousand of our fellow citizens were attacks on all of us. There was that spirit of altruism and concern for others which is at the heart of a moral community.

The United States is also a religious community

In saying that the United States is (or at least has been) a religious community, I am relying on sociologist Robert Bellah's notion of "civil religion." The United States, Bellah argues in a famous essay written in the 1960s,[27] has had a civil religion from its

---

[27] "Civil Religion in America," *Daedalus*, Winter 1967; reprinted in Bellah, *Beyond Belief* (New York: Harper and Row, 1976).

earliest days, a religion accurately reflected in the inaugural addresses of the American presidents, every one of which contains a reference to God. This God is not a specifically Christian God, even though most Americans have always been Christian; presidential addresses never mention Jesus Christ or the Trinity. Rather, the God of the American civil religion is a nondenominational God having at best a moderately biblical flavor. One of the functions of this God is to bless and protect America, to guide it on its historical progress.

But God is not simply a patron who always promotes the interests of his American client, no matter how ill-behaved the latter may be. He is a God of righteousness, and he demands righteousness from the United States. It follows that he is a judge, a judge who will reward the United States for its righteousness, yet punish it for its sins. The nation has a divine protector, yes; but at the same time, the nation stands under judgment. The very best articulation of the articles of this American civil religion, says Bellah, is to be found in Abraham Lincoln's Second Inaugural Address, where the president talks about the sufferings of the Civil War as God's punishment for America's long sin of slavery.

For the individual American, the national civil religion is not an alternative to the religion of a particular church — as though one had to choose between it and, say, Methodism. No, you can have both at once. You cannot, of course, be a Methodist and a Catholic at the same time, but you can simultaneously be both a Methodist or a Catholic as well as an adherent to the national faith. There is, by definition, nothing in the American civil religion incompatible with any particular religion that flourishes in the United States. Ideally, no matter what particular churches we may worship at, we can all worship the God who keeps a watchful eye on the United States.

Chapter 10

A Protestant Nation
Becomes Judeo-Christian

To understand better this thing called the American moral community, let us turn now to a historical account of its founding and development, giving particular attention to its religious dimension.

Before the American Revolution, a number of colonies were the homes of established churches, churches that received taxpayer support and other special privileges, e.g., the Anglican Church in Virginia and the Congregational Church in Massachusetts and Connecticut. In the seventeenth century, some persecution of non-established religions took place. Massachusetts exiled Roger Williams and Anne Hutchinson to what became Rhode Island and, a few years later, put to death a small number of Quakers who had entered the Bay Colony from Rhode Island. But for the most part, nonestablished churches were tolerated in the colonial era. This meant that those belonging to these lesser churches were members of the colonial community, but in places like Virginia and Massachusetts, they were second-class members, marginal members.

Established state churches give way
to an unofficial national religion

With the coming of the Revolution, established churches disappeared in some places (in Virginia, for example, at the initiative of Thomas Jefferson and James Madison), while fading away, without fully disappearing, in others. Massachusetts, for instance, did not totally abolish taxpayer support of its fading establishment (which, by that date, included both Congregational and Unitarian churches) until the second quarter of the nineteenth century. But whatever remnants of state establishments may have remained in the new republican era, the nation as a whole had no established church. The First Amendment to the Constitution made it clear that the federal government would support no official religion.

But even if the United States had no official religion, it did have an unofficial one. If it had no formal faith, it had an informal one. If it had no government-supported national religion, it had a privately supported national religion. This informal, unofficial national religion may be called "generic Protestantism." The nation was not just a political community; it was a religious community — a kind of church in the strict sociological sense of the word *church*, a religious body to which virtually the entire nation belonged.

The Protestant tent, of course, was exceedingly capacious; it covered a wide and very diverse range of individual churches, from Particular Baptists at one end of the spectrum to Unitarians at the other. Of course, individual churches disputed with one another, often intensely. But there remained a generic Protestantism on which all agreed. The articles of this generic creed were few; for, of course, nothing could be included in the generic creed that would give offense to any particular church. Most of these were positive articles: that God existed; that the Bible was the word of God and the rule of faith for Christians; that Jesus was sent by God to teach mankind, by word and example, the way to Heaven; that the moral code taught by Jesus was the highest and best morality; that there was life after death; that, in the next life, the saints would live with God.

American Protestantism was
united in its animus toward Rome

But there was at least one great negative article: that the Church of Rome was a false church, that the pope was a fraud, that the religion taught by Rome and its pope was a terrible distortion of true Christianity. Protestants could not agree among themselves as to what "true Christianity" was, but they could all agree on one thing: whatever it was, it was not Roman Catholicism.

A thousand examples can be found of this taken-for-granted bias against Catholicism, but one of the most striking is William Ellery Channing's 1836 "Letter on Catholicism." Channing, who may be called the father of American Unitarianism, was among the most liberal Protestants of his age. No one was more tolerant; no one made a greater effort at sympathetically understanding the point of view of persons who differed from him in opinion. And hardly any American Protestants were friendlier to Catholics. Channing maintained a personal friendship with the Catholic Bishop of Boston; he led the respectable Protestants of Boston in denouncing and atoning for the burning, by a Protestant anti-Catholic mob, of a Catholic convent in the Boston suburb of Charlestown; and in 1829, he wrote a long and very sympathetic essay on the life and writings of the Catholic Archbishop of Cambrai (France), François Fénelon (1651-1751).

If any Protestant of this early American period might have been expected to hold a favorable — or at least a fair-minded — view of the Catholic religion, it would be Channing. But even Channing was not able to rise above the standard Protestant prejudices of the day, saying of Catholicism, "The creation of dark times, it cannot stand before the light" — that is, the light of modern enlightenment and spiritual progress.[28]

---

[28] *The Works of William E. Channing, D.D.* (Boston: American Unitarian Association, 1886), 471.

Another striking example, also from liberal Boston, can be found in the career of Orestes Brownson, the most important intellectual convert to Catholicism in nineteenth-century America. Prior to his conversion, Brownson had played an important role in the Boston Unitarian and Transcendentalist scene, a friend of Channing and Emerson and Theodore Parker, among many others. But when, in 1844, he converted to Catholicism, it was as if he had fallen off the edge of the earth. No matter how tolerant these intellectual New England gentlemen were, and no matter what sympathy they had for medieval and Renaissance Catholic art (a sympathy that was rapidly growing at this time), they just could not take seriously a modern man who embraced Catholicism. It was clear that he had destroyed his intellect, that he no longer had anything to say that any thinking person would care to waste his time hearing.

The Anglo roots of early
American anti-Catholicism

To appreciate how traditional and how deeply rooted American anti-Catholicism was, it will be helpful briefly to review its history; which includes reviewing its history in England, for the prehistory of American anti-Catholicism was to be found in English anti-Catholicism.

Anti-Catholicism was an old thing in the Anglo-American world, going back to the reign of Henry VIII in the sixteenth century. The king himself, despite his rebellion against Rome, held Catholic views with regard both to doctrine and to the sacraments, and he was even Catholic in his opposition to a married clergy. (How ironic that Henry, who married six times himself, was unwilling to allow priests to marry even once!) But he was decidedly un-Catholic in at least two things: his rejection of the pope's authority and his destruction of monasticism. And those who remained fully Catholic (like Thomas More) — not semi-Catholic, like the king — were considered enemies of the realm and could be punished with death.

Anti-Catholicism grew apace during the reign of Henry's only son, the boy-king Edward VI. At Edward's death (while he was still a teenager) a pro-Catholic reaction took place under Queen Mary (daughter of Henry by his first wife, the Catholic Catherine of Aragon); but her strenuous persecution of Protestants — a persecution that won her the infamous title "Bloody Mary" — confirmed them in their intense anti-Catholicism.

The next ruler, Elizabeth (Henry's daughter by his second wife, Anne Boleyn), restored Protestantism. And soon thereafter, the pope declared her to be of illegitimate birth and therefore no true ruler of England; the pope, in effect, was encouraging rebellion against the queen. Not surprisingly, Elizabeth made the practice of Catholicism illegal and put to death missionary priests who came into England from the Continent. She also put to death Mary Stuart ("Mary Queen of Scots"), for Mary was a Catholic who perhaps had a better legal claim to the throne than Elizabeth. Mary was suspected of trying to seize the throne, and the Catholics of England were considered accomplices to treason. Catholics were also suspected of a willingness to rise against Elizabeth in the event of an invasion by Phillip II of Spain — a rising that was averted when Phillip's famous *Armada* came to grief in 1588.

Early in the next reign, that of James I (the Protestant son of Mary Stuart), the very worst Protestant suspicions against Catholics were confirmed in spades when the "Gunpowder Plot" was revealed. Guy Fawkes and a number of other discontented Catholics, bitterly disappointed that the new king had failed to ease the Elizabethan anti-Catholic policies, despite pre-coronation hints that he would do so, planned to blow up the Parliament building at a moment when the king and both houses were present. A great quantity of gunpowder in the basement was discovered at the last moment, thus averting a simultaneous assassination of the entire

Protestant leadership of the kingdom.[29] Could there any longer be doubt in the mind of the average English Protestant that Catholics were, almost by their very nature, treacherous and anti-English?

The next king, Charles I (son of James I), was believed by the more thoroughgoing Protestants (that is, the Presbyterians and other "Puritans") to be an aspirant to tyranny, as well as sympathetic to Catholicism. Civil war broke out; the king lost and had his head chopped off in 1649. Cromwell and the Commonwealth followed, which meant that, for more than ten years, England was ruled by the most Protestant of the Protestants, by the most anti-Catholic of the anti-Catholics. The now-settled Protestant conviction that Catholics were essentially anti-English and pro-tyranny served to justify Cromwell and his lieutenants in their brutal repression of the Catholics of Ireland, including the mass slaughter of Drogheda.[30]

In 1660, the monarchy was restored, and although the king, Charles II (son of the executed "martyr" Charles I), was sympathetic to Catholicism and would eventually, in 1685, be received into the Church on his deathbed, this did little to mitigate Protestant anti-Catholic prejudices. If anything, it stimulated them; for Protestants feared, not without some cause, that the king hoped to restore the fortunes of English Catholicism and that he was ready to do so with the help of the great national enemy, Louis XIV of France.

When the Great Fire of London broke out in 1666, destroying most of the city of London, it was commonly — although quite

[29] A highly readable account of the plot can be found in Antonia Fraser, *Faith and Treason: The Story of the Gunpowder Plot* (Doubleday Anchor Books, 1996).

[30] English forces led by Oliver Cromwell killed as many as four thousand residents of the Irish town of Drogheda in 1649 as punishment for Northern Irish insurgency.

erroneously — believed that Catholics had deliberately set the fire. When, some years later, the Monument was erected to commemorate the fire, an inscription on the Monument reiterated this slander in stone; after all, this is the kind of thing Protestants had come to expect from Catholics. A furious "witch hunt" of Catholics began in the 1670s when rumors of a "popish plot" swept the country, and thirteen guiltless Catholics (about half of them Jesuits) plus one Protestant were sent to the gallows.[31]

Anti-Catholicism in England reached its summit in the 1680s and '90s. In 1685, James II succeeded his brother, who died without a legitimate heir. Unlike his politically shrewd elder brother, James did not wait until reaching his deathbed to enter the Church. He became a Catholic, an openly declared Catholic at that, many years before ascending the throne. Protestants quite naturally dreaded the thought of a Catholic king, but they consoled themselves that his only children, Mary and Anne, had been

[31] An amusing anecdote symbolizes the anti-Catholicism of the reign of Charles II. The king may have been fundamentally Catholic in sympathies, but these sympathies did not extend to Catholic teachings on the duties of chastity and marital fidelity. The king had always been quite a ladies' man, and his tendencies in this direction were not curtailed when he married the Portuguese Catholic princess, Catherine of Braganza. While on the throne, he had a series of mistresses; and, as befits one who believed, as he did, in religious toleration, some of these mistresses were Catholic and some Protestant. One of them was the leading stage actress of the day, Nell Gwynn. One day, when Nell was leaving the palace following an assignation with the king, her closed carriage was stopped and surrounded by a mob of angry Protestants, shouting, "Death to the Catholic whore! Death to the Catholic whore!" The situation was dangerous, but the great actress rose to the occasion. She emerged from the carriage. "Be at ease, good people, be at ease!" she declared in her best Drury Lane manner. " 'Tis not the Catholic whore; 'tis the Protestant whore." Whereupon the mob, satisfied at the king's rectitude, peacefully dispersed.

raised Protestant; so James's successor would be religiously correct. Then the king, a widower, married again, this time to a young Catholic princess from Italy, Mary of Modena. Mary bore him a child, a boy, who was, of course, baptized a Catholic; and according to English law, the son of a monarch takes precedence over the daughters, even though the latter may be older. So England was scheduled to have yet another Catholic king upon the death of James, and after that a probably indefinite series of Catholic kings.

This would never do. Protestant unhappiness with this situation was manifested in a sensational rumor that soon began circulating: that Mary had not really given birth to a son; rather, a non-royal baby had been smuggled into Mary's room in a warming-pan, and now this fraudulent baby, in order to secure a Catholic succession, was being presented to the nation as the king's son. So treacherous were Catholics, believed much of the country, that they would stoop even to a cheap trick like this.

Imprudent politician that he was, James then handed his Protestant opponents a sword to use against him. He began removing Protestants from office and, in spite of a law prohibiting it, appointed a considerable number of his fellow Catholics to civil and military posts. He reformed the English army in Ireland so that it was now officered by Catholic commanders. He even engineered a Catholic takeover of Magdelen College in Oxford. He then made his fatal mistake when he issued a "declaration of indulgence," a royal decree suspending laws restricting religious freedom for Catholics and Nonconformists (Protestants, in almost all cases Puritans, who did not conform to the Church of England).

This was unacceptable to the Nonconformists, the most intensely anti-Catholic of all Protestants; they would rather remain unfree than win their freedom in company with Catholics. It was also unacceptable to the Church of England, which insisted that the law should continue to discriminate against both Catholic and Nonconformist. A number of bishops disobeyed the king's command that his declaration should be read from the pulpit of all churches, and when the king had them prosecuted, the jury acquitted them. Now the dam burst. The enemies of the king invited William of Orange (the husband of James's daughter Mary) into England; the commander of James's army, his old friend John Churchill (the ancestor of Winston Churchill), deserted the king; James fled the kingdom to France (1688); and the Parliament, declaring that the king's flight was tantamount to abdication, presented the crown to William and Mary (1689). After James's unsuccessful attempt to regain his throne with the aid of Louis XIV, the game was up.

This was the so-called "Bloodless Revolution" or "Glorious Revolution." A king had been removed because — so the standard justification ran — he was a would-be tyrant bent on imposing the system of papist superstition and ecclesiastical tyranny on the good Protestant people of England, and what is more, he tried to do it with the help of the nation's great enemy, Louis XIV of France.

A terrible repression now fell on the Irish Catholics. Things had been bad enough after their defeat by Cromwell. Now things suddenly got much worse as the regime of "penal laws" was introduced, a regime that lasted for a century and more, reducing the average Catholic to a condition of misery and virtual slavery. "Was this not cruel?" one might ask English Protestants of the time. "Yes," they would reply, "but what else are we to do with people who, by the very nature of their religion, are superstitious, traitorous, and pro-tyranny?"[32]

---

[32] The degree of anti-Catholicism at this time can be measured by the attitude of John Locke, good friend of the Protestant political leader, the Earl of Shaftesbury, and author of the standard philosophical justification of the Glorious Revolution, *The Second Treatise of Government*. Locke was not a fanatic Protestant who felt a visceral hatred for Catholics.

The Decline and Fall of the Catholic Church in America

After the Glorious Revolution, the few English Catholics who remained hardly dared to show their heads for the next century or so. When in 1745 to 1746, Charles Edward Stuart (the "Young Pretender," known in Scottish sentimental legend as "Bonnie Prince Charlie") invaded England with a small army of Highlanders, there was no English Catholic rising to support him. They had been thoroughly whipped. In the eighteenth century, the wickedness of Catholics was a taken-for-granted truth among most Englishmen, but the fear of Catholicism waned; for who could fear an enemy who had been so totally crushed? And yet, so deeply rooted was anti-Catholicism in the English Protestant psyche, that even as late as 1780, the old ferocious bigotry could break out again in the Lord Gordon Riots.[33]

It was not until 1829 — nearly a century and a half after the final defeat of Catholicism in the Glorious Revolution — that anti-Catholic prejudice had abated sufficiently for Parliament to

Rather, he was very much a religious moderate, a latitudinarian who strongly disapproved of what he called religious "enthusiasm" (see "Of Enthusiasm," in his *Essay Concerning Human Understanding*, Bk. 4, ch. 19). Thus, he was a great champion of religious toleration. Yet his toleration did not extend to Catholics. Obviously speaking of the Catholic Church, he said, "That church can have no right to be tolerated by the magistrate which is constituted upon such a bottom that all those who enter into it do thereby *ipso facto* deliver themselves up to the protection and service of another prince," i.e., the pope (*A Letter Concerning Toleration* [Indianapolis: Bobbs-Merrill, 1950], 51; first published in English in 1691). Mild-mannered though he was, both by temperament and by conviction, even Locke was anti-Catholic; even Locke felt that being a good Catholic and being a good Englishman were contradictory attributes.

[33] A mob of some sixty thousand burned down Catholic homes and buildings in London, killing hundreds, in protest of religious tolerations laws favorable to Catholics. These riots play a major role in the Dickens novel *Barnaby Rudge*.

pass a law granting so-called "Catholic Emancipation," which gave the Catholics of Great Britain (including Ireland) the right to vote and to hold civil and military office. And even at that late date, there was strong opposition to this measure; getting it passed in Parliament was no easy matter. When emancipation had first been suggested by the prime minister, the Duke of Wellington, a few years earlier, it was blocked by the opposition of King George III, who, in his increasingly rare lucid moments, was able to remember his anti-Catholic prejudices. The king held that to agree to full civil equality for Catholics would be a violation of his coronation oath, which required him to defend the Church of England.

English anti-Catholicism
crosses the Atlantic

This profound English anti-Catholicism came to America with the English settlers of the seventeenth and eighteenth centuries. This was particularly true in the northern colonies, above all in New England, where Puritans dominated. All English Protestants, regardless of specific denomination, were, of course, anti-Catholic; but the more thoroughgoing their Protestantism, the more anti-Catholic they were likely to be. These northern Protestants represented, in words Edmund Burke would utter in 1775, "the dissidence of dissent and the Protestantism of the Protestant religion."[34] Hence, they were quite thoroughly anti-Catholic.

By the time of the American Revolution, more radical forms of Protestantism had spread even to the southern states — not Congregationalism, which never flourished outside New England, but Baptist and Methodist churches. On average, then, the Protestant "temperature" of the new republic was much higher than it was in England. For in England, the great majority of people still

[34] Burke's "Speech on Conciliation with America."

belonged to the established church, which was far less intensely Protestant than were the dissenting churches — Congregationalists, Presbyterians, Baptists, Quakers, and Methodists — while in the United States, almost everybody with a religious affiliation belonged to a dissenting church. So if anti-Catholicism was a strong prejudice in England, it was even a stronger prejudice in America.

From the beginning, then, anti-Catholicism was part of the cultural legacy that the new republic inherited from the mother country — along with its language, its literature, its religion, its education, its spirit of commerce, its laws, and its basic constitutional structure. It was deeply dyed into the American fabric, and it would take the better part of two centuries to eliminate it.

For that matter, it is not totally eliminated even to this day. Among certain Protestant fundamentalist sects, one can find that the old anti-Catholicism is still alive and well: the pope is still the anti-Christ, and the Church of Rome still the whore of Babylon. One of the "fundamentals" of classic Protestantism, especially of its Anglo-American variety, has always been the belief that Catholicism is a false and wicked religion, a vile betrayal of Christianity and a danger to the nation.[35]

[35] The classic statement of what came to be called Protestant fundamentalism was given in a twelve-volume work initiated in 1909, titled *The Fundamentals*. These volumes were a collection of scores of essays that did battle against the many enemies of traditional Protestantism: modern philosophy, Darwinism, the higher criticism of the Bible, liberal or modernistic Protestantism, Mormonism, Christian Science, and, of course, Catholicism. The two anti-Catholicism essays contained in the volumes are titled "Is Romanism Christianity?" and "Rome, the Antagonist of the Nation." A four-volume edition of this work, slightly abridged, was published in 1917 under the title *The Fundamentals: A Testimony to the Truth*. This work was republished by Baker Books of Grand Rapids, Michigan, in 1998.

A Protestant Nation Becomes Judeo-Christian

Catholic and Jewish immigrants
enter the national community

Generic Protestantism was the unofficial national religion of the United States prior to the first great influx of Catholic immigrants, many of them refugees from the Irish famine, about the middle of the nineteenth century. Given this unofficial religion, Catholics could expect to be no more than marginal members of the national community. The same was true of the even smaller numbers of Jews, secularists, and other non-Protestants. It was also true of the Mormons, who, although perhaps Protestant in some very loose sense of that word, put themselves outside the generic Protestant church by their shocking beliefs and practices: their claim that Joseph Smith was a God-inspired prophet, their amendment to the biblical canon (the Book of Mormon), and, most shocking of all, their polygamy.

The mid-century influx of Catholics to the United States — especially to the urban centers of the Northeast, where, in a short time, they became a significant fraction of the population and an important political force — did nothing, at least in the short run, to alter the boundaries of the national church. Just the opposite: it hardened those boundaries; it gave Protestants a sharper sense than ever of their common Protestant identity. It was one thing to belong to an anti-Catholic religion when Catholicism was little more than an abstraction, the religion of the distant pope of Rome. It was something else when large numbers of Catholics were living just across the railroad tracks and threatening to take over city hall. No doubt these American Catholics would have to be recognized as members of the national community — but they were marginal members, triply marginal: first as Catholics, second as immigrants, third as poor. The line between Protestantism and Catholicism was no longer an abstract theological line; now it was a concrete sociological line dividing "real" Americans from marginal Americans.

The Decline and Fall of the Catholic Church in America

No sooner had the nation begun gradually to assimilate the Irish Catholics than a newer, bigger, and even more exotic flow of immigrants came into the United States. Beginning in the 1880s and continuing for thirty years, until the outbreak of World War I, Catholics from Italy and the Slavic countries, as well as Jews from the Russian Empire, flooded into America. The earlier Irish may have looked strange to American Protestant eyes, but at least they spoke English (almost all of them), and in their homeland they had had some experience of popular government and the common law. But look at these people from southern and eastern Europe — no English language; no common law; scant, if any, experience with democracy.

And although the Irish, Italians, and Poles adhered to a perverse form of Christianity, at least it was a form of Christianity. The Jews, on the other hand, were introducing an ancient non-Christian religion to the United States. Not perfectly new perhaps, since some German Jews had come into the country earlier in the nineteenth century, and some Portuguese and Spanish Jews had been here since the colonial era. But these earlier Jews had been very small in number, hardly noticeable, nothing to worry about. Besides, by now they were Westernized, modernized; they didn't have a "Jewish" ethnic style; they were not redolent of the ghetto. These newer eastern Jews, by contrast, were too numerous to ignore, and they were very "Jewish" indeed.

What was to be done? Were the boundaries of the national community to be expanded to take these new immigrants in as full-fledged members, as first-class citizens? Well, not yet. Perhaps someday, but not today. In view of the great numbers of non-Protestants now in the country, it was perhaps unrealistic to expect that the American national community could remain permanently a Protestant community. But these people would have to become more Americanized before they could be granted full membership. In the meantime, they would be relegated to the margins while the unofficial national church would be kept generically Protestant.

The national moral community
struggles to accept Catholics and Jews

If the first generation of immigrants could be successfully excluded from full membership in the national community, this policy of exclusion became increasingly difficult to maintain with their children and grandchildren. For one thing, the latter were no longer immigrants; for another, most of them soon ceased to be poor. (Upward mobility was particularly rapid among the Jews; the Catholic groups moved upward more slowly, but just as surely.) The only discordant note remaining was their religion. How long could native-born, law-abiding, well-educated, middle-class Americans be excluded from full membership in the national community simply because of their religion? Something had to give; and when it did, the United States, if it wished to remain a religious community, would have to redefine the content of the unofficial national religion.

One possible way of doing it would be to switch from a generic Protestant basis to a generic Christian basis. This would give us a national religion suitable for both Protestants and Catholics, who together made up the overwhelming majority of the American population; it would also be suitable for Mormons and Eastern Orthodox Christians.

But it would be unsuitable for Jews — a fatal objection. The Jews were small in numbers: at their peak, no more than 4 percent of the total United States population, as opposed to the 25 percent that the Catholics came to represent. (Today, this Jewish share is only a little above 2 percent.) But the Jews were hardly any more objectionable than the Catholics; if the latter were to be welcomed in, why not the former? Besides, the Jews had Americanized quickly, more quickly than any other immigrant group, rising rapidly into the middle classes sooner than the Irish, Italians, or Slavs. They became highly educated and adopted American political, social, and economic values. Even in religion, they had semi-Americanized, most of them abandoning the exotic Orthodox form of their faith and adopting instead the more modernized Conservative or Reform forms.

Moreover, Jews were coming to have an influence in American life beyond what might have been expected on the basis of their numbers alone. Their high levels of education and income, along with their outstanding achievements in law, medicine, science, scholarship, journalism, and the arts (especially popular entertainment: Hollywood and Broadway), made it absurd to claim that they would have to remain marginal or second-class members of American society. They were unlikely to put up with this quietly — in striking contrast, say, to black Americans, who, for nearly a century after the Civil War, made few effective protests against their treatment as third-class Americans.

The religious community
is renamed to include Jews

So a solution would have to be found that would allow Jews as well as Catholics to become full members of the national community, to become "real" Americans. The solution was to redefine our hitherto generically Protestant national religion, not as generic Christianity, but rather as generic *Judeo-Christianity*. Thus, in the 1930s and 1940s, new expressions began to appear in speeches and in print: references were increasingly made to "our Judeo-Christian heritage" and "our Judeo-Christian traditions."

The experience of the Great Depression and, even more, the experience of World War II impressed a deep sense of national solidarity on the American people. It was now relatively easy to feel we were all in the same boat, regardless of our many distinct religions; and since we had all prayed to the same God to get us through depression and war, it was easy to feel that we all shared a common faith. By the 1950s, *Judeo-Christian* had become a common — or rather, canonical — adjective. Equally canonical had become references to the American people as being made up of "Protestants, Catholics, and Jews" — our national religious trinity. In other words, the unofficial national religion had been successfully redefined.

Emotionally, it had not been easy to redefine the national faith. Evidence for this is the fact that it must have been clear from about the middle of the nineteenth century that the redefinition would eventually have to take place, yet it was not successfully done until the middle of the twentieth century. Intellectually, however, only a few modifications were called for. No more nasty slights against the papacy would be allowed. References to the Bible would have to have a degree of ambiguity in them, so as not to accent the fact that Christians counted both testaments in their Bible, while Jews counted only the older testament. References to Jesus would have to be very discreet; it would not be enough to avoid mentioning his divinity, which, even in the era of generic Protestantism, had been avoided out of respect for the Unitarians; now, in order not to offend Jews, one would have to avoid claiming that Jesus was anything more than a first-class ethical teacher and role model. But the rest of the old generic Protestantism could be retained: God, God's providence, the (ambiguous) Bible, the Ten Commandments, life after death. The consensus would be "thinner," but still substantial.

Chapter 11

The End of the Judeo-Christian Era

This new national faith, so long in preparation, enjoyed rather a short run on the stage. Its golden age was the immediate postwar period, especially the 1950s; the age of the baby boom, the expanding suburbs, the Cold War, Ozzie and Harriet, Elvis, and the Montgomery bus boycott was also the age of the celebration of our "Judeo-Christian heritage."

The United States Supreme Court announced the end of this Judeo-Christian era in the summer of 1962, when, in *Engle v. Vitale*, it ruled that the Constitution prohibited officially sponsored prayer in public schools. The ban was implied, reasoned the court, by the No-Establishment Clause of the First Amendment. This book is not the place to discuss the legal aspects of this decision, a decision that still causes political tempers to boil nearly half a century after the event. Instead, I want to discuss some of its sociological aspects.

Viewed sociologically, the prayer decision was a recognition by the court that *not all* citizens of the United States are religious believers. If the United States had truly been, as the prevailing national religion assumed, a Judeo-Christian nation, there would have been no objection to the practice of school prayer, at least no objection in principle. There might, of course, have been objections to this or that particular prayer; but the court did not ban a particular prayer; it banned all prayer.

Enter secularism
and John Dewey, its prophet

The truth is that, by the early 1960s, American society contained another non-negligible group in addition to Protestants, Catholics, and Jews. These were the unbelievers, the secularists, the naturalists, the atheists and agnostics. They can be called by a variety of names, but they all come down to the same thing: these people were neither Christians nor Jews nor members of any other religious faith (if they happened to be Jews, they were so in an ethnic sense only). They did not believe in prayer; they did not believe in life after death; they did not believe that morality is in any way founded upon the nature or will of God. Indeed they doubted God's very existence. They believed that the universe, including its human element, is to be explained, to the degree it can be explained at all, in purely naturalistic terms. In short, they rejected the consensus that formed the basis of the short-lived Judeo-Christian national faith.

These secularists were not like the atheists of old. Old-fashioned American atheists were akin to the classical "village atheist," that is, they were negative and destructive, mainly concerned with denying what believers believed; and if, in the course of this denial, they shocked religious believers, so much the better.[36] Those secularists more typical of the twentieth century, on the other hand, tended to be positive, constructive. They were not about to waste time denying the supernatural; rather, they took that denial for

---

[36] A famous example of the old-fashioned atheist was Clarence Darrow, the great defense attorney who defended, among others, Eugene Debs, Leopold and Loeb, and John Scopes (of "Monkey Trial" fame). In his autobiography, *The Story of My Life*, Darrow is not at all shy about putting on display his skeptical and sarcastic attitude toward Christianity and the Bible. His book was originally published in New York by Charles Scribner's Sons in 1932; it was republished in New York by the Da Capo Press in 1996.

granted and moved on to giving a naturalistic account of the world and human life.

The model secularist in the first half of the twentieth century, the great prophet of modern American secularism, was the philosopher John Dewey (1859-1952). Dewey wrote an immense number of books and essays about a vast range of philosophical subjects, including metaphysics, epistemology, logic, psychology, sociology, politics, education, ethics, and aesthetics. He constructed a world-model that made no appeal to God or the supernatural; a world-model put together out of purely naturalistic materials. But his denial of God's existence was always merely implicit; he never took the trouble to write antitheistic tracts. (Dewey would never have written, for instance, a work like that written by his philosophical contemporary, Bertrand Russell, "Why I Am Not a Christian.") He was writing for a readership that took it for granted that these subjects could be discussed without bringing God in, either because there is no God or because God was irrelevant to serious philosophical discussion.

Dewey's influence was enormous and his writings widely read (although not for their literary charm, for they have none; Dewey was a tedious writer). Dewey's writings were read because they expressed the ideas and sentiments of a large class of intellectual Americans. These people felt no need for God, nor did they need anyone to prove to them that God was an outmoded idea. But as they saw it, it was not enough simply to reject God. That may have been fine for pioneer secularists and naturalists of earlier generations, the village atheists; but it was not good enough for them. For they were no longer pioneers; they were settlers; they intended to live normal human lives within the borders of naturalism. A merely negative naturalism would not be able to compete successfully with traditional supernaturalism, no matter how far behind the times the latter might be. A positive, sophisticated naturalism was needed, one that could explain the world and human experience in a more coherent and comprehensive way than supernaturalism could. In the eyes of his readers, it was this kind of explanation Dewey provided.

Why intellectuals have tended to be secularists

This naturalism/secularism of the first half of the twentieth century was not a mass phenomenon; it was pretty much confined to a highly educated elite. It was not found among the working and middle classes; it was not found even among most sections of the affluent classes. Rather, it was a worldview found, when found at all, among intellectuals and academics, especially academics at the nation's leading universities.

Why this was so is difficult to understand. There had not always been this natural affinity between intellectualism and religious disbelief. Until after the Civil War, in fact, American intellectuals took religious belief quite seriously.

Very tentatively, let me suggest a few explanations.

For one, many modern American intellectuals have been affiliated with great research universities. This means they have mastered a vast body of genuine knowledge; and this knowledge, modern science being what it is, has no supernatural component. Neither the natural sciences nor the social sciences explain anything in terms of supernatural forces. Original works of literature and the fine arts do, of course, contain many references to the supernatural (think of Dante as a classic example), but professors who are historians and critics of literature and the arts are able to do their work without bringing God into the picture. Now, it is not surprising that men and women whose daily life is spent explaining things in nonsupernaturalistic terms would come to believe in the total adequacy of nonsupernaturalistic explanations.

For another, these academics are people endowed with what may be called hyperdeveloped organs of intellectual curiosity. For most human beings, the intellect is a means to an end, a tool to assist them in living their lives. For academic intellectuals, by contrast, the activity of intellect is, to a very large degree, an end in itself. Their curiosity is so overwhelming that knowledge is valued for its own sake, quite apart from any practical end it might be applied to; indeed, it is often valued even if it is certain that it will turn out to be quite useless.

Moreover, this curiosity is, for the most part, directed toward the empirical world, the world that can be apprehended by the senses. A naturalistic point of view, so the scientific history of the last few hundred years has shown, is very helpful in satisfying this curiosity. A supernaturalistic point of view, on the other hand, is not. There was a time, of course, a few centuries back, when the latter statement was not true; supernaturalistic premises were very helpful, for example, to Kepler, Newton, and Linnaeus. But this is no longer the case.

Third, intellectuals are very good at rational argument, at constructing rational proofs for the positions they hold. As a result, generally speaking, they are not receptive to the notion that we are entitled to assert propositions on the basis of "intuition" or "faith." But hardly anyone offers rational proofs for supernaturalism; and when these "proofs" are examined, they usually turn out not to be very persuasive to scientifically trained minds.[37]

Of course, in saying this, I am not unmindful that there is a long tradition in Christian theology and philosophy, especially Catholic theology and philosophy, which holds that faith and reason can be reconciled; that the discoveries of reason can never contradict the doctrines of faith and that the doctrines of faith can often, if not always, be proven by reason. This tradition goes back at least to Justin Martyr in the second century and includes such

---

[37] Take, for example, the "Cottingley Fairies," a 1917 photographic hoax that attracted the attention of noted spiritualists of the day, such as Arthur Conan Doyle.

notables as Augustine, Anselm, and Aquinas, not to mention Pope John Paul II, who reiterated this ancient idea of the harmony of faith and reason in his 1998 encyclical letter *Fides et Ratio.*

Despite this tradition, however, in actual practice, very few Christians, including Catholics, have ever adhered to their faith for purely rational reasons. Nor does the tradition hold that one's adherence ought to be *purely* rational. It has held that faith is a gift of grace; that rational considerations may pave the way for the reception of this gift; and that further rational considerations may confirm the truth of certain doctrines of faith. But it has never taught that Christians ought to receive the teachings of faith as the conclusion of a syllogism whose premises are established purely by reason.

So my point remains: Academic intellectuals like to have (or so they claim) solid reasons for accepting a conclusion. When they see religious believers motivated by something apart from rational proof, they respond with skepticism. This is a skepticism that can be overcome, but it is nonetheless the normal starting point of the modern academic intellectual when it comes to religious belief.

Fourth, the audience to which academic intellectuals present their proofs is made up of people who come from a wide variety of religious and philosophical backgrounds. Now, generally speaking, in order to communicate with the world, you can adopt either of two strategies. One, you can translate your message into the idiom with which each of your particular audiences will feel most at home; in other words, one version of the message for Buddhists, another for Hindus, a third for Communists, et cetera, *ad infinitum.* The second strategy is to deliver it in a common language that everyone understands.

Obviously this latter strategy is the more practical choice; hence, it is the one that intellectuals have embraced for their communications to the world. But this common language will of necessity have to avoid supernaturalism, for not all particular audiences accept supernaturalism, and those who do accept it often have conflicting supernaturalistic theories. It is far easier for intellectuals to do their work by avoiding the language of supernaturalism. By default, then, naturalism has become the *lingua franca* of the intellectual world.

Finally, although, according to standard versions of cultural history, the "myth of progress" was exploded by the horrible battlefield experiences of World War I and the postwar rise of homicidal totalitarianism in Russia and Germany, nonetheless the myth continued to flourish in the United States, perhaps because America never came close to experiencing totalitarianism and avoided the worst horrors of the two world wars. At all events, in America, the "exploded" myth is still subscribed to, more or less unconsciously, by the average man and woman in the street. The argument that something is better because it is newer, ridiculous though it is outside the narrow fields of scientific discovery and technical invention, continues to be a very persuasive one when addressed to Americans. Now, an implication of this myth is the proposition that historically more recent ideas are better and truer than older ideas. So if you subscribe to the general myth of progress, you will more than likely subscribe to this special theory of intellectual progress as well. Look at the last thousand years of European and American history, and you will see that supernaturalism is old, and naturalism is new; that religion is old and secularism new. Therefore, naturalism and secularism must be truer and better.[38]

Other cultural factors feed the growth of secularism

If the factors just described account for the prominence of secularism and naturalism in the life of twentieth-century American

---

[38] Ironically, since the myth of progress is now out of date, it must — on its own premises — be false. But, of course, this logic does little to impair the myth's cogency among those who have not heard that it is out of date.

intellectuals, two further factors account for a sudden, rapid spurt in the size of the secularist constituency in the years following World War II.

• *The great intellectual migration.* One of these two factors was the influx, during the 1930s and early '40s, of outstanding European philosophers and social scientists, refugees from Nazism. Not all of these, to be sure, were secularists, but many, if not most of them, were. Especially important in this respect were those refugees who had been connected with the Frankfurt School, which attempted to blend Freudianism with Marxism: such eminent personages as Erich Fromm, Theodor Adorno, and Max Horkheimer. Many of these transplanted intellectuals were offered safe harbor at New York's New School for Social Research, but others were spread around the country (Ernst Cassirer, for instance, was at Yale, Albert Einstein at Princeton).[39]

In those days, European naturalism was much more overt, much more out-of-the-closet, than American naturalism. The tradition of European naturalism and secularism went back to the eighteenth-century Enlightenment; many public battles had been fought in the interim; European secularists felt very comfortable about being open in their beliefs. American naturalists, by contrast, were reluctant to give offense to their religious neighbors; and although their worldview clearly implied a rejection of theism,

---

[39] For a fine report on this migration insofar as it involved intellectuals from Germany and Central Europe, see *The Intellectual Migration: Europe and America, 1930-1960*, a collection of studies and first-person accounts edited by Donald Fleming and Bernard Bailyn (Cambridge: Harvard University Press, 1969). Another book along these lines, although, in this case, not limiting itself to Germans and Central Europeans, is *Illustrious Immigrants: The Intellectual Migration from Europe, 1930/41* (Chicago: 1968), written by Laura Fermi, herself one of these "illustrious immigrants," the wife of the Nobel Prize winner, the physicist Enrico Fermi.

they abstained from underlining this point. They may have been atheists, but they were not "shouting atheists."

For example (once again), John Dewey: An atheistic naturalism is the backdrop for all his thought, but he seems to have been reluctant to cause pain to religious believers by making explicit denunciations of their beliefs; a reluctance that derived in part, I think it is clear, from his goal of influencing the schoolteacher profession with his ideas on "progressive education." The great majority of American public-school teachers were believing Christians; so why antagonize them, thereby inciting them to turn away from what Dewey believed to be his good education ideas? The European refugee scholars would have felt little of Dewey's scruples or cautions; hence, they were able to teach their American counterparts how to express their naturalism more frankly.

The influence of the Europeans was considerable, and this for three reasons. For one thing, their talents and achievements were very great. For another, they tended to be concentrated in and around New York City, which was then, even more than now, the intellectual center of American life and the home of the publishing industry. Third, some of them at least were masters of the era's two greatest intellectual fashions, Marxism and Freudianism; and they had mastered these fashions in a sophisticated way, eliminating much of the crudeness found in the vulgar popularizers of Marx and Freud; they were not mere Marxists and Freudians, they were neo-Marxists and neo-Freudians and, best of all, neo-Marxist-Freudians.

• *The higher-education explosion.* A second factor was the rapid expansion of American higher education in the aftermath of World War II, an expansion provoked in large measure by the GI Bill of Rights, which transformed college-going in America from an elite privilege to something approaching a mass phenomenon. But if there were more college students, there would have to be more college teachers; which meant there would have to be more scholars trained in graduate schools; which, in turn, meant there would have to be more graduate-school professors. In short, the student population explosion produced a population explosion in the professoriate. But it was precisely the professoriate that was the chief bearer of the secularist-naturalist subculture.

By about 1960, then, although the great majority of Americans were religious believers, a very small but influential minority were nonbelievers, and the time had come when they could no longer be ignored. One could no longer pretend that they did not exist or that their numbers and importance were so minimal that they virtually did not exist. Nor could one pretend that these unbelievers did not mind being semi-excluded from the national community. They would have to be recognized and incorporated. In 1962, the Supreme Court provided the act of recognition. It would now be up to society at large to incorporate them into the national community.

Chapter 12

Secularists Win a Place
in the National Religion

Secularism and naturalism, as we saw in the last chapter, became increasingly significant factors in American cultural life during the first half of the twentieth century; and by the end of the 1950s — thanks to the intellectual migration from Europe and the tremendous postwar expansion of higher education — they were very significant factors indeed.

Yet because these American secularists were neither Christians nor Jews (although almost all of them were either ex-Christians or ex-Jews), they could not be part of the unofficial national religion, the national Judeo-Christian consensus. In an America that defined itself in religious terms, they could be no more than marginal members of the national community, second-class Americans. But this was an absurd state of affairs. Here was a class made up mostly of intellectuals; with hardly any exceptions, a respectable and law-abiding class; a class extremely influential in the worlds of science, scholarship, art, and politics. How could such people be classified as marginal members of the national community? Perhaps so long as they were minuscule in numbers, we might get away with so classifying them; but by 1960, their numbers, although still relatively small, were far from minuscule, and they were growing every year.

The Decline and Fall of the Catholic Church in America

Something would have to give. And this something, clearly, was the Judeo-Christian definition of the national community, since there was no likelihood that the now-large secularist class would either fade away or suddenly get religion.

The time had come to expand the boundaries of the national community once again, to redefine the content of the national moral-religious consensus. Just as the hitherto Protestant nation had redefined itself in order to open the doors to Catholics and Jews, so the Judeo-Christian nation would have to redefine itself to open the doors to secularists. Henceforth the American national community would have to admit agnostics and atheists as first-class members.

It was this redefinition that was, in effect, sanctioned by the United States Supreme Court in its 1962 *Engel v. Vitale* decision banning school prayer. "It is neither sacrilegious nor antireligious," wrote Justice Hugo Black for the 7-0 majority, "to say that each separate government in this country should stay out of the business of writing or sanctioning official prayers and leave that purely religious function to the people themselves and to those the people choose to look to for religious guidance."

Why did the Court not find occasion to announce this constitutional principle fifty or seventy-five years earlier? Because the time was not socially ripe for announcing it. In those earlier days, Catholics and Jews had not yet been fully incorporated into the national community; it was still far too early to worry about a small number of unbelievers. But by 1962, the Catholics and Jews had been welcomed in, and the unbelievers had grown both more numerous and more important. It was generally conceded that Catholics and Jews had a right not to be offended by specifically Protestant prayers in a public-school classroom. But unbelievers, too, now had a right not to be offended. Prayer in public schools, even if that prayer were so artfully and nondenominationally designed as to give no offense to members of this or that particular faith, necessarily gives offense to secularists; and if secularists were full members of the national community, we should not be giving offense to them; we should respect their objections. And the only way of respecting their objections was to ban state-sponsored prayer from public schools altogether.

Whatever the legal casuistry that led to the Court ruling, this was the social reality that lay behind it.

Was this a truly revolutionary shift?

The prayer decision, as I said, was a way of declaring that unbelievers are full members of the national community, no longer merely marginal members.

But what kind of national community now remained? If the national community had always been a religion-based community, if it had always been a kind of *de facto* national church, what was it now? Clearly it could no longer be a national church if secularists were full-fledged members. For what kind of church (except for the Unitarians, a rare and special case) explicitly welcomes professed atheists as members? What religious common denominator can there be between theists and non-theists? Now that America was a Judeo-Christian-secularist community, it would have to be defined in nonreligious terms.

At first glance, this task of redefinition seems to imply a major cultural revolution. After all, going from a religion-based national community to a nonreligious one seemed a much bigger leap than the earlier transition from a Protestant community to a Judeo-Christian one.

It was a sense of how revolutionary this leap could be that caused such great alarm among religious conservatives at the time of the Court decision (and to this day: witness the fact that they are still pushing for a prayer amendment to the Constitution, four decades later). Of course, these conservatives do not usually formulate the reasons for their alarm in precisely these terms. Often they talk as though they believe that the mumbled and inattentive recitation of prayer in school would serve, in a direct and unmediated way, to prevent delinquency and immorality among the young. Since this seems unlikely to be true, it is easy to laugh at these sociologically simplistic religious conservatives; and a good many laughs have indeed been had at their expense.

But behind their simplistic formulations, there lies, I suggest, a more profound insight, one not easily dismissed. At an intuitive and inarticulate level, they understood that the fundamental basis of American society had shifted. What had been a religious community for nearly two centuries — that is, for the entire history of the republic — was to be such no longer. And so fundamental a shift was bound, sooner or later, to have grave moral consequences, both for the young and for everyone else.

But was the shift really as great as it might have looked to religious conservatives? Was it really all that revolutionary?

In his mid-seventies, John Dewey published a short book titled *A Common Faith* (New Haven: Yale University Press, 1934). In it, he argued in favor of a nonsupernaturalistic conception of religion. He made a distinction between "religion" and "the religious," i.e., between particular religions (such as Christianity) and a religious attitude; and he emphatically rejected the notion that religions have a monopoly on the religious attitude. In fact, he said just the opposite: in the modern world, religions are often the foes of the religious attitude. Belief in the supernatural, said Dewey, draws religious attention away from the realm of natural things — the realm in which we actually live and move and have our being. To counter supernaturalism, Dewey urged a sense of "natural piety" — an attitude of submission toward the universe as a whole combined with an active pursuit of the ideal values the universe makes possible: beauty, truth, work, repose, affection, and brotherhood.

In his attempt to rescue the religious attitude from supernaturalists on the one hand and garden-variety anti-supernaturalists on the other, Dewey would even permit us to continue using the word *God* — provided we used it to refer, not to some imaginary supernatural supreme being, but to the great complex of ideal values that we pursue here in this world of nature.

His view is summed up in the book's concluding sentences — one of the few places, by the way, in Dewey's normally turgid prose where he rises to the level of something like eloquence:

> We who now live are parts of a humanity that extends into the remote past, a humanity that has interacted with nature. The things in civilization we most prize are not of ourselves. They exist by grace of the doings and sufferings of the continuous human community in which we are a link. Ours is the responsibility of conserving, transmitting, rectifying, and expanding the heritage of values we have received that those who come after us may receive it more solid and secure, more widely accessible and more generously shared than we have received it. Here are all the elements for a religious faith that shall not be confined to sect, class, or race. Such a faith has always been implicitly the common faith of mankind. It remains to make it explicit and militant.[40]

If Dewey is correct, then a naturalistic view of the world has at least the potential for being religious. This being so, would it not have been possible, in the wake of the Supreme Court's 1962 prayer decision, to redefine the American national community without abandoning its religious dimension? Could the hitherto Judeo-Christian national religion not have been broadened into a Theist-Non-theist national religion? A newly certified "Religion of Humanity and Nature" (as we may call Dewey's proposed religion) could join the previously certified religions of Protestantism,

---

[40] *A Common Faith*, 87.

The Decline and Fall of the Catholic Church in America

Catholicism, and Judaism in constituting a new unofficial national church. "We may not agree on certain details," the members of this broad (indeed, very broad) church could say, "such as whether God exists, whether there is life after death, et cetera. But we agree on a number of major issues: the importance of beauty, truth, and goodness, and the importance of cultivating a pious attitude toward nature and human life."

Well, although such a redefinition was theoretically conceivable, it was practically impossible. Dewey's idea of a Religion of Humanity and Nature, enunciated nearly three decades prior to the Supreme Court decision, never caught on. American secularists of the first half of the twentieth century may have regarded Dewey as a wise leader on many questions, but not on this one. The trouble was, they did not think of themselves as being religious in an unconventional manner; they thought of themselves as being nonreligious. An illustration of this can be found in Sidney Hook's reaction to Dewey's book. Perhaps no philosopher was a greater fan of Dewey than was Hook, yet Hook told Dewey that he strongly disagreed with Dewey's attempt to rehabilitate the word *God* by giving it a meaning acceptable to naturalists.

Any hope for a Theistic-Non-theistic national religion was nothing but a pipe dream. The incorporation of secularists as full-fledged members did indeed signal a revolutionary change in the American national community — as the Catholic Church would be surprised (and unprepared) to discover when it let down its ghetto walls and engaged that community in the 1960s.

Part IV

The Deeper Problem
of Catholic Identity

Chapter 13

Church, Sect, Denomination: Three Kinds of Religious Body

In the first part of this book, we looked at the great disruption of American Catholicism that took place in the late 1960s, a disruption, as I contended, that was the result of three converging factors: Vatican II, the end of the Catholic "ghetto," and the great American cultural revolution of the '60s and '70s. All by itself, each of these factors held great potential for disruption, but the simultaneous occurrence of all three was overwhelmingly disruptive for Catholicism in the United States. In the second part of the book, we looked at the philosophical underpinnings of the cultural revolution, and in the third part, at the national moral-religious community and its eventual need to incorporate religious nonbelievers.

In this fourth part, after the necessary detour we took in the second and third parts, we return to our main subject, American Catholicism. We will do so by examining the concepts of a *denomination* and a *denominational mentality*. For it is my contention that great numbers of American Catholics, perhaps even the majority of them, developed, beginning in the 1960s, what I shall be calling a denominational mentality; and yet the Catholic religion is not a religion of the denominational type. Hence, there is a contradiction, a potentially fatal contradiction, at the heart of American

The Decline and Fall of the Catholic Church in America

Catholicism today: a nondenominational religion peopled by members and leaders with a denominational frame of mind.

Another way of putting this: My purpose in this part of the book is to argue that the problems facing American Catholicism run much deeper than the first part of the book suggested. There it was argued that the great decline of the American Church was the result of "bad luck" — the bad luck that three debilitating factors happened to converge. If this had been the whole story, we might reasonably hope for a gradual recovery as decades go by and these three events fade into the past: much the way an individual gradually recovers from an illness. But the current Catholic malaise has much deeper roots than mere bad luck, and it will take more than time alone to produce healing.

That is, if it ever heals: it is not inconceivable that American Catholicism, if it continues on its present course, might eventually disappear from the American scene.

The Reformation introduced
new kinds of churches

The Protestant Reformation produced two completely new, and radically different, kinds of religious bodies, organized along two quite different lines. On the one hand were the "territorial" or "national" churches, e.g., the Anglican Church in England; the Lutheran Church in many parts of northern Germany and Scandinavia; the Reformed Church in the northern part of the Low Countries and in parts of Switzerland and Germany; and the Presbyterian Church in Scotland. On the other hand were the "gathered" churches, e.g., the Baptists, the Quakers, the Mennonites, the Independents, and (much later, beginning in the eighteenth century) the Methodists.

The first kind of church, the national or territorial, embraced the entire body politic. Everyone who was the subject of a certain prince or the citizen of a certain republic was included as a member of the church. It may be that a person did not become an official member of the church until the moment of Baptism; but since Baptism was performed in infancy, in practice everyone in the realm was born into the church. There was nothing voluntary about church membership. By contrast, the second kind of church, the gathered church, was purely voluntary. You were not born into it; you joined it. It was a free association of like-minded individuals who felt themselves called by God; people wanted to join together with other "saints" in the worship of God.

Apart from the principle of membership, there were other striking differences between these two kinds of religious bodies. First, of course, was size: the territorial church was large, the gathered small. Second was the degree of religious intensity: on average, it was far higher in the gathered than in the territorial church. This is easy to understand, since the territorial church was made up of "saints" at one extreme, of criminals at the other, and of all shades of lukewarmness in between; the gathered church was made up of "saints" only — that is, of persons who took their religion very seriously. For if they did not, why would they go to the trouble (a trouble that often involved risk of persecution) of leaving the established church and joining a small and very demanding religious group?[41]

---

[41] Religion may be compared, in this sense, to music. Almost all humans have some love of music: they like to listen to it, and they sometimes like to hum or whistle or sing a tune, even if they do not do this very well. But only a small fraction of the human race has an intense love of music, so intense that they are willing to devote much of their lives to it: they become professional musicians, or, at a minimum, they become frequent and habitual listeners at concerts, operas, et cetera. Let us call the first group musical amateurs and the second musical virtuosi. Almost everyone has some love of religion, but only a few have a love of it that is so intense that they feel compelled to devote their lives to it. This is the difference between "religious amateurs" (which is what most of us are) and "religious

A third difference had to do with their attitude toward persecution. Territorial churches had a strong tendency to persecute. Sometimes the persecution was relatively mild — fines for attendance at unauthorized worship or nonattendance at authorized worship, for example — and sometimes it was severe, up to and including the death penalty. But this tendency to persecution, although deplorable from our latter-day point of view, was quite understandable in the context of the times. After all, the church was the nation at prayer; hence, those who broke ranks with the church were breaking ranks with the nation; dissenters from the nation's religion were nothing less than enemies of the prince or the republic. A heretic was not merely a heretic; he was also a traitor. Small wonder that governmental authorities would want to repress them, violently if need be.

By contrast, gathered churches were opposed to persecution. Being small and weak, they had no power to persecute others; and only if they lived under a regime that abstained from persecution could they hope to flourish. Historically speaking, the first great champions of religious liberty were not eighteenth-century Enlightenment types like Voltaire and Thomas Jefferson, but these sixteenth- and seventeenth-century Protestant sects, such as the Independents (or Congregationalists, as they came to be called), the Baptists, and the Quakers. In America, the first champion of religious liberty was Roger Williams, the minister from Salem who founded Rhode Island after being expelled from Massachusetts.[42]

virtuosi" (which is what only a few — the "saints" — are). In Catholicism, the virtuosi have commonly been drawn to the priesthood and the religious life; in Protestantism, the virtuosi have commonly been drawn to the gathered churches.

[42] Williams is usually credited with being the founder of the Baptist movement in America, which, in a way, he was. But he was not a Baptist for long. He was more of a "seeker" than a Baptist. Credit for founding the Baptist movement in America should more fairly be given to John Clarke of Newport.

This brings us to a crucial feature that both varieties of Reformation churches had in common. Both claimed a monopoly of religious truth. Both claimed to be the one true faith, the one true church of God.[43] They could allow that other churches (e.g., the Church of Rome and the various gathered churches) had portions of the truth, yes, but admixed with important and vicious errors.

Another way of putting this is to say that both kinds of churches, territorial and gathered, were *theologically* intolerant. Oddly enough, this intolerance justified their diametrically opposite attitudes toward political and legal toleration. The national church believed its monopoly of truth gave it the right to persecute; for why should religious error be given room to flourish? Conversely, gathered churches felt that their monopoly of truth gave them the right to demand a regime of religious liberty; for why should religious truth be crushed simply because it was the privilege of a politically weak minority?

The concept of the denomination develops in the United States

At the end of the nineteenth and beginning of the twentieth centuries, this old distinction between territorial and gathered churches came to play an important analytic role in German sociology and historiography, especially in the writings of Max Weber and Ernst Troeltsch. For short, they called the territorial-church type a *church* and the gathered-church type a *sect*.[44]

---

[43] The territorial churches usually put territorial limits on this claim. For example, the Church of England did not claim to be the only true church on a worldwide basis; it merely claimed to be the only true church in England, allowing that other Protestant bodies might represent the true church in other countries. These various national true churches were seen as national branches of the one catholic church of Christ.

[44] This terminology is perhaps not the most desirable, for, in common speech, the word *sect* is often used pejoratively. But

The Decline and Fall of the Catholic Church in America

For Troeltsch, church and sect were two of the three types of religion, the third being mysticism. Religion of the church type was that of the masses; religion of the sect type was that of a selective religious elite; religion of the mystical type was that of the religious virtuoso, the solitary individual face-to-face with God.

Almost from the beginning, Christianity had been a combination of all three types. During the ages of early and medieval Christianity, all three managed to remain — in a somewhat unstable mix — within the boundaries of the Catholic Church, which was, at different levels and for different people, simultaneously a mass religion (church), an elite religion (sect), and an individual religion (mysticism). One of the remarkable achievements of medieval Catholicism, and indeed, of ancient and modern Catholicism as well, was to keep all three of these approaches to religion under one "big tent." The ecstatic mystic did not separate himself from the monastic community, nor did the monks separate themselves from ordinary Catholics, while these ordinary Catholics regarded the monks and the mystics as belonging to the same religion as they did. The explosion of the Protestant Reformation, however, decomposed this mix, differentiated its elements, and produced nonoverlapping forms of churchly, sectarian, and mystical religion.[45]

For Weber, the church-sect distinction was essential to the development of his famous "Protestant ethic" thesis, formulated and defended in his classic work, *The Protestant Ethic and the Spirit of*

there is little we can do about this, since, in the world of sociology, *sect* has long been a standard term. All we can do is to remember that, when the word is used here, the intention is to use it descriptively, not pejoratively.

[45] For Troeltsch's discussion of the church-versus-sect difference, see his work *The Social Teachings of the Christian Churches*, Olive Wyon, trans. (Louisville: Westminster/John Knox Press), Vol. 1, 331-343. For his discussion of mysticism, see Vol. 2, 691 ff.

Capitalism.[46] It was not among the Protestant *churches*, such as the Anglicans and Lutherans, that the so-called Protestant economic ethic developed; rather, it was among the *sects*. Thus (contrary to a popular misunderstanding of Weber's thesis), the mentality that led to the creation of the modern business system did not originate among Protestants in general, but among sectarian Protestants, members of the gathered churches. The nineteenth-century Industrial Revolution was the product of a mentality Weber called "the spirit of capitalism," and this spirit, in turn, was nothing but an eighteenth-century secularization of the seventeenth-century economic ethic of the Protestant sects. Thus, the Industrial Revolution was the grandchild, so to speak, of the gathered churches: the Baptists, the Congregationalists, the Quakers, and so forth, all of whom were strongly influenced by the theology of John Calvin.

When Weber's sociological ideas began to catch on in the United States in the 1930s and 1940s, following publication of a book written by Talcott Parsons (one of Weber's great American followers), *The Structure of Social Action* (New York: McGraw-Hill, 1937), American sociologists naturally wished to put his church-sect typology to use. The trouble was, the typology did not fit the American religious scene very well. The "sect" half of the typology fit just fine, since the United States, more than any other country in the world, abounded in sects, as it does to this day. But the "church" half would not do at all, since the United States did not have any churches; that is, it did not have any religious body that came anywhere close to embracing the entire population.

True enough, the United States contained a number of religions that had been churches back in Europe — the Episcopal Church (England), the Presbyterian Church (Scotland), the Lutheran

---

[46] Originally published in German in 1904, it appeared in an English translation by Talcott Parsons (New York: Charles Scribner's Sons, 1930).

Church (Scandinavia, parts of Germany), the Reformed Church (the Netherlands), and, of course, the Catholic Church (France, Italy, Spain, Portugal, Poland, and elsewhere). But whatever they may have been in Europe, these were not churches — in Weber's sense of the word — here in the United States. It was also true that the United States had a number of religious bodies that, during the colonial era, had been churches even here on the western shore of the Atlantic, e.g., the Episcopal Church in Virginia and the Congregational Church in Massachusetts and Connecticut. But these had long since ceased to be churches even within the boundaries of their own states.

If the most striking characteristic of a church is that it embraces virtually the entire population, then the nearest things to a church in twentieth-century America were the Southern Baptists among whites in many Southern states and the Mormons in Utah. But even these instances were far from being true churches. For one thing, these religions did not embrace everyone in their territory. Many people in Utah were not Mormons, while many whites and all blacks were left outside the Southern Baptist churches. For another, both Southern Baptists and Mormons, despite their vast size, had certain traits[47] marking them as sects or near-sects, for they had started out as sects and they still bore traces of their sectarian heritage.

So what were American sociologists to do with Weber's typology? Should they simply discard it, toss it out as a bit of European rubbish not applicable to the New World? They were reluctant to do so, since the sect half of the typology served very well in the analysis of American gathered churches. Instead, they modified

[47] For example, the Southern Baptist insistence that one must undergo a conversion (or "born again") experience before being baptized and counted as a true Christian; or the Mormon expectation that members donate ten percent of their gross income to the church.

the typology by adding a third type of religious organization: the *denomination* — a type that included all the mainline Protestant churches: the Episcopal, the Presbyterian, the Methodist, most Lutherans, and some Baptist churches.

If we put aside the fact that any particular denomination includes only a small fraction of the total American population, it otherwise resembles a church in many ways. In admitting members, it is not very selective. It usually practices infant Baptism. Its members are commonly born into the denomination, not converted into it (although, it should be noted, the rate of conversion is higher than it would be in a real church, since, for reasons we will note later, many people switch as adults from one Protestant denomination to another). The average level of religious intensity among its members is not high. American denominations are either former churches reduced in size or former sects reduced in intensity.

There is one other feature, however, that clearly sets denominations apart from both churches and sects — and it is this feature that will be the focus of attention in this part of the book: *theological* tolerance.

Chapter 14

The Denominational Mentality

Both church and sect, we have seen, claimed to be the one true faith. Each claimed that, outside its boundaries, salvation was either impossible or at least extraordinarily difficult. If you wanted to be saved, if you wanted to spend eternity in Heaven and not in Hell, your best bet was to become a member of this one true faith.

By contrast, the denomination made no such claim. From the denominational point of view — the point of view I will henceforth refer to as the "denominational mentality" or the "denominational attitude" — no religion could claim a monopoly on truth; in fact, it would be arrogant to make such a claim. Rather, there were many routes to religious truth, many versions of the same ultimate truth. If we picture truth as the summit of a high mountain, diverse religions are following various paths to that summit: different roads, same goal. None is completely perfect, but all possess some degree of perfection. Thus, religions must be tolerant of one another. Indeed they should be more than simply tolerant; they should be positively friendly; they should cooperate with one another. Ideally, society's diverse faiths should be related to one another as coequal members of a great religious federation.

In principle, if the denominational mentality were carried to its logical conclusion, this religious federation would be worldwide — embracing Christians, Jews, Muslims, Buddhists, Hindus, et cetera. But in practice it has normally been limited to the nearby neighborhood, to churches whose members have frequent contact with one another. Thus, when the United States was a virtually all-Protestant nation, the denominational mentality was prepared to embrace all varieties of Protestantism. Roman Catholicism (not to mention more exotic forms of religion) was still beyond the pale. But when, by the early twentieth century, Catholics and Jews had migrated into the United States in large numbers, the denominational mentality was ready to welcome these new faiths to the neighborhood, with the result that the United States was increasingly spoken of, not as a Protestant nation, but as a "Judeo-Christian" nation. And today, when many Muslims are found in the United States,[48] the denominational mentality is ready to welcome them as well.

Some groups resisted
the denominational mentality

Of course, not all religions were prepared to return the denominational mentality's tolerant embrace. "No one has a monopoly of religious truth," it says. "All religions are approximately equally true, approximately equally good. Let each of us, therefore, worship God in the church, synagogue, or mosque of his or her choice. And let us collectively join in a grand religious federation." But some religions responded to this invitation with, "No, thank you. We have the truth, and you do not. So why should we join your federation?" This is the response given by the Protestant churches

---

[48] "Many," yes, but who knows how many? Unfortunately (from a sociological point of view) the U.S. Census Bureau has no question on its decennial census forms about religious affiliation. "While no one knows how many Muslims live in the U.S. — estimates span 1.2 million to 10 million — their numbers are growing fast" (Laurent Belsie, "America's Elusive Minority," from *The Christian Science Monitor*, October 7, 2002).

that are either sects or near-sects. And for a long time, it was the response given by the Catholic Church.

To the denominational mentality, this is a shocking response, for it shows that those who make this response are intolerant; and the denominational mentality can tolerate almost anything in religion except intolerance.

Thus, for a long time (until the 1960s), Protestants with a denominational mentality, despite their principled tolerance, and despite their standing invitation to include Catholicism in the great American religious federation, strongly disapproved of Catholicism. But this disapproval was not because they considered Catholicism a false religion. That may have been the attitude of their Protestant forebears way back in the days closer to the Reformation; but no more. These latter-day Protestants with a denominational mentality considered Catholicism to be no more false than any other religion, and therefore just as true as any other religion. No, their objection was that Catholicism was intolerant; in its arrogant claim to be the one true church, it was insulting its neighbors, perhaps even threatening them.[49]

[49] Probably the most conspicuous Protestant example of this viewpoint in the 1950s was New York Methodist Bishop G. Bromley Oxnam (1891-1963). One of the founding fathers of the Federal Council of Churches, Oxnam was a big name in liberal Protestantism (he once made the cover of *Time* magazine) at a time when liberal Protestantism was in something of a slump. He remained a great believer in the Social Gospel during an era when the neo-orthodoxy of Reinhold Niebuhr was riding high. He had no objection to Catholics, if only they could learn to behave themselves like good, tolerant Americans, instead of insisting that theirs was the one true religion.

One example (of many) of his critique of Catholic intolerance was a presentation he made at a 1951 panel discussion sponsored by the Harvard Law School Forum. The topic was "Public Aid to Parochial Education," which Bishop Oxnam unsurprisingly opposed, predicting that if Catholic schools were to be given taxpayer support, all Catholic schoolchildren

The Decline and Fall of the Catholic Church in America

But about thirty-five years ago, in the aftermath of Vatican II and the dismantling of the Catholic quasi-ghetto, American Catholicism did an abrupt about-face. At long last, most Catholics began to adopt the denominational mentality of most of their Protestant neighbors. They became theologically tolerant. To be sure, there was no official announcement to this effect. The National Conference of Catholic Bishops did not issue a statement renouncing their traditional one-true-faith claim. But the new attitude, the denominational attitude, was suddenly found everywhere in the Catholic community. It was certainly widespread among the laity; and it was almost equally widespread among ordinary priests; while bishops, although more circumspect in their manifestation of this attitude, did little or nothing to resist its presence among laypersons and lower clergy. Catholics abandoned their old "arrogance," their old claim to religious superiority. Instead they were happy to be members of a now-respectable American religion, neither better nor worse than the religions that met in other churches and synagogues in town.

Unfortunately (that is, from the viewpoint of Protestants and Catholics having a denominational attitude), conservative Protestant religions have been unable to achieve a similar about-face. By

would be withdrawn from public schools. These children would no longer routinely associate with their Protestant and Jewish peers, and in Catholic schools they would be subjected to Vatican-approved propaganda that would indoctrinate them as to the "evils" of such things as freedom of the press and religious freedom. They would be told that it was the duty of the state to protect the interests of the "true" religion. Further, the whole business of winning state aid for Catholic education may simply be a way of laying the groundwork for the creation in the United States of a Catholic political party that would take its marching orders from Rome just as surely as Communist parties take their marching orders from Moscow. The text of Oxnam's presentation can be found online at the website of the Harvard Law School Forum.

"conservative" religions here, I have in mind, e.g., the Southern Baptists, the Assemblies of God and other Pentecostalists, the Missouri Synod Lutherans, the Mormons, and the Jehovah's Witnesses. These have retained their sectarian or quasi-sectarian mentality; that is, they continue to hold that theirs is the one true faith. As the denominational mentality sees it, these sectarians remain incorrigibly intolerant, and such intolerance is seen as an affront to their neighbors and a threat to American democracy, which thrives on a spirit of tolerance. This explains why the great religious division in the United States nowadays is no longer the old Catholic-Protestant division, but, rather, the division between liberal Protestants and conservative Protestants.[50]

Liberal Protestants have the denominational mentality, while conservatives have a more or less sectarian mentality; and neither can very well tolerate the other. This intolerance is deeply rooted on both sides, since the conservatives pride themselves on their theological intolerance, while the liberals pride themselves on their intolerance of intolerance.

As long as the ancient Protestant-versus-Catholic division remained viable and conspicuous, the Protestant-versus-Protestant division remained in the shade; no matter how poor an opinion each side had of the other, both agreed that Romanism was far worse. But once Catholics adopted the denominational mentality in the 1960s, liberal Protestants no longer had any significant quarrel with Catholicism. The Protestant-versus-Catholic division soon lost its prominence, and the liberal-Protestant-versus-conservative-Protestant division emerged as the major religious division in American life.

---

[50] For purposes of this discussion, I am counting such groups as the Mormons and the Jehovah's Witnesses as Protestant, even though there are some who would contend that they belong to a fourth class of Christian religions, neither Orthodox nor Catholic nor Protestant.

The Decline and Fall of the Catholic Church in America

The denominational mentality offers attractive benefits

The great advantage to the denominational mentality, that which has most caused it to thrive in this country, is that it suits a pluralistic society like the United States. The fundamental problem of any such society is this: How can we live in peace with one another? In a country as vast and heterogeneous as the United States, it is a huge problem. Yet one of the great achievements of American history is that we have been relatively successful in solving this problem of peace-despite-diversity.

But how could Americans live in peace with one another if everyone was full of the sectarian spirit? In that case, we would continually be making negative judgments about the religions of most of our neighbors. There is an old story (which sounds too good to be true) told about Cardinal Manning, the Catholic Archbishop of Westminster during much of the Victorian age. One evening following a public event, he and an Anglican bishop found themselves sharing a cab. "How appropriate that we should be riding in the same cab," said the Anglican. "After all, we both serve God." "Very true," the cardinal replied, "you in your way, I in His." As a witticism, this kind of thing is all very well, but it is anything but a formula for establishing good relations among neighbors.

In a great commercial-industrial society like ours, the dominant mentality is pragmatic. The fundamental question we tend to ask about anything is not, "Is it true?" but rather, "Does it work?" And the great thing about denominationalism in the United States is precisely this: *it has worked* — at least so far. It has worked at minimizing social friction, at allowing people who belong to different faiths to live in peace with one another. American denominationalism has allowed us, despite an immense variety of religious beliefs, to live, not just without civil war and persecution, but virtually without tension. Here in America, thank God, religion has never been a major source of conflict and social disorder.

In saying this, I do not mean to suggest that the United States has been completely free from religion-based conflict. Not at all. Catholics, as I point out elsewhere in this book, were long subject to prejudice and discrimination; and so were Jews. In the 1830s, a Catholic convent was burned down in Charlestown, Massachusetts, by a Protestant mob. Probably the single worst instance of religious intolerance and violence in American history was the lynching of the founder of the Mormons, Joseph Smith, along with his brother Hyram, on June 27, 1844, in Carthage, Illinois, not far from the Mormon settlement at Nauvoo. It was this lynching that impelled the Mormons to pull up stakes and, under the new leadership of Brigham Young, head west, finally settling in Utah, a thousand miles or more from angry, intolerant mobs.

Even today, the United States is not totally free from religious conflict. The current "culture war" (which we will examine later in the book) is a kind of religious conflict: on the one side, conservative Protestants and Catholics and Jews; on the other, nonreligious secularists along with liberal Protestants and Catholics and Jews. So it is true that America has experienced religious conflict. But this has been almost as nothing when compared with our one truly serious form of intergroup conflict: racial conflict. This is a very sad record of serious conflict, having produced, among other things, a terrible civil war. Our religious history has nothing to compare with it. And in no small measure, it is the spirit of denominationalism that can be given credit for this relatively good record.

And if denominationalism has led to social peace and harmony, it has led to other benefits as well, for from social peace and harmony, many good things flow. Most obviously, a lack of religious conflict has been good for the American economy. To a very great degree, although perhaps not perfectly, buyers and sellers, employers and employees, have been able to disregard the religious affiliation (or nonaffiliation) of the people with whom they do business. With few exceptions, consumer and labor markets have been able to operate without the distortion of religious prejudice and tension. In the worlds of professional sports, popular entertainment, and high culture, Americans have rarely objected to athletes or artists because of their religion. If they can hit home runs, if they can sing, if they can act, if they can make us laugh, if they can write a good work of fiction or drama, they have been generally well-received by American audiences, regardless of whether they have been Protestant or Catholic or Jewish or atheist.

Small wonder, therefore, that our business, political, and academic elites, those especially responsible for maintaining social peace and harmony, approve of denominationalism and the denominational mentality. They like it so much that they find it difficult to imagine any other religious regime.

Chapter 15

Harmony Before Doctrine:
Forging Denominational Consensus

In the two preceding chapters, I first defined the nature of denominationalism and the denominational mentality, and next I gave an account of some of the many benefits that have accrued to American society from it. In this chapter, I want to make explicit a concept that has been implied in the two preceding chapters: the concept of a *denominational consensus*. I am setting the stage in this chapter for the four succeeding chapters, in which, reversing course, I will attempt to show the *disadvantages* of the denominational mentality.

Picture the beliefs of religion A and religion B as represented by two circles. To the extent that A and B agree in their beliefs, these two circles intersect. But A has certain beliefs that fall outside the intersection, and so (in all probability) has B. So our two circles end up producing three segments: on one side, a segment containing the beliefs of A that are not shared by B; on the other, a second segment containing the beliefs of B that are not shared by A; and finally (in the middle) an intersecting segment containing beliefs shared by A and B. Let us call these shared beliefs a "denominational consensus."

When two or more churches adopt a denominational attitude toward one another, they embrace a principle that says, "The doctrines we hold in common are far more important to us than those that divide us." In other words, the intersection of their two sets of beliefs — i.e., their denominational consensus — becomes more important than the beliefs that are peculiar to each; or, to revert to our image, the left- and right-hand segments fade in importance, while the center, intersecting segment becomes of paramount importance.

I say it *becomes* of paramount importance, as though this were a result of the adoption of a denominational attitude. Perhaps, however, it would be more correct to say that the causal relation operates the other way around: from the fact that the intersecting beliefs are felt to be more important, it follows that these two religions are able to adopt a denominational attitude toward one another. Whatever the causal relationship may be, the two things go together — a denominational attitude and the view that the beliefs the two religions share are more important than the beliefs on which they differ.

This is a point of view very alien to those who belong to what they consider to be the one true religion. They feel that their *entire* doctrinal system is important. They do not look at their belief system as hierarchically arranged in such a way that some beliefs are really important, others far less important, and others downright trivial. Thus, they do not feel free to downplay some beliefs and to jettison others for the sake of reaching ecumenical agreement. For them, the distinction between essential and nonessential beliefs makes no sense.

This is not to say that they fail to recognize the fact that they share beliefs with other religions; it is just that they do not consider these shared beliefs to be significantly more important than the beliefs they do *not* share with others. All their beliefs are essential; otherwise why would their one true religion have insisted on all these beliefs? Belief in the divinity of Christ, for instance, is not less essential than belief in the existence of God. This belief in

Christ's divinity is not something that traditional Catholics or Southern Baptists are willing to de-emphasize for the sake of getting along with people who do not share this belief; they are not willing to count it as a "peripheral," as opposed to a "core," belief of their religion. People with this one-true-religion mentality, then, are not the kind of people who will work at producing a denominational consensus.

But nowadays, of course, there are plenty of Catholics for whom it is the most natural thing in the world to make a distinction between core and peripheral beliefs. Belief in God is a core belief, for this is something all Christians and all religious believers share. Belief in the divinity of Christ is non-core, for it is a belief that both our non-Christian neighbors and even many of our (liberal) Christian neighbors do not share. And belief in the Virgin Birth is downright marginal, for who believes in this nowadays except the most unenlightened members of the Christian community, i.e., religious conservatives, whose opinions do not have to be respected, both because of their lack of enlightenment and because of their intolerance of those who do not share their views?

Two degrees of consensus: thick and thin

Now, doctrinal consensus among denomination runs in degrees. Let us distinguish between a "thick" consensus and a "thin" consensus. These should be viewed as opposite ends of a spectrum, with every degree of intermediate thickness or thinness lying between the extremes. In a thick consensus, the parties have a great deal in common, a long list of doctrinal articles they agree on. In a thin consensus, the parties have very little in common, only a few things they agree on. Four things follow once we recognize this distinction between thick and thin.

• *More difference means thinner consensus.* The greater the differences among parties to a denominational consensus (DC), the

thinner the consensus will be. Traditional Methodists and Presbyterians, for instance, agree on a lot of things; a consensus between
them would be thick. But if, say, the Unitarians became a third
party to the consensus, the content of the consensus would suddenly become very thin, since there are not many articles of faith
that Unitarians, Presbyterians, and Methodists hold in common.

• *The denominational center of gravity shifts.* As a DC thins out
to take in more and more groups — first some Protestants, then all
Protestants, then all Christians, then all Christians and Jews, and
finally, everybody — somewhere along the line, a shift takes place
in what may be called the "denominational center of gravity." Let
us say religions X and Y (two very similar, highly doctrinal religions) have adopted denominational attitudes toward one another. Because of their similarity, the DC between the two will be
very thick. The central doctrines of each faith will also be central
in the consensus. When they say, as denominationalists must, that
"what we have in common is more important than what divides
us," this common denominator will include all, or almost all, of
the traditionally important doctrines of each faith.

But as the denominational circle expands, as more and more
groups are taken in, the consensus grows thinner and thinner. By
the time the consensus reaches the thin end of the spectrum,
many of the traditionally important doctrines of religions X and Y
will have been left out of the consensus. When Presbyterians,
Methodists, and Unitarians, for instance, adopt denominational
attitudes toward one another, the resulting DC will omit such doctrines as the Trinity, the Incarnation, and the atonement — all of
them essential to Methodism and Presbyterianism, but rejected by
Unitarianism.

• *The lowest-doctrine religion benefits most.* In the construction
of a DC, the religion that believes the least has a certain advantage.
Let us suppose that the creed of religion X has ten articles (belief

in God plus nine others); and let us suppose that the creed of religion Z has a single article only (belief in God). The resulting DC between the two will therefore have only one article: belief in God. In creating a DC between the two religions, religion X will have to check 90 percent of its belief system at the door; religion Z, on the other hand, will be able to bring its entire belief system in.

Now, unlike this hypothetical example, in the real world, it will rarely happen that the faith of one of the participating religions will end up being the common faith of the entire denominational community. More usually, all participants will have to check parts of their creeds at the door. Nonetheless, the principle illustrated by the example holds — namely, that those religions that believe the least will be able to bring a greater percentage of their beliefs into the consensus, while those that believe the most will have to leave a greater percentage outside.

• *High-doctrine religions are devalued.* Since the denominational mentality holds that the things we agree on are more important than the things we disagree on, it follows that doctrines left outside the consensus become, at least by implication, matters of secondary importance. Further, it follows that this impact will fall disproportionately on religions with high doctrinal content. To return to the example given in the previous paragraph, 90 percent of the creed of religion X will be demoted to a status of secondary importance, while the entire creed of religion Z will retain its primary-importance status. Creation of a DC, in short, will have more of a negative impact on the creeds of high-doctrine religions than it will on those of low-doctrine religions.

Catholicism inevitably suffers
in a denominational consensus

If the principles we just examined are true, it would be fatal, at least in the long run, for Catholicism to become part of a thin DC.

The Decline and Fall of the Catholic Church in America

Catholicism is a high-doctrine religion. Entering into a DC with many forms of religion, some of them of a low-doctrine character, Catholicism would have to check many of its typical beliefs at the door. On the principle that what we share in common is more important than what divides us, the beliefs left outside the consensus — beliefs, for instance, relative to the Trinity, the Incarnation, the Resurrection, the Virgin Mary, and the papacy — would be seriously devalued in importance.

On the same principle, Catholicism's center of doctrinal gravity would shift. Most doctrines that were traditionally at the heart of the Faith would, now being matters of secondary importance, shift to the periphery.

Catholicism would no longer be the same religion it has been for many centuries. For all practical purposes, it would cease to exist — even though there would be a modern denomination going by the old name.

Let us entertain a hypothetical possibility that in reality has been a sociological and historical impossibility: that American Catholicism had become part of the American DC in the early part of the twentieth century. If that had happened, Catholics would have had to compromise, through de-emphasis, certain Catholic ideas — e.g., the veneration of the Virgin Mary and the role of the pope, for Protestants were quite unwilling to accept these ideas. But they could have retained the great bulk of Catholic doctrine. For at that time, American Protestantism was still largely orthodox according to a Catholic understanding of orthodoxy; that is, Protestants still accepted the ancient Faith of the Church in its substantial doctrinal content and were still, for the most part, morally orthodox. Entering into a DC with them would, of course, have required that Catholics de-emphasize the bans on divorce and contraception, but otherwise Catholics and Protestants were pretty much in agreement as to what the Ten Commandments required. They could have had a "thick" DC.

The content of the DC would have been what C. S. Lewis called "mere Christianity."[51]

But in reality, it did not become possible for American Catholicism to enter into a DC with Protestantism until the final third of the twentieth century, and by that time, the mainline Protestants — under the influence of liberal Protestantism, which, in turn, was being powerfully influenced by the new secularism of the 1960s — were beginning a radical turn away from ancient Christian orthodoxy. On the doctrinal side, as the last decades of the twentieth century played out, many theologians and ministers and ordinary laypersons were openly skeptical of traditional doctrines, such as the divinity of Christ, the Virgin Birth, and the Resurrection of Christ, among others. And on the moral side, these same people were developing tolerant attitudes toward extramarital sex, cohabitation, abortion, and homosexuality. Traditional Christianity was being hollowed out.

For Catholics to attempt a DC with Protestants of this kind, they would have to de-emphasize, and thus compromise, much of the central content of their Faith. Nothing more than a very thin consensus could be achieved. Yet it was precisely at this moment, a moment when mainline Protestantism was commencing a historic retreat from Christian orthodoxy, that millions of Catholics decided to enter into a DC with their Protestant brothers and sisters. The result, quite unsurprisingly, has been a retreat from orthodoxy on the part of many Catholics.

[51] It is interesting that Lewis's famous book originated in BBC radio talks given during World War II — in other words, at a time when British Protestantism, like American, was still rather orthodox. Since British Protestantism, like mainline American Protestantism, has drifted away from orthodoxy, Lewis could not have written such a book today and claimed that it represented "the belief that has been common to nearly all Christians at all times" (*Mere Christianity* [New York: Macmillan, 1960], 6).

A DC between Catholics and fundamentalist
Protestants has been hard to achieve

But among the more "fundamentalist" churches, i.e., Evangelicals and Pentecostals, orthodoxy has remained strong; hence, there was a possibility — at all events, an abstract possibility — that a thick "mere Christianity" DC could be worked out between Catholics and these conservative Protestants. But practically speaking, such a DC has, to date, proven impossible, despite a number of earnest efforts.

For one, Rev. Pat Robertson made an attempt to bring the two sides together politically, when his immensely influential political operation, the Christian Coalition, attempted to spin off a Catholic counterpart, the Catholic Alliance. But the Alliance has never really caught on, its membership numbers being minuscule in comparison with the membership of the Coalition. For another, in the May 1994, issue of the magazine *First Things*, a statement appeared from a group called "Evangelicals and Catholics Together." The statement stressed the beliefs and values and interests that are held in common by the two religious communities, and it was signed by many prominent figures from both camps — and yet, little has come of it. They might be allied on many moral and social issues, but, to date, neither ordinary Catholics nor ordinary Evangelicals seem ready to embrace one another as sharers of a common faith.

There are three reasons for this, I suggest:

• Precisely because Evangelicals are so traditional, many of them cling to the old Protestant tradition that sees Catholicism as a perversion of Christianity.

• Catholics are naturally reluctant to embrace a class of Protestants who continue to hold old anti-Catholicism prejudices.

• Since they are now members of the American cultural mainstream, Catholics, by and large, share the mainstream prejudice against Evangelicals and Pentecostals: that is, they view them as ignorant, narrow-minded, intolerant, and often fanatical.

So if Catholics were to enter into a denominational consensus with fellow Christians, those fellow Christians could be no other than the Protestants from the mainline denominations; and these are denominations increasingly dominated by liberal Protestants, who are, of course, low-doctrine Protestants. Hence, a DC with these people would have to be a thin consensus. That is to say, Catholics, as members of a high-doctrine faith, would have to de-emphasize many of the essential beliefs of the Catholic religion.

DCs with non-Christians threaten to thin the consensus even further

The situation has grown even worse from the point of view of Catholics who would like to see the ancient doctrines of their Faith retained. For, in the last few decades, there has been a great influx into the United States of persons from East and South and Western Asia, persons adhering to religious faiths that are not Christian or Jewish: Buddhists and Hindus and Muslims. A religious DC that includes *all* faiths held by Americans, then, would have to be so broad and so thin that it would have about it nothing specifically Christian or Jewish or Buddhist or Hindu or Islamic. It would have to emphasize what is common to these faiths and de-emphasize everything else. It would not be Christianity-in-general or even Judeo-Christianity-in-general. It would be religion-in-general.

When I say the thinning out of Catholic teaching was bound to happen once Catholics try to enter into a DC with their fellow-Americans, I do not mean, of course, that the pope and the bishops would give this thinning-out their official stamp of approval. What I am talking about here is Catholicism as it exists in the minds of ordinary believers, not as it exists in the minds of the bishops, the official defenders of orthodoxy. Once rank-and-file Catholics embrace a thin DC, it becomes impossible for them to continue to believe in their traditional high-doctrine religion. They may continue to go to church on Sundays, and they may continue to call themselves Catholic; but their Catholicism will have been evacuated of almost all its doctrinal content.

And it is not just laypersons I have in mind here. Anecdotal evidence suggests the clergy have been affected as well. I remind the reader of my comments about the quality of sermons in Catholic churches in recent decades. Have homilists talked in a specifically Catholic way? Or have they instead spoken about (thin) Christianity-in-general? Or have they spoken about (even thinner) religion-in-general? I doubt that priests on average have been as willing as their parishioners to adopt the denominational mentality, but many of them do not lag far behind their parishioners.

The DC leads to religious indifferentism

I should add that not all American bishops are free of the denominational mentality. In 2002, a joint committee of Jewish and Catholic leaders, including some bishops on the Catholic half of the committee, issued a double statement (one Jewish, the other Catholic) on the vexing question of Christian attempts to convert Jews to Christianity. The Catholic statement said, in short, that there was no theological justification for Christians attempting to convert Jews, for Judaism was a religion revealed by God and thus valid before the coming of Christianity (another religion revealed by God), and it remains a valid religion after the coming of Christianity. As for the "Great Commission" found at the end of the Gospel of Matthew ("Go, make disciples of all nations, baptizing them in the name of the Father and the Son and the Holy Spirit"): Christians comply with this imperative when they *inform* Jews about Christianity; there is no call to go beyond the giving of information, no need to attempt persuasion or conversion. The

Catholic bishops who made this statement were not speaking for the United States Conference of Catholic Bishops (USCCB), yet they were not far from doing so; for their half of the joint Jewish-Catholic committee was a task force created by the USCCB.

This Catholic statement, needless to say, had scant justification in doctrine or tradition or theology, but it was perfectly justified from the point of view of the denominational mentality. In other words, it was an *American* statement, not a *Catholic* statement. And it opens the possibility for a series of further statements. If there is no need to convert Jews today, there will be no need to convert Protestants tomorrow, nor any need to convert Muslims and Buddhists and Hindus the day after tomorrow. And perhaps on the day after that, there will be no need to attempt the conversion of sincere agnostics and atheists. Of course, some quasi-theological justification will be needed for these further retrenchments on the Great Commission, but these will easily be found by any halfway-clever Catholic who is driven, not by his high-doctrine Faith, but by a low-doctrine DC.

An amusing side note of this episode is that, in telling Catholics that they need no longer make any attempts to convert Jews, the statement is telling them that they must not do what they were not doing in any case! When did American Catholics last undertake a mission to convert American Jews? For that matter, when did they last undertake a mission to convert anybody? With very rare exceptions, American Catholics are not in the conversion business. And why should this be a surprise? For it makes no sense for people holding the denominational mentality to attempt to convert anyone from religion X to religion Y. After all, are not all religions equally good, equally valid?

Some Christians — e.g., Evangelical and Pentecostal Protestants, and quasi-Christians like Mormons and Jehovah's Witnesses — still make an effort to convert others, including Catholics and Jews, to their faith. And they often succeed. They have "picked off" many Catholics, especially those who came to the United States from Latin America. And they have even converted some Jews — causing great distress in the Jewish community, which tends to regard evangelization efforts, not as well-meaning attempts to share truth (or Truth), but as attacks — quite intolerant and un-American attacks. These would-be converters do not play by the rules of the DC game; they do not hold a denominational mentality. They are convinced that they hold the unique true faith. This is a conviction few American Catholics hold today.

Let me stress that none of the above happens overnight. The logical implication of an abstract principle is one thing; the psychological and social realization of this logical implication is quite something else. The former is instantaneous; the latter may take years, decades, even centuries to come to pass. And in some cases, it will not come to pass at all; some counterforce may make it practically impossible for the logical implications of a position to get worked out. Logic, after all, is not the only force in the world. What I am contending, then, is not that the logical implications of a principle always get realized in fact, but rather that they always *tend* to get realized.

In the next chapter we will look at some of the effects a thin DC has had, and will tend to have, on American Catholicism.

Chapter 16

The Denominational Mentality
Weakens Church Loyalty

In the preceding chapter, after describing what I mean by a denominational consensus, I adumbrated some of the disadvantages for Catholicism that are bound to arise from such a consensus and the denominational mentality that goes with it. In this chapter and the three succeeding ones, I will examine the disadvantages of the denominational mentality in a more detailed and systematic way. These are disadvantages for *any* religion, but they are *a fortiori* disadvantages for Catholicism.

The question of the advantages and disadvantages of denominationalism is, of course, a question of a pragmatic type. The antidenominationalist might dismiss it by saying, "This is the wrong question to ask. Do not ask if denominationalism has any disadvantages. Ask if it is true or false." This is a theological question, however, and my focus is not theological, but sociological. I propose, therefore, to leave the question of truth alone — other than to concede this: that it is a question of the first importance. If I do not try to answer it, it is because it is out of my territory, not because I consider it an insignificant matter.

Back to my question, then: Does the denominational mentality, despite its many obvious advantages, have any offsetting disadvantages? I believe it does, if not for society as a whole, then at least for the denominations that adopt it. This mentality, I want to argue, will eventually, if persisted in, prove lethal to the American Catholic Church, just as it is currently proving lethal to many Protestant denominations.

First of all, it weakens church loyalty. If there were a certain food product you loved to eat on a regular basis — pork pies, let us say — and there was only one market or restaurant in a twenty-five-mile radius that sold it, you would make a point of going to that one outlet. If, on the other hand, every market and restaurant in the region sold pork pies, and if all the pies were approximately equally tasty and nutritious, and if they all sold for approximately the same price, you would not especially care which outlet you shopped at, and you would tend to go to the one nearest at hand.

So it is with loyalty to churches of the denominational type; or better, so it is with persons having the denominational mentality. If you are a religious person, even moderately so, and you believe that religion X has a monopoly on truth and salvation, then you will be sure to belong to religion X, even if it takes a lot of trouble to travel to its religious services and participate in its religious life. In other words, you will have a high degree of loyalty to religion X. If, on the other hand, you believe that no religion has a monopoly on truth and salvation, if you believe that all religions, or at least most religions, have an approximately equal grasp on these things, it will not make much difference to you which religion you belong to. For all, or at least most, will seem equally good.

Of course, there are other motives for church loyalty apart from truth. Perhaps, for instance, you grew up in a certain church; or perhaps it was the church of your parents and grandparents; or perhaps you like the personality of the pastor at your church; or perhaps the music is especially beautiful at your church; or perhaps it is located just around the corner from your house, easy to walk to on Sunday morning; and so on. But there is no motive for loyalty quite so strong as the belief that yours is the one true church. As long as you believe that, you will almost certainly remain loyal — even if you do not like your pastor, even if the music is awful, even if you have to travel all the way across town on Sunday morning. Who cares, as long as your church does what no other church can do: supply you with truth and promise you salvation?

One of the great tests of religious loyalty is how people react to the prospect of their children marrying outside the current family religion. For those holding the conviction that theirs is the one true faith — e.g., Catholics in the old days, Mormons and Orthodox Jews today — such a prospect is something to dread. If their child marries outside the fold, he will be cut off from truth and perhaps eventually from salvation. What could be more dreadful? Such people take loyalty precautions early in the lives of their children, drilling into them the idea that theirs is the true faith, that it is unthinkable that they should marry outside the faith. Usually this indoctrination works. Sometimes, however, it does not, and the result is a painful family scene when the children announce their plans to marry outside the faith.

By contrast, for those having the denominational point of view, marriage outside the family religion is no big deal. And if persons with a denominational outlook are able to smile on out-marriage, even more are they able to take in stride lesser acts of apparent disloyalty — like switching from one church to another. You were a Methodist in Elm City, let us say, but now you have moved to Oak Grove and you have become a Presbyterian. Why not? Back in Elm City, most of your friends were Methodists and you liked the pastor. Here most of your friends are Presbyterian, and you truly enjoy the sermons given by the pastor of their church. Mind, you have nothing against the Methodists; they are fine people; you have no regrets that you used to be one of them. Nor do you have anything against the Methodist Church, a fine institution. But the Presbyterian Church is just as good, and in Oak Grove you happen to feel more comfortable with the Presbyterians.

The Decline and Fall of the Catholic Church in America

Or maybe you are still living in Elm City, but your socioeconomic situation has improved over the years. When you were relatively poor, so were most of your friends and neighbors, and they belonged to the local Methodist church; so it certainly made sense for you to belong. But now you are relatively rich, and so are your new friends and neighbors, and they belong to the local Episcopal church; so you should, too.

In the last analysis, the denominational mentality says, it is all the same, is it not? Does God really care which church you belong to, as long as you belong to some church and, more important, lead a decent life? But this attitude is irreconcilable with the Catholic Church's definition of itself.

Chapter 17

The Denominational Mentality
Causes Membership Decline

A second problem arising from the denominational mentality is that the denomination affected by it — or perhaps I should say, *in*fected by it, since, from the point of view of the ecclesiastical organization, it is a kind of disease — will eventually decline in membership. At first, this decline will be relative; that is, the denominational church will not grow as rapidly as nondenominational churches, and it will shrink as a percentage of society's overall population. But in time, the decline will be absolute; that is, the denomination in question will actually be reduced in numbers.

The denominational mentality hinders
church recruitment and retention

If a church, like any other organization, is not to shrink in numbers, it will have to recruit new members on an ongoing basis. Old members are constantly dropping off the rolls: some because they have quit, others because they have died. To maintain its numerical strength, therefore, the church will have to recruit one new member for every member who has resigned or died. And if it is to grow in numbers, it will have to recruit more than one. A complementary strategy is to encourage members not to quit. The more the church can retain its old members, the less pressure there is to recruit new ones. Recruitment and retention, then: these are two efforts a church must attend to if it is to grow numerically, or at least if it is not to shrink in numbers. But both efforts are seriously damaged by the denominational mentality.

Consider retention first. In the preceding chapter, we saw how the denominational mentality, with its broad and genial tolerance, its readiness to consider all religions (or at least all forms of Christianity) approximately as good as all others, reduces loyalty to any particular religion. But if my loyalty to a church is significantly reduced, the chances of my remaining a member of it will also be significantly reduced. If it really makes no difference, just as long as I belong to *some* church, then the odds are greatly reduced that I will remain a lifetime member of my current church.

But it is not just a question of deciding to remain a member myself. Retention is also a question of how hard I will try to encourage others to remain members. Clearly, if I have a denominational mentality, I will not work at this as hard as I might otherwise do. If it really makes no difference which church a person belongs to, why should I persuade my friend or my neighbor not to switch churches? If all religions are equal, if, therefore, his or her spiritual well-being will not be jeopardized by switching churches, why engage in the hard work of persuasion? Why not just say, "We will miss you here on Sundays, but good luck in your new church"?

And now consider recruitment. Religions have two main ways of recruiting new members: one is by winning converts, the other by passing the faith to one's children. Some (the Jehovah's Witnesses, for instance) rely heavily on winning converts. Others (the Catholic Church is a good example) rely mainly on passing the faith on to the children.

Those having the opposite of a denominational mentality, believing that their religion is the one true faith, will obviously make a strenuous effort to pass the faith on to their children. To leave the faith would be to jeopardize one's salvation, and they certainly would not want that to happen to their children. Those, on the other hand, who have the denominational mentality will make a far less strenuous effort to pass their particular religion on to their children. No doubt they would be pleased if their children decided, when adults, to belong to the same church they did. But in the end, since all churches are equally pleasing in the sight of God, they would be satisfied — happy even — to see their children practicing religion in *any* church. The intergenerational dropout rate will thus be far higher for churches having a denominational mentality.

When it comes to conversions, it is a mixed picture. For denominations, there are two kinds of converts: those switching from one church to another, and those converted from an unchurched status to a church-membership status. Denominations will find it relatively easy to gain a lot of the former kind, but nearly impossible to gain the latter.

In a world permeated with the denominational mentality, there will be an abundance of religion-switchers. Without any great effort on its part, therefore, religion X will get its fair share of the switchers. All it has to do is remain passive: put out the welcome mat and wait; they will show up because they are shopping around for a new church. If it is lucky, the church will get enough switchers-in to make up for the switchers-out.

But when it comes to the other kind of conversion — the winning of the hitherto unchurched — it is a completely different story. Here a passive strategy will not work. With only rare exceptions, the unchurched will not come knocking at the church door, asking to be taken in. Instead, the church will have to go knocking on their doors: perhaps even literally (as the Jehovah's Witnesses and Mormons do). It will have to make an aggressive outreach effort.

The Decline and Fall of the Catholic Church in America

But will a church full of the spirit of denominationalism make such an outreach? Not likely. Churches that believe (really believe, not just believe in a lip-service kind of way) that they possess the one true faith will quite naturally want to share this with others; they will make the outreach effort. But a denominational church? Why should it go to the bother? Since all religions are equally good, why not let some other church make the effort?

And since all are equally good, who is to say that the condition of the unchurched is seriously inferior to the condition of the churched? Who knows? Maybe the unchurched person is "spiritual but not religious" (as a popular expression of the day has it). Maybe he or she has a private relationship with God, one not mediated through any church community, and perhaps this is just as worthwhile as the relationship with God experienced by the typical church member.

In sum, when the denominational churches are compared with the "one-true-religion" churches, the former will do more poorly at both essential tasks, retention and recruitment.

This can be seen in the twentieth-century history of American denominationalism. The Protestant denominations (the so-called "mainline" churches — the United Church of Christ, the Episcopal Church, the Presbyterian Church of the USA, the Evangelical Lutheran Church of America, the American Baptists) have shrunk in size, at first in their percentage of the total population, and eventually in absolute numbers. Meanwhile, the more conservative and sectarian churches (Southern Baptists, Mormons, Assemblies of God, Jehovah's Witnesses) have grown. The history of Methodism is very instructive on this point. As long as a sectarian spirit prevailed in it, it grew; but when, beginning in the early twentieth century, it was invaded by a spirit of denominationalism, it began to decline; so that today, when it is one of the mainline churches, it, like the rest of them, is shrinking in absolute numbers.

Misleading numbers: evaluating the impact
of denominationalism on Catholic membership

At this point, someone will object that the American Catholic Church does not conform to this pattern. It will be pointed out that I have asserted that Catholicism, starting immediately after Vatican II, gave up its "closed" status and became one more American denomination, permeated by the denominational mentality — widely so at the level of the laity and significantly so even at the clerical level. But if this is so, then, on the theory I have been defending in this chapter, Catholicism should be declining in numbers. But in fact, it is gaining in numbers, while retaining its percentage of the overall American population.

The truth is that American Catholicism *has* declined in numbers, just as one would expect it to do, given its denominational status, yet this decline has been masked by two factors. One is the very loose and liberal manner in which the number of American Catholics is computed. If you have been baptized as a Catholic, you will be counted as a Catholic, even if your religion is now a matter of complete indifference to you, even if you have not darkened a church door for years or decades. When counting Catholics, no serious attempt is made to distinguish between "real" Catholics (those, let us say, who commonly go to church on Sundays) and merely "nominal" Catholics (those for whom Catholicism is no longer a matter of importance). In the post–Vatican II era, who can doubt that the number of real Catholics has dropped while the number of nominal Catholics has greatly increased? If the Catholic-counters counted only real Catholics, it would be evident that the numerical strength of the American Catholic Church has dropped dramatically in the last thirty-five years.

The other masking factor is the immense number of Latin Americans, almost all of them at least nominally Catholic, who have migrated into the United States in the last generation. These Latino Catholics do not constitute evidence that the American

The Decline and Fall of the Catholic Church in America

Catholic Church is making strong retention or recruitment efforts. They do not count as "retainees," since they are not old members who were retained. They are old members of the Catholic Church, yes, but not old members of the American Catholic Church. And they do not count as "recruits" either, since they were not converted to Catholicism. They were already Catholics before arriving here.

There has been plenty of "slippage" in the Catholicism of these immigrants. Many of them are far less Catholic here than they would have been in the old country. For in the old country, Catholicism permeated the culture, something it is far from doing in the United States. In a Catholicism-permeated culture, it is hard not to be Catholic, no matter how slight one's private religious impulses may be. In a largely secularized culture, such as America's, it is the easiest thing in the world for a person of weak religious impulses not to be Catholic. What is more, many Latinos with stronger private religious impulses have, since coming to the United States, switched to Evangelical and Pentecostalist forms of Protestantism, the same switch that has been taking place in many of their old countries.

The truth is, the Catholic Church in the United States has done a relatively poor job of maintaining the Catholicism of its newly arrived Latino members. This is in striking contrast to the excellent job the Church did of maintaining the Catholicism of its earlier immigrants of European background — the Irish, the Quebecois, the Italians, the Germans, the Poles and other Slavs. There are two reasons for this contrast. One is that the older groups brought lots of their own priests and nuns along with them — from Ireland, from Italy, and so forth — whereas the Latino groups have brought relatively few. The other reason is that these Latino groups began in large numbers at precisely the moment when the American Catholic Church was losing its self-confidence and adopting a denominational mentality. Why make a strenuous effort to maintain the Catholicism of Latino immigrants if Catholicism were not the uniquely true faith? By contrast, the European immigrants came to America when the denominational mentality had no hold on American Catholics; at a moment when Catholics were thoroughly convinced that they possessed the one true faith. Quite naturally, then, every effort was made to maintain the Catholicism of these older immigrants and their children.

The American Church needs to get a true understanding of its dwindling numbers

When we compare the number of Catholics today with the number forty years ago, we should, if we want to compare apples with apples, subtract millions of nominal Catholics and millions of Latino immigrant Catholics, and then we will get a clearer picture of what kind of job the American Catholic Church has done in retaining old members and recruiting new ones, and we will see that it has done a poor job: a poor job of passing the Faith on to children, and an equally poor job of retaining baptized Catholics as active members of the Church.

But this poor job is exactly what you would expect in a church that has been affected — or *infected* — by the denominational mentality. American Catholicism is traveling down the road earlier traveled by mainline American Protestantism: a road that terminates, it seems likely, in something resembling extinction.

Chapter 18

The Denominational Mentality
Destroys the Dogmatic Principle

All religions include a certain element of faith. That is to say, a religion makes no sense unless its adherents believe a few things about God or the gods, about the universe, about what happens to the soul following death, and so forth. In many religions, however, this faith element is a minor thing in comparison with the ritual element. For instance, in most religions that we used to call "primitive" (it is politically incorrect to call them that nowadays), the ritual is elaborate, and the doctrines are few. The priest is one who, after long training, has acquired great ceremonial expertise. His theological expertise, by contrast, is minimal, simply because there is not much theology to be expert about.

In many ancient religions, moreover, beliefs were held largely as matters of personal opinion. The ancient Greeks developed a large and wonderful mythology about gods, demigods, and heroes — a mythology we still find fascinating today. But these stories were not dogmas; they were not articles in a creed; you did not have to believe them unless you felt like it. Perhaps the only belief in Greek religion that had a truly dogmatic character about it — that is, the only belief you could get in trouble for rejecting — was the belief in the existence of the gods. Atheism the Greeks disapproved of. But even with regard to this mandatory belief, it did not really matter what you believed *about* the gods, so long as you believed they existed. You could believe in one God or hundreds; you could be a monotheist on Monday, Wednesday, and Friday and a polytheist on Tuesday and Thursday; you could accept the popular myths about the gods or reject them; you could reject some as undignified while accepting others.

Christianity is essentially and distinctively a dogmatic religion

Well, Christianity is a very different breed of cat. It is a highly dogmatic religion; at least it had always been so until the emergence of liberal Protestantism in the nineteenth century; and even today it remains so in most of its branches — in Catholicism, in Orthodoxy, in Evangelical and Pentecostalist Protestantism. In Christianity, the belief element has been as important as the ritual element, perhaps even more important. And it is not just that Christianity proposes a lot of beliefs to the consideration of its followers; these are *official* beliefs, beliefs you have to subscribe to if you wish to be a member in good standing — in a word, dogmas.

This explains why Christianity, unlike almost any other religion in human history, has employed creeds. The early Church informally adopted the so-called Apostles' Creed; more formally, creeds were adopted at the councils of Nicea (fourth century) and Chalcedon (fifth century). In the Reformation era of the sixteenth and seventeenth centuries, the newly organized Protestant churches adopted creeds: the Augsburg Confession of the Lutherans; the Thirty-nine Articles of the Anglicans; the Westminster Confession of the Presbyterians. Not to be outdone, the Catholics during this era adopted the so-called "Creed of Pius IV" at the Counter-Reformation Council of Trent (sixteenth century). This list is only a small fraction of the many statements of dogma that Christian churches have issued in the more than 1,900 years of Christian history.

To the degree that your thinking is inspired by the dogmatic principle, you will be sensitive to the presence of religious beliefs that differ from your own. You will notice differences, even small differences, between the beliefs held by your church and those held by some rival church. Witness as just one example the dogmatic conflicts between Catholics and Protestants in the Reformation era. Some of these had to do with quite obvious differences in belief, e.g., those relating to the papacy, Catholics considering the pope to be the Vicar of Christ, Protestants viewing him as the antichrist. But other differences — having to do with the atonement, with justification, and with the mode in which Christ is present in the Eucharist — were so subtle that those of us living a few centuries later have a hard time, even after close inspection, seeing just what the differences were. Yet sixteenth-century dogmatists were able, not only to see the differences, but to feel that these small and subtle distinctions, these infinitesimal nuances, were matters of exceedingly great importance, so important that it was worth provoking a rupture in European civilization.

Those whose thinking, on the other hand, is inspired by the denominational principle tend to ignore theological differences between churches, especially subtle differences. "This is not worth fighting about," says the denominational mentality. "It is ridiculous for churches to denounce one another because of nearly invisible doctrinal differences on matters such as justification, the Eucharist, and even the divinity of Christ. That way lies animosity, conflict, social division. Let us focus instead on what unites us, not what divides us. Let us focus on what we have in common, which is so much more important than what is distinctive to each." In other words, the spirit of denominationalism is flatly incompatible with the spirit of dogmatism.[52]

---

[52] Persons with an antidogmatic mentality have always had great fun when telling the story of the earliest Church councils,

Denominationalism is incompatible
with Christian dogmatism

The denominational principle, therefore, tends toward the production of nondogmatic religion. It does not arrive at this conclusion all at once, of course, but it moves inevitably in that direction. For such is the inherent logic of denominationalism. If we consider all religions to be equally worthy, if we consider all sincere believers to be equally honorable, then how can we continue to place emphasis on those dogmas that distinguish our religion from others? For such an emphasis means that we consider our religion to be truer than others, and if truer, then better. But to claim that our religion is better and truer than the other fellow's is inconsistent with the basic premise of denominationalism.

Thoroughgoing denominationalists, therefore, will renounce dogmatism altogether. This does not mean that they will necessarily renounce holding all religious opinions; but they will hold these as private conjectures only, not as definite truths; they will not adhere to them in a dogmatic spirit. If, for instance, you are a true denominationalist with a nostalgic attachment to traditional Christian teachings, you may well be inclined to believe that Jesus really did rise bodily from the dead; but you will not feel sure of this; you will not even want to feel sure of it; and, above all, you will not be tempted to insist that you are right and the person who denies this is wrong. At most, belief in the Resurrection will be your "personal opinion," little more than a subjective preference, like your preference for chocolate ice cream over vanilla. When it comes to ice cream, you do not insist that chocolate-lovers are right and vanilla-lovers wrong; you simply enjoy your chocolate quietly while allowing the other fellow to enjoy his vanilla.

> which saw ferocious disputes over exceedingly fine points of doctrine, mere *iotas*. But from the point of view of a person with a dogmatic mentality, these were exactly the kinds of dispute the Church Fathers should have had. Iotas *matter*.

If denominationalism in religion implies a nondogmatic attitude, the converse is also true: a nondogmatic attitude in religion implies denominationalism. If we believe nothing dogmatically, if our articles of faith are no more than personal preferences, then it becomes impossible for us to disapprove of someone else for disagreeing with one of our beliefs. All beliefs and belief-systems will be approximately equal in merit.

The inherent contradiction
of denominationalism

Here, however, we should take note of something of a contradiction that enters into the attitudes of many nondogmatic denominationalists. They hold no dogmas — except for the "dogma" that one should hold no dogmas. They consider all religions to be equal — except for those religions that do not consider all religions equal. In practice, nondogmatic denominationalists, who are prepared to give their approval to all sincere believers, often disapprove of those who sincerely disbelieve in denominationalism and nondogmatism. Thus, in the contemporary world of American religion, many liberal Protestants (and many liberal Catholics, I may add), although full of the spirit of tolerant denominationalism, disapprove of fundamentalists and other sectarian Protestants.

From the denominationalist point of view, the trouble with fundamentalists and other sectarians is not that they hold a number of beliefs, but that they hold them in a dogmatic, exclusive, and intolerant mode; they hold them in such a way as to say, "We are right, and you are wrong." If, by contrast, they were to hold them in such a way as to say, "These just happen to be our customary beliefs, so we like to reiterate them in church every Sunday. But please don't worry; we are not claiming that we're right and you are wrong" — this would be completely compatible with the denominational spirit.

Chapter 19

The Denominational Mentality
Erodes Orthodoxy

Orthodoxy, a transliteration from the Greek, means "right teaching" or "correct teaching." *Heresy* (or *heterodoxy*) is the opposite of *orthodoxy*, meaning "wrong teaching" or "incorrect teaching." The fact that these words originated among ancient Greek Christians reminds us that Christianity, from the very beginning, thought it important to make sharp dogmatic distinctions.

The word *heresy* is difficult to use nowadays. For one thing, it is historically associated with the old *odium theologicum*; it calls to mind the kind of religious persecution we thought we had safely put behind us. For another, the word has often been used in the twentieth century ironically and honorifically, as a term of praise for those who have the independence and courage to be nonconformist in their opinions. I hope I will be permitted to use the word *heresy* here in a way that is neither hateful nor honorific. I need a word to refer to opinions that deviate from orthodox Christian belief, especially orthodox Catholic belief. I suppose I could keep saying *unorthodox*, but this, in addition to being rather awkward when used again and again, is exposed to some of the same objections raised regarding *heresy*. In this chapter, I propose to use the word *heresy*, therefore, along with its adjectival and adverbial variants, in a technical, nonjudgmental sense. My intention is simply to *describe* contemporary American heretics; I have no wish to condemn or to praise them.

A dogmatic religion that permits
heresy is a contradiction in terms

A dogmatic religion has no choice but to be intolerant of heresy, at least heresy that emerges within its own ranks. A church that tolerates in-house heresy will soon find that it has plenty of it; and a church rife with heresy, a church in which the holding of heterodox opinions is a normal state of affairs, can no longer be considered a dogmatic church.

Every so often, Vatican authorities discipline a theologian for holding unorthodox views on some moral or doctrinal question — for example, the well-known dissidents Hans Kung, Charles Curran, and Tissa Balisuraya. Inevitably this leads to an uproar of protest in liberal Catholic circles. Sometimes the protesters claim the Vatican has made a mistake — that the theologian's views are in fact not heretical. More commonly, however, the protest is grounded on the idea that the Vatican really should not be in the heresy-hunting business at all; that it should be willing to allow freedom of theological opinion (even heretical opinion) in the Church, just as we allow freedom of political opinion in a liberal and democratic society.

But how can the Church do this without ceasing to be a dogmatic church? A dogmatic religion that does not punish heresy is nothing less than a contradiction in terms. Or if it is not a contradiction in terms, on the very first day it adopts this nonenforcement policy (for these things take time to reveal their full implications), it will become such in relatively short order.

What sociologists say about deviance in general holds true here as well, for heresy is simply a form of cognitive deviance; that is to say, it is a form of intellectual nonconformity. Just as a society has rules that prohibit certain kinds of behavior (bank robbery, for instance), so it has rules that prohibit certain kinds of opinion as well. Even a very liberal society, such as our own American society, will have at least a few of these required beliefs. Americans are not allowed to believe that we would be better off if ruled by a Nazi or a Communist dictatorship; nor are we allowed to believe that the earth is flat, or that George Washington is not really dead but is sleeping in a mountain cave and will return to lead us when we really need him. Of course, someone who holds such deviant beliefs will not be imprisoned or fined; but he will be ridiculed or held in contempt, and these are forms of punishment.

In any society that has rules (and every society, whether a church or a baseball team or a great nation like the United States, necessarily has rules), a certain amount of deviance — rule-breaking — is bound to occur from time to time. By punishing deviance, society vindicates its rules and keeps most potential deviants on the conforming side of the line. But if society fails to punish deviants, if it tolerates rule-breakers — whether these rule-breakers be bank robbers or heretics — over time, this policy of tolerant inaction is tantamount to repeal of the rule: implicit repeal by process of gradual erosion. The absence of a red light is tantamount to a green light.

The denominational mentality, being "soft" on the dogmatic aspect of religion, is reluctant to punish in-house heretics. If we have decided to soft-pedal dogma, does it really make sense to get into the business of bringing charges of heresy, of punishing the unorthodox by throwing them out of their professorships and pastorates? This is a nasty and unpleasant business. It becomes nastier and more unpleasant still when carried on against someone who is a decent person, whose unorthodox views seem well intentioned, and who will often be a personal colleague and friend of those whose task it is to enforce the requirements of orthodoxy. A person with a strongly dogmatic mind will perhaps rise to the challenge, saying (as Aristotle did when he criticized the Platonists),

The Decline and Fall of the Catholic Church in America

"We love our friends, but we love the truth more." A person less in love with the dogmatic side of religion (in other words, a person with a denominational mentality) will recoil from the task.

Besides, says the denominational mentality, does it make sense to go to war with heretics in our own ranks when we are so tolerant toward heretics in churches other than our own? The essence of denominationalism, remember, is a friendly tolerance toward persons of other faiths, no matter how much they depart from what we consider to be orthodoxy. Of course, we might want to maintain a slightly stricter standard for those in our own church than for those in other churches, just as we have stricter moral standards for members of our own family than we have for members of our neighbor's family. But "slightly stricter" standards are one thing, diametrically opposite standards something else. If the rule is "Anything goes" when we think about our neighbor's church, how can the rule be "Nothing is permitted but the strictest orthodoxy" when thinking about our own?

The full implications of this tolerance of in-house heresy will not immediately reveal themselves. At the outset, the heresies will be moderate ones, and they will be put forward in a discreet manner, e.g., in classroom lectures to graduate students of theology or in theological journals with a tiny circulation. Heresy in a church will not begin with someone shouting from the rooftops, "Jesus Christ is a fine man, but he is not divine." Yet once it is realized that discreet, moderate heretics are being left unmolested, bolder and more radical ones will step forward, and then those who are bolder and more radical still, and so forth; until finally those who deny the most fundamental Christian doctrines will be able to say their piece in a quite public way and get away with it. The once-dogmatic religion will have ceased being dogmatic.

This is a slippery slope that liberal Protestant denominations have slid down again and again. Their denominational mentality made them reluctant to get into the distasteful business of squelching the moderate heretics in their midst, with the result that eventually — in some churches sooner, in others later — they were playing host to a mass of radical heretics. Except, of course, that by this time, these "heretics" were not heretics anymore, since official dogma had virtually collapsed, and where there is no official dogma, there can be no heretical deviations from that dogma.

A religion that tolerates heresy will also tolerate secularism

If it is true, as I have argued, that the denominational mentality leads both to a weakening of the dogmatic principle and to a tolerance of in-house heretics, then what is the attitude of this mentality toward outright secularists — those who are not only non-Christian, but non-theistic, those who quite simply reject any religious belief?

The answer, once again, is tolerance. If we respect everyone's theological opinion, how can we condemn disbelief in God? That, too, is a theological opinion, is it not? All the arguments that can be adduced in favor of tolerating religious diversity and heresy apply here as well. If the atheist or agnostic in question is sincere, intellectually honest, and morally decent, how can we regard his belief as something deserving of condemnation? And can we suppose God really cares? Can we suppose that God is pained or made indignant because some law-abiding citizen is skeptical of his existence? Religious unbelief is simply one more theological opinion in a society in which people hold a wide range of theological opinions. It may not be *our* opinion, but so what? Theological opinions held by churches other than our own or by heretics in our own church — these are not our opinions either, but we, with our denominational mentality, are quite content to respect them. So why should atheism and agnosticism not be included in the circle of our genial tolerance?

The Decline and Fall of the Catholic Church in America

At first glance, the line separating theism from non-theism may seem wider and more definite than that separating one variety of theism from another. The former looks like a difference in kind, the latter only a difference in degree. A spirit of toleration was bound to expand until it finally embraced all degrees of theism. But is there not something like a firebreak between theism and non-theism? Is it not natural for the denominational mentality to come to a halt at this firebreak?

Well, yes, it may have seemed natural to halt when this line was first reached. But earlier in the history of the denominational mentality, it seemed quite natural to halt at certain previous lines of division; they, too, once looked like firebreaks. American Protestants could, for instance, tolerate all forms of Protestantism, but there was a great gulf fixed between Protestantism and Catholicism; surely it would feel "unnatural" to cross that line. Yet cross it they eventually did. But if Protestants could learn to tolerate Catholicism, surely there must be a firebreak between Christianity-in-general and Judaism; we could never truly tolerate the latter, could we? And yet we have done so. Further, we have come to tolerate Mormons and Jehovah's Witnesses; and as American demography changes, we are learning to tolerate such hitherto strange religions as Islam and Buddhism and Hinduism. In the last analysis, the denominational mentality recognizes no firebreaks.

Moreover, this conclusion is not simply an inference from the denominational principle or from previous history. It is now a fact of experience. As recently as forty or fifty years ago, unbelief was still a shocking and scandalous thing to Americans. The Supreme Court's *Engel v. Vitale* decision of 1962 (the decision declaring mandatory student prayer in public schools to be unconstitutional) was a turning point; or, to return to the metaphor I have been using, it was the moment we began leaping over the firebreak. Today in America, unbelief is still fairly unusual, the United States being just about the most theistic of modernized nations;

but it is no longer shocking and scandalous; it is no longer seen as an offense to good morals or good manners.[53] If you choose to be an atheist or an agnostic, fine; we respect your choice just as much as we respect the choices of those who elect to be Presbyterian or Greek Orthodox. As an atheist or agnostic, you belong to a cognitive minority, true enough; but so do the Presbyterians and Greek Orthodox. America is a nation of cognitive minorities. Being a cognitive minority, however, is not the same as being cognitively deviant.

At this point in the dialectic of denominationalism, we arrive at what looks very much like a *reductio ad absurdum*. What began as friendly toleration of the other fellow's religion has ended in friendly toleration of the other fellow's nonreligion — or even irreligion. What began with a search for a doctrinal common denominator has ended with abandonment of the idea that there must be any doctrinal common denominator at all.

What does this mean for American Catholicism? If Catholics adopt, as they largely have done, the denominational mentality, they will have set their foot on the very slippery slope that leads to toleration of agnosticism and atheism. And by *toleration* here I mean religious indifferentism: the belief that all theories about the ultimate nature of reality and the ultimate meaning of life are approximately equally worthwhile. I mean the belief that Catholicism is good, and so is Protestantism, and so is Judaism, and so is Islam, and so is agnosticism, and so is atheism; and, moreover, they are roughly equally as good as one another. That is where the logic

---

[53] I have been a college philosophy teacher since 1963. In my early years, there may have been, for all I know, a few atheists in my classroom. But no one ever openly declared his atheism during class discussion. Such a declaration would have astonished most hearers, probably including me. But nowadays I am not surprised to hear two or three such declarations every semester; and if any students are astonished at these declarations, they have the good form to conceal their astonishment.

of the denominational mentality takes us. And that, more to point, is a *terminus ad quem* thoroughly incompatible with a dogmatic religion like Catholicism. If American Catholics adopt this mentality in a widespread way, the Church in America will be doomed.

Part V

The Search for a
National Moral Consensus

Chapter 20

Experimenting with a National
Religion Based on Morality

American secularists, as we saw earlier, were unwilling to follow
John Dewey in his proposal for a Religion of Humanity and Nature; a proposal that, despite its naturalistic and atheistic content,
would have gone so far as to permit the continued use of the word
God — that word, of course, having been suitably redefined. And
needless to say, American religious believers never dreamed of accepting Dewey's proposal for a "common faith." Thus Dewey's proposal of the mid-1930s came to nothing. It was certainly no longer
around when the Supreme Court prayer decision of 1962 signaled
that the Judeo-Christian consensus was at an end and that secularists would now have to be welcomed as full-fledged members of
the national community.

Could America adopt
a purely *moral* national faith?

So what was to be done after 1962 and the prayer decision? If
the United States was to continue to be a moral community, and
not simply a utilitarian association, this community could no longer have a religious basis; for secularists, now entitled to full membership in the community, would not join their fellow Americans
in affirming even a thin religious consensus. They would veto a

religious basis for this community just as surely as Christians would veto an atheistic basis.

But could not everybody agree on a purely *moral* basis? Could not everybody, whether a religious believer or an unbeliever, agree for example that murder is wrong and that democracy is good? Religious believers, if they wished, could go a step further (in private, so to speak) and ground this morality on religion, while unbelievers could simply affirm the morality without reference to a transcendent foundation. For what difference did it make what this common morality was grounded upon, if anything at all, so long as there was consensus about it?

And was this really such a big step from the previous Judeo-Christian consensus? Was it, in fact, not the logical next step, and rather a small step at that? After all, by the time the prayer decision was handed down in 1962, the unofficial American national religion — the Judeo-Christian religion — had already been largely stripped of its doctrinal content and become almost a purely moral faith. Just about the only doctrinal point the many varieties of American Jews and Christians could agree on was that God exists. But even here there was much less than full agreement; for although everyone could agree on the verbal formula ("God exists"), there was considerable disagreement as to precisely how *God* should be defined.

Yet, despite the thinness of the doctrinal consensus, there was still, in those pre-1962 days, a relatively thick *moral* consensus. Everybody agreed that lying, cheating, stealing, robbery, rape, and murder were wrong. Everyone believed in democracy and the rule of law. Everyone believed that education and honest hard work were good things. Monogamous marriage was a good thing; divorce, although sometimes unavoidable, was rather a bad thing. There was disagreement about the moral gravity of premarital sex, some holding that it was terribly wrong, others viewing it as a merely venial sin, if not a peccadillo; but there was a general belief that it was wrong. And, of course, unmarried cohabitation was clearly wrong; abortion was criminally wrong; and homosexuality was unspeakably wrong. In the early 1960s, abortionists were still being prosecuted, and undercover cops were still laying traps for homosexual men who solicited other men in public places.

Another way of putting this is to say that, by the 1950s, the national religion had pretty nearly arrived at the point at which Matthew Arnold, the great Victorian poet and critic, had arrived three-quarters of a century earlier. Arnold — in an attempt to preserve what he regarded as the essential core of biblical religion when its peripheral doctrines (its "overbeliefs," as he called them) were under severe attack from natural science and German biblical criticism — had defined religion as "morality touched by emotion." And he had defined God as "the Eternal not-ourselves that makes for righteousness." In other words, the essence of religion was morality; and the only doctrinal belief of any importance was the belief that there is some power in reality (popularly known as God) that supports us in our efforts to lead morally good lives.

But if religion was almost entirely a matter of morality, then it seems that bringing nonbelievers into the national community would not be the dramatic change religious conservatives supposed at first glance. As long as atheists and agnostics subscribed to the common American moral code, what was the problem? They were subscribing to the essence — the moral essence — of the national faith, were they not? True enough, under the new dispensation, we would have to drop references to God, and that would be sure to cause a certain amount of sentimental heartburn. But consider this: God had already been demoted to a kind of second-rank position in the national faith. That is, God's role was to support morality; it was not the role of morality to lead the nation to God. So if the Judeo-Christian national faith consisted, in a sense, of moral decency plus God as a reinforcement, the new national faith — the tripartite Judeo-Christian-secularist faith — would consist in a sense of decency alone. Would this be such a big change?

As we will see shortly, yes, it would be a big change. This is not because a purely moral basis of community would be impossible in theory; nor even because it would be impossible in practice, given the right cultural conditions; but because it would be impossible in actual American practice, given the cultural conditions that prevailed in the United States beginning in the 1960s.

America achieved a thin moral consensus by trimming the Judeo-Christian moral code

I have been arguing both sides of the question, the question being this: In the absence of a religious consensus, could the United States, beginning in the early 1960s, retain its moral consensus? And since a moral consensus is an indispensable condition for moral community, this question, of course, entails the further question: Could the United States continue to exist as a moral community? Or would it be reduced to the level of a purely utilitarian association?

Clearly the transition from a Judeo-Christian national community to a believer-plus-secularist community would require, not just the dropping of all religious doctrine, but also a "thinning out" of moral doctrine, since some parts of the hitherto national moral consensus had been derived from biblical teachings. But how far would this thinning out have to be carried? How much of the older moral code would have to be deleted to get down to a moral code common to theists and non-theists?

Complicating this issue was the fact that there was much moral diversity among non-theists — far more than among theists. Christianity, after all, was originally a breakaway from Judaism; Protestantism was a breakaway from medieval Catholicism; and the younger Protestant churches were breakaways from the older ones. No matter how much the Judeo-Christian religions had diverged from one another, they all had a common theological ancestry; and this meant that, like biological species with a common evolutionary root, they tended to resemble one another. They were homologous, and the resemblance was especially striking in their moral codes. Hence, not a great deal of thinning out had been needed in order to find a common code acceptable to Protestants, Catholics, and Jews. For instance, they all agreed on the authoritativeness of the Ten Commandments — even though Catholics might number them differently from Protestants and Jews, and even though the various faiths might give somewhat different interpretations to this or that commandment.

By contrast, non-theists had much less of a common philosophical ancestry. They had no sacred books. They had no canonical prophets. They all revered Darwin, of course. Many of the highbrows among them were fans of John Dewey. Many of the middlebrows were fans of Bertrand Russell (the Russell of the popular works, e.g., "Why I Am Not a Christian," not the Russell of the esoteric works in mathematics, logic, and epistemology). Many of the radicals were devotees of Karl Marx. Some few were fans of Nietzsche. Yet many others were equally uninterested in Dewey, Russell, Marx, or Nietzsche. They had no common creed, no common morality; and the closest thing to a common ancestry among them was that most of them were philosophically descended from the eighteenth-century Enlightenment. Yet even this was not true of all of them, for many were culturally descended from that great anti-Enlightenment movement, Romanticism.

To create a new American moral consensus, then, it would not be possible to accommodate the secularists as a bloc, since they did not constitute a bloc; they constituted many more or less independent blocs. An American moral consensus, then, would have to involve an accommodation with all these blocs, at least with all the really significant ones.

The Decline and Fall of the Catholic Church in America

One thing should have been clear from the beginning, that is, from the moment the national moral community ceased to be a Judeo-Christian community and was faced with the need of reconstructing a community that would include both believers and nonbelievers. It should have been clear that many religion-based elements of American morality would have to go. They could continue to be part of one's private morality, of course, but they could no longer be insisted on as part of the quasi-official public morality. For how could a religious morality, or any portion of a religious morality, be an element in a common national morality embraced by religious and nonreligious citizens alike?

I say this *should* have been clear — and yet it was not. And why not? Because many people were unaware of just how dependent the American moral consensus had been on the Judeo-Christian religious tradition. This is not to say that some people did not pay lip service to the great impact of this tradition; they paid such lip service all the time. But not many, except perhaps a few religious conservatives, had seriously thought through what was bound to happen once the American moral consensus was deprived of its biblical foundations.

Let us make a list of what logically was bound to go — and we will see how strikingly this corresponds to what in fact *did* go over the next few decades.

• *Sexual morality in general.* The strict code of sexual morality would have to go. Every society needs a sexual code, of course, and this will always be more or less restrictive, never permitting absolute sexual license. But few codes have been as restrictive as those connected with traditional Judaism, Catholicism, and Protestantism; few have rated chastity at quite so high a value. The chances that secularists, in constructing a sexual code on nonreligious grounds, would come up with an equally strict code were zero. Thus a "sexual revolution" was bound to be a result of a new consensus morality that leaves religion out of the picture; which is to say, among other things, that the traditional taboo on fornication would have to be considerably relaxed.

• *Cohabitation.* The taboo on unmarried cohabitation would also have to go. This is an obvious corollary of the sexual revolution. It makes little sense to permit unmarried people to have sex if we are not equally prepared to allow them to live openly together without being married.

• *Out-of-wedlock births.* Here is another corollary of the sexual revolution. If unmarried sex is permitted, it is bound to happen that there will be a certain number of out-of-wedlock pregnancies, some intended, some not. If we permit the antecedent (unmarried sex), then how can we censure the consequent (out-of-wedlock births)?

• *Divorce.* Negative attitudes toward divorce would have to go, as well as laws meant to enforce those attitudes. Here is yet another corollary of the sexual revolution. The revolution means that adults should be free to choose — and free to reject — sexual partners. But marriage, involving as it does a promise of fidelity, is a restriction on that freedom. Now, there is, of course, nothing wrong with that restriction, provided it is voluntarily accepted. But when the marriage has become an unhappy one, when the partners are yoked together, not by mutual consent, but by the forces of law and public opinion, there is no voluntariness; the principle of sexual freedom has been violated. In the world of the sexual revolution, both law and public opinion will have to recognize the right of a marriage partner to walk out of a marriage whenever he or she chooses. In other words, we would need "no-fault" divorce laws and the removal of the stigma that hitherto attached to divorce. Both law and public opinion will have to regard divorce as a legitimate personal choice.

• *Abortion*. Here is still another corollary of the sexual revolution. What sense does it make to have a regime of sexual freedom if it is not at the same time a regime of easy abortion?

• *Homosexuality*. If we permit a high degree of sexual freedom, how can this reasonably be confined to heterosexuals? For traditional religious believers, homosexuality may well be the "abomination" that the Bible calls it. But how can it be assigned that valuation by nonbelievers in the absence of a good secular reason for the traditional detestation of homosexuality? In fact, homosexuality is a kind of test case for sexual freedom. If we refuse to extend this freedom to homosexuals, it shows we are still smuggling religious considerations into our moral code. On the other hand, if we permit homosexuality, which religious believers have always regarded as an especially obnoxious form of sexual deviance, it shows we have finally developed a religion-free sexual code. (The desacralization of the American moral code would extend beyond sex — to suicide, for instance — but sex was its most obvious field of application.)

And, of course, all these should-have-been-foreseeable consequences did, in fact, come about. Once secularists, in all their bewildering moral variety, entered the national community on an equal footing with religious believers, and once it became plain that we could not have a national moral code that was unacceptable to these secularists, the sexual revolution of the 1960s and '70s followed. Within a dozen years following the 1962 prayer decision, this sexual revolution had led to an explosion of premarital sex and cohabitation, an epidemic of out-of-wedlock births, no-fault divorce laws and a skyrocketing divorce rate, the legalization and widespread moral acceptance of abortion, and the beginnings and rapid progress of the homosexual movement.

I do not mean to suggest that welcoming secularists as full-fledged members of the national moral community was the *only* factor that led to the sexual revolution. It was an indispensable factor, a *sine qua non*, but there were, of course, other factors. Earlier I talked about some of them: the philosophical preconditions of moral relativism and ethical emotivism (or "choice-ism"); the generalized rebellion against authority that arose in the 1960s in connection with social protests against racism and the war in Vietnam; not to mention the "affluent society" that middle-class Americans and their children lived in during the two decades following World War II.

Evaluating the candidates for a new moral code

But secularist demands for a reform of the American moral code could not be confined to specific details, like no-fault divorce, homosexuality, and abortion. It was a matter of general principles as well. It is inevitable that thoughtful people will attempt to reduce their many moral rules to a small number of abstract principles from which these rules may be derived, perhaps even to a single abstract principle. Kant had done this with his Categorical Imperative;[54] Bentham had done the same with his Greatest Happiness Principle;[55] and Jesus had done the same when he reduced the law to two principles: love God with all your heart, mind, soul, and strength, and love your neighbor as yourself.

Moreover, this reduction to a small number of abstract principles is not simply a manifestation of philosophical tidiness. It is indispensable for purposes of instruction and polemic. If you are teaching a moral code to followers or to children, it will not be enough to list innumerable detailed rules. You will want to teach them the general principles from which those rules can be derived.

[54] Kant, *Groundwork of the Metaphysics of Morals*, H. J. Paton, trans. (New York: Harper Torchbooks, 1964), 88.

[55] Bentham, *An Introduction to the Principles of Morals and Legislation*, ch. 1, sect. 2; also Bentham, *A Fragment on Government*, preface, 2.

If you do not, they will not really understand the spirit informing the rules; worse still, they will not know how to respond to a situation for which they cannot remember a specific rule. Likewise, if you are defending your moral code before an audience of foes or skeptics, you will not be able to confine your defense to particular items; your audience will challenge the principles that lie behind those items.

Thus it was that in the post-1962 era, as "negotiations" proceeded for the development of a new post-theistic moral consensus, secularists learned to defend their specific ethical rules with appeals to abstract principles. (I propose to refer to moral debates between religious believers and secularists as "negotiations," as though the two sides were trying to arrive at a mutually agreeable consensus as to what the moral code should be for the American moral community. I realize these debates were not really negotiations, but they were something *like* negotiations. It is, I believe, a helpful metaphor.)

Now, a number of famous philosophical principles — principles that did not commit one to any religious beliefs — *might* have been appealed to by the secularists, but they were generally ignored. What were these principles?

• *Natural law.* There was the natural-law principle, first enunciated in the ancient world by the Stoics,[56] then carried on by Christian theologians — especially Catholic theologians, most notably Thomas Aquinas (1225-1274), an Italian Catholic priest, member of the Dominican Order, and professor of theology at the University of Paris. But this theory held little attraction for secularists. Even though natural-law theory teaches that it is entirely possible for humans to discern the difference between right and wrong without need of divine revelation, still it has a kind of

[56] The Stoic school was founded by Zeno of Citium in about 300 B.C.

incidental religious flavor to it. The Stoics, after all, taught that the rules of morality were ultimately based on God or Nature or Reason (three names for the same ultimate reality); and Catholic theologians had incorporated natural-law theory into the Catholic moral system.

• *Categorical Imperative*. Again, an attempt might have been made to base secular morality on the ethical theory of Immanuel Kant. His ultimate Categorical Imperative could be expressed several ways. One of these was: Act on universal principles only; in other words, act according to rules that you can consistently will to be rules for everyone's actions; make no special exceptions for yourself or your friends. Another was: Always treat humanity, whether in yourself or in others, as an *end* (something intrinsically valuable), never merely as a *means* (something instrumentally valuable only). But Kant, although an Enlightenment rationalist, and therefore presumably "liberated" from the Christianity of his childhood, carried a lot of Christian baggage with him. When examined in detail, his specific moral opinions pretty much coincide with Christian views, and Christian views moreover of the strictest kind, i.e., of the Pietistic kind.[57] This included Christian views on sexual questions. These comments on homosexual conduct were typical of Kant's views on sexuality: "This practice . . . is contrary to the ends of humanity. . . . The self is degraded below the level of animals, and humanity is dishonored."[58] And although he did not base morality on belief in God, he did the reverse, which, from a secularist point of view, would be just as bad: that is,

---

[57] Pietism was a German Protestant evangelical movement, analogous to Puritanism and Methodism in the English-speaking world. It began in the second half of the seventeenth century and was still going strong when Kant was a boy. He grew up in a Pietistic family and attended a Pietistic grammar school.

[58] Kant, *Lectures on Ethics* (Indianapolis: Hackett, 2002), 170.

he based belief in God on morality, teaching that the person who attempts to lead a morally good life will inevitably find himself believing in God. Clearly, Kant would not pass muster with secularists.

• *Utilitarianism*. Closer to being acceptable to secularists was the Utilitarianism of Jeremy Bentham (1748-1832) and his many followers, including John Stuart Mill (1806-1873), who produced a more sophisticated form of Utilitarianism. At least Bentham and his followers had the merit, from the secularist point of view, of leaving God quite out of the picture. The trouble, however, from the point of view of American secularists of the 1960s and '70s, was that Utilitarians tended to give priority to society over the individual. In asking what is morally right, they were, in effect, asking: "What's best for society as a whole?" Of course, society is made up of individuals, so in posing the question this way, they were not totally disregarding the interests of individuals. Nonetheless their emphasis was social rather than individualistic. But this clashed with the secularist temper of the 1960s and '70s — a temper that was radically individualistic, emphasizing the right to personal freedom, the right to "do your own thing."

Something all three of the above philosophies have in common is their conviction that the rules of morality are *objective* truths; they are not merely man-made conventions. But by the 1960s, American secularism was not in a mood to embrace the idea of objective or absolute moral truths. Morality, as many secularists, especially the young among them, saw it, was largely a matter of personal preference: "You choose your moral code, I'll choose mine, and we'll respect one another's right to choose." What was needed, then, was a theory that justified what may be called the "Personal Liberty Principle" (PLP).

In their "negotiations" with theists, as both sides attempted to grope their way toward a new American moral consensus, it was the PLP that most secularists clung to as their nonnegotiable demand. "This should keep all parties happy," they said, "since it allows everyone to be quite free to lead the life of his choosing, whether that life be puritanical or libertine or something in between. If you disapprove of cohabitation or abortion, fine; don't do either one. At the same time, those who approve of such things should be allowed to act on their convictions. What could be more tolerant? What could be more reasonable as a basis for a common American morality?"

Chapter 21

Evolution of the Personal Liberty Principle

The ground for the ready reception among secularists of the PLP had been prepared by a couple of intellectual fashions that flourished earlier in the century, fashions discussed earlier: cultural relativism and ethical emotivism. Both served to undermine the idea that there is an objective moral law. Both led to the conclusion that moral rules and values are, in the last analysis, simply matters of personal preference.

I do not mean to suggest that these ideas, or indeed any ideas, all by themselves, were enough to convert American secularists to a new way of thinking. People, after all, are not pure thinking machines. When we change our way of thinking, we need a motive for change, and the motive usually arises from the circumstances in our lives. Much depends on our friends, our foes, our jobs, our lack of jobs, et cetera. Before a conversion in our thinking takes place, we have to be ripe for conversion. Still, ripeness is not all. Once we become ripe, new ideas have to be presented to us before we can adopt them.

My argument, then, is this: In the two decades from the mid-1940s to the mid-1960s, Americans, especially younger ones, were ripe for the ethical theories being promoted by the cultural relativists and the logical positivists. America's splendid nineteenth-century isolation from the rest of the world had ended; the world was growing smaller; and ordinary Americans were becoming increasingly aware of the world's great cultural diversity. Even at home, we were growing more aware and more respectful of the diversity within our own boundaries. The United States had long been a nation in which the "normal" person was white and Protestant. But now Catholics and Jews had transformed themselves into real Americans, and even blacks were knocking at the door. Normality would have to be redefined; it would have to admit of variety. "White Protestant" would henceforth be only one way of being an American, one of many ways.

The prosperity of the post–World War II decades increased this awareness of diversity still further. More money meant more choices, choices not just of consumer goods, but of lifestyles. If you were rich enough — and more and more Americans were becoming at least moderately rich — you did not have to remain passive as the larger society imposed a way of life on you; you could actively choose your own way of life.

Clearly, in this postwar era, we were now living in a world in which it was vitally important that we be tolerant of one another. The need for tolerance was underlined by the fact that we had just been through two dreadful world wars, wars largely the result of national, racial, and religious intolerance. The need for tolerance was further underlined by the ominous fact that the threat of nuclear catastrophe was hanging over everyone. If the human race was to survive, we would have to keep our heads; we would have to avoid fanaticism; we would have to learn tolerance.

In such a social and economic environment, the theories of the cultural relativists and ethical emotivists were very plausible. Moral codes, both schools of thought agreed, were man-made things. For the relativists, they were social creations; for the emotivists, individual preferences. But either way, they were human inventions; they had no warrant beyond human preference, either collective or individual; they had not descended from Heaven, from Mount Sinai, or (as Kant would have it) from some impersonal and universal power of Reason. The lesson that seemed to follow from these two theories was the lesson of *tolerance*, precisely the lesson needed at this critical juncture of American history. If your moral code is just as human as mine, if mine is no more rooted in God or eternity than yours, then it follows (does it not?) that I should tolerate your way of life and you mine. By getting rid of the notion that we have a monopoly on moral truth, we can avoid the temptation to oppress others.

Which theory works better: relativism or emotivism?

But if cultural relativists and emotivists were correct in their agreed-upon assertion that moral rules are simply man-made creations, a further question arose: Which of the two theories, relativist or emotivist, should we adopt as the better?

If we opt for cultural relativism, we are opting for a conformist morality. We are saying that the rules of society should have authority over the individual; that the individual should subordinate his wishes and choices to the collective choices made by society as a whole. This option had a great deal of plausibility during World War II. After all, a great war cannot be fought effectively when a spirit of individualism is running rampant. An individual might prefer not risking his life in combat or making certain home-front sacrifices for the sake of the war effort; but in wartime, such individual wishes have to be subordinated to the wishes of the whole. If the nation was to win the war, the authority of the nation would have to be paramount; individuals would have to conform, regardless of personal preferences.

But what about after the war? Further, what about questions of personal morality; questions, for instance, having to do with sexual conduct? Why should I have to obey rules of society that tell me it is a naughty thing to go to bed with my girlfriend? It is easy enough to see why society should have authority over the individual when it comes to the war effort, but far less so when it comes to sex.

The further the United States moved away from the World War II years, the less plausible it seemed to argue that society's collective moral preferences were entitled to take priority over the moral preferences of the individual. The principle of social priority implied that good conduct was nothing more than conformity — conformity to the arbitrary will of society; or rather, conformity to the will of society's conservative and timid majority, for it is this majority that makes and enforces the moral rules of society. Nonetheless, the conformist momentum of the 1940s carried over into the 1950s, which was, for the most part, a decade of moral conformity. This enabled the cultural-relativist theory of morality to retain its plausibility; it comported well with the conformist spirit of the age.

But the sound of distant thunder could be heard. High school and college commencement speakers of the 1950s routinely denounced the spirit of conformism, even when the speakers themselves were great conformists and would be shocked if anyone seriously acted on these denunciations. So popular were commencement denunciations of conformism that we may almost say that it became an act of conformism to denounce conformism. Conspicuous nonconformists were celebrated by popular culture, especially among the young: Elvis Presley, Marlon Brando of *The Wild One*, James Dean of *Rebel without a Cause*, and, among the somewhat more literate division of the young, the San Francisco Beats — Ginsburg, Kerouac, and the others.

Something was about to explode.

The explosion took place in the mid-1960s. A generation of young people arrived on the American scene asking this question: "If moral rules are arbitrary preferences, not mandated by God or Nature or Reason, why should the preferences of society take priority over my own individual preferences? What is society, after all, but a collection of individuals? And why should the wishes of those individuals, many of them old and stupid, be morally more significant than the wishes of the individual, namely, myself?"

No good answer could be given, especially at a moment in American history when the authority of collective society was suffering a crisis of legitimacy. As noted in an earlier chapter, the black civil-rights movement had persuaded virtually everyone, above all the young, that American society had a long and vicious history of racism. Critics of the Vietnam War were increasingly successful at persuading the public — again, especially its younger sections — that the war was unwise and immoral. Now, if society was wrong about race and war, why should we imagine that it would be right about other things? About sex, for instance? Or about drugs?

A third way: John Stuart Mill and the
birth of the Personal Liberty Principle

Of course, there would have to be some limits to the right to design one's personal morality. After all, we cannot have people designing a personal code that permits them to rape, rob, commit murder, et cetera. That would lead to social chaos, violent anarchy, a war of all against all, a Hobbesian state of nature in which life would be solitary, poor, nasty, brutish, and short. And so, in the minds of secularists, especially secularists of the younger generation, what seemed a reasonable limitation evolved: "You can design or adopt whatever moral code you like — with the proviso that your conduct under that code will not cause harm to other people." This, in a nutshell, is the Personal Liberty Principle (or PLP as I have called it).

The PLP had been given its classical enunciation a century earlier by the English philosopher, economist, political scientist, and sociologist John Stuart Mill in his book *On Liberty* (1859).

Society, Mill said, should maximize the freedom of adult individuals to speak, act, and associate as they please, with this one proviso: *so long as they do not cause harm to others*. And how was society to maximize personal liberty? Simply by leaving people alone, by not interfering with their conduct, either by law or by the pressure of public opinion.

> The object of this essay [Mill famously declares in his opening chapter] is to assert one very simple principle, as entitled to govern absolutely the dealings of society with the individual in the way of compulsion and control, whether the means used be physical force in the form of legal penalties, or the moral coercion of public opinion. That principle is that the sole end for which mankind is warranted, individually or collectively, in interfering with the liberty of action of any of their number, is self-protection. That the only purpose for which power can be rightfully exercised over any member of a civilized community, against his will is to prevent harm to others. His own good, either physical or moral, is not a sufficient warrant. . . . The only part of the conduct of anyone, for which he is amenable to society, is that which concerns others. In the part which merely concerns himself, his independence is, of right, absolute. Over himself, over his own body and mind, the individual is sovereign.[59]

How was society to maximize personal liberty? Simply by leaving people alone, by not interfering with their conduct, either by law or by public opinion. The good society would be one in which everybody is thoroughly tolerant of everybody else (always, of course, with the no-harm-to-others exception). Harm to self would

---

[59] Mill, *On Liberty* in *Utilitarianism, Liberty, and Representative Government* (New York: Dutton, 1951), 95-96.

be permitted; otherwise a paternalistic alibi might be cooked up for all sorts of interference with freedom. Given this legally and socially tolerant atmosphere, diversity would flourish, diversity of opinion and conduct and association.

And diversity, said Mill, is a good thing, a very good thing. Why? Because it gives members of a society an enriched menu of options available to them; and with more options to choose from, we are more likely to discover true opinions and good modes of living.

Take opinions, for instance. The more opinions there are on a certain topic — a topic, say, of religion or politics or natural science — the more likely it is that at least one of these opinions will be the *true* opinion; and this true opinion having been discovered by some especially insightful thinker, the rest of us can then embrace it. But the fewer opinions there are, the more likely it will be that none of them is true, which means that society as a whole will have to go without the truth on that particular question. Of course, when there is complete freedom of opinion, many of the opinions that emerge, perhaps even most of them, will be false; but that is a price worth paying to get at the truth.

Or take conduct. When someone lives an unconventional kind of life, he is conducting what Mill calls an "experiment in living," rather akin to a scientific experiment. The more freedom of conduct there is in society, the more these experiments in living will take place; and these experiments can prove instructive to the rest of us, whether they turn out well or badly.[60]

---

[60] Mill, among other things, was one of the great economists of his day, and his economic theory was that of classical free-market liberalism, according to which, economic progress is made only through commercial competition. In this competition, some enterprises succeed, and others fail. These business failures are a price society pays — a price well worth paying — for economic progress. It seems likely that this was Mill's model for what he had to say about the desirability of

Mill's classic defense of the PLP was written more than a century before it was needed by the secularists of the cultural revolution of the 1960s and '70s. Mill expressed their central idea perfectly — the idea, namely, that we should be free to do whatever we like, provided we do not hurt others. Small wonder his book remains in print today, nearly 150 years after it was written, and remains in print in popular paperback editions. For the book continues to say what the typical moralist of the secularist kind wants to hear.

Beyond Mill, to the modern moral PLP

It is worth noting, however, that there are two rather distinct interpretations that can be given to the PLP. One interpretation (let us call it the moral PLP) says that conduct is morally permissible or right, so long as it does not hurt others. The other interpretation (let us call it the social PLP) does not concern itself with moral rightness or wrongness. It simply concerns itself with the limits of social control over the opinions and conduct of individuals. It does not go so far as to say that conduct is morally permissible so long as it does not hurt others; it simply says that we should not interfere with such conduct, regardless of whether it is moral or immoral.

Mill's own interpretation was of this latter kind; that is, he was a defender of the *social* PLP, not the moral PLP. In *On Liberty*, he does not discuss the morality of individual conduct; he simply discusses the limits that society should observe in placing restrictions on that conduct. If we wish to see Mill's discussion of individual morality, we have to read his *Utilitarianism*, written a few years

diversity in opinions and modes of living. Let ideas and modes of living compete in the markets of opinion and morality, and the best ideas and the best modes of living will eventually be victorious — just as the best business firms emerge victorious after competition in the commercial free market.

after *On Liberty*. Putting the two works together, we can see, I be-lieve, that Mill would have insisted that society has no right to in-terfere with a great deal of conduct that he himself would consider immoral.[61]

I think it is clear to any observer of the American scene that most of today's PLP enthusiasts, especially those of the younger generation, take Mill's principle and carry it beyond where he himself intended to go: that is to say, they are defenders of the *moral* PLP; they hold that conduct is morally permissible so long as it does not harm others.[62] This is because they define morality in

[61] On the other hand, it can be argued that Mill, despite his in-tentions, actually is offering a moral interpretation of PLP in *On Liberty*. For as a Benthamite or Utilitarian, and therefore a believer in the Greatest Happiness Principle, he holds that conduct is morally good whenever it contributes to the well-being of society as a whole. But in *On Liberty*, he argues that morally bad conduct — my neighbor's habitual drunkenness, let us say — contributes to the well-being of society by serv-ing as an instructive example of how *not* to lead one's life. Thus, immoral conduct (habitual drunkenness) is at the same time morally good conduct (in that it contributes to the well-being of society). This is only one of a number of inconsisten-cies that can be found in Mill's philosophy. The most famous of these is to be found in his *Utilitarianism*, where he asserts that in estimating the goodness of an action, only pleasure counts, but then goes on to assert that *quality* of pleasure counts, too. In both cases cited here, his inconsistency arises from a contradiction between his Benthamite theory and his moral intuitions. And this reminds one of yet another of Mill's inconsistencies: on the one hand, as a theorist, he did not believe in the possibility of moral intuition; on the other hand, as a very decent person ("the saint of Rationalism," Gladstone called him), he was chock full of very fine moral intuitions.

[62] Of course, if you are defender of the moral PLP, you will also be a defender of the social PLP; for the former implies the lat-ter, although the latter does not imply the former. If you think conduct is morally permissible or right insofar as it does not

such a way that it has to do with conduct only insofar as it impacts on others. Insofar as it impacts on me, an act may be wise or foolish, admirable or unadmirable, but it is neither moral nor immoral. If I get drunk tonight in the quiet of my home, this may be very disgusting and very stupid, but, provided it does not produce harm to others, it is not immoral.

In defining morality in this way, they are departing from the teaching of both traditional moral philosophy and traditional moral theology. The ancient Greek philosophers held that cowardice and intemperance — two vices that are the opposites of the cardinal virtues of courage and temperance — are immoral in and of themselves, quite apart from any hurtful impact they may have on others. And Catholic moralists have always taught, for example, that drunkenness and masturbation are sinful, quite apart from any hurtful impact they may have on others. That so many of today's Americans define morality as having to do with interpersonal relations only is either the cause of the popularity of the PLP or the effect of that popularity; probably a combination of both.

hurt others, you will also think that society has no business interfering with such right conduct; but it is possible to believe that certain conduct is morally wrong — homosexual intercourse, for instance — while at the same time believing that society should not prohibit that conduct.

Chapter 22

The Inevitable Culture War

At the time of the Supreme Court's prayer decision of 1962, the United States had not yet switched from the conformism of the '50s to the anti-conformism of the late '60s, although it was on the verge of doing so.

If we use our imaginations to go back to that moment, trying to picture to ourselves how big a shift would be involved in putting together a new moral consensus — a consensus that would include secularists as well as Jews and Christians — the shift would not seem, at first glance, to be all that great. For if Christians and Jews subscribed to a religion-based moral code, and secularists subscribed to a conformity-based code, then the two sides, it would seem, could readily arrive at a consensus. The dominant code of the day, the code of the great majority, was pretty much the same for both sides; it is just that the two sides conformed to the code for different reasons — the religious majority because they believed it was the will of God, the secularist minority because they believed that one should conform to the prevailing social code.

But a few years after the 1962 decision, the situation had changed completely. Among secularists, moral conformism was out, moral individualism and the PLP were in. In formulating a new moral consensus, the two major parties to the negotiations no longer came to the table with nearly identical moral codes.[63] The religious party still had its customary code, more or less biblical in origin, but now the secularist party had embraced a minimal code, nothing more than the PLP. The religious party still had a long list of "thou shalts" and "thou shalt nots," while the secularist party had reduced its morality to a single commandment, which could be formulated in a number of different but equivalent ways: Thou shalt be tolerant; thou shalt not be judgmental; thou shalt permit others to do whatever they want (provided they do not harm anybody).

Two methods of reaching a moral compromise

By the beginning of the '70s, the gap between the two parties was immense. How, then, was a moral consensus to be achieved? Some compromise would have to be worked out. In this case, as with every compromise, there were two ways of achieving it: the "half a loaf" (HAL) method and the "least common denominator" (LCD) method.

• *HAL*. In the HAL method, neither side gets what it wants in full; instead, each gets approximately half of what it wants and goes without the other half. This is the method of compromise typical of collective-bargaining agreements between labor and management. The union, for example, wants a 10-percent pay increase, while management wants to give no more than a 2-percent increase; in the end, they agree to a pay increase of about 5 or 6 percent; thus, both sides walk away with something like half a loaf.

---

[63] In speaking here of "negotiations," I am, of course, speaking metaphorically, not literally. There was no moment at which official bargaining teams representing the secularist and religious communities met at a table and tried to hammer out an agreement on a new moral code. But the public debates about morality that began in the 1960s, and continue today, were *like* collective-bargaining negotiations.

• *LCD*. In the LCD method, the two sides go with their points of agreement, disregarding everything on which they disagree. This is the way friends choose which movie to see. You want to see either movie A, B, or C, but not D or E. Your friend wants to see either C, D, or E, but has no wish to see A or B. So your compromise is to see movie C.

Another way of describing the LCD method is as the "veto" method. Parties to an LCD compromise normally arrive at their mutually agreeable choice by allowing one another to veto certain possible options; those options still in play after all vetoes have been exercised are the ones the parties agree on. In the example just given, you vetoed D and E, while your friend vetoed A and B. That left C as the only option still in play. So you went to see movie C.

Sometimes there is little difference between the two methods. For instance, when two parties each want two things, one of which they want in common; and as a result, each party gets half of what it wants while having to do without the other half. Such a compromise can equally be described as HAL *and* LCD.

But at other times, there is a significant difference between the two. Let us say one party wants many things, and the other wants only one thing. For instance, you want items 1 through 10 on a list; your friend wants item 3 only, and is opposed to all other items on the list. So, since 3 is the only item you both agree on, the two of you choose item 3 and omit the other nine. In this case, your friend has a strong veto, having vetoed 90 percent of your preferences, while having no burden of renunciation, getting 100 percent of what he wanted. You, by contrast, did not exercise any veto at all, and you have a heavy burden of renunciation, having to give up 90 percent of your wishes.

Of course, no one is likely to adhere to the LCD method of compromise very long if he constantly has to bear the heavy burden of renunciation all alone. Imagine management saying to the union: "You want a 10-percent pay increase, and we want to give you only 1 percent. Since we both agree that you should get at least 1 percent, let us leave it at that." No wonder labor-management negotiations prefer the HAL method.

Thus, there are two ways of arriving at a compromise: in one way (HAL), the parties split the difference and arrive at an agreed-upon middle ground; in the other (LCD), the parties veto all options they find objectionable and agree on the non-vetoed items.

The moral negotiations break down

Up until the 1960s — that is, prior to the moment it became necessary and appropriate to include secularists as full-fledged members of the national community — Americans, when arriving at a religious and moral consensus, always used the LCD, or veto, method. The first Protestant consensus was based on what all Protestants, from Calvinists to Unitarians, held in common: for instance, the existence of God, the authority of the Bible, the importance of Jesus, life after death, and a certain moral code. And the later and thinner Judeo-Christian consensus was based on what all Christians and Jews held in common: the existence of God, the authority of the Bible (even though the contents of the Bible would be differently defined among Protestants, Catholics, and Jews), life after death, and a certain moral code. Anything that any party to the consensus had strong objections to would have to be left out of the consensus.

It would be natural, therefore, for the LCD method to be used in this case as well. But this method, remember, gives an advantage to the party that has a short list of demands, since it must place only a small number of its demands outside the consensus, perhaps none at all; whereas the party that has a long list of demands finds that reaching consensus forces it to leave many of its demands outside.

In the negotiations about the new moral consensus — negotiations that began in the mid-1960s and have continued to this day, still unresolved — the bargaining stance of the secularist party has been this: "Freedom and tolerance are the only values we can all agree on. If we adopt a morality with any greater content than this, we are bound to give offense to at least some members of the national community. The PLP, on the other hand, will offend no one — not even you religious believers, since you, too, believe in freedom and tolerance, don't you? If you want to have a personal morality that goes beyond tolerance, fine; according to our proposed terms for the new consensus, you are free to do so, provided you adopt this morality as a private choice only, as something you won't impose on others. What could be more reasonable?"

Those in the religious party have had two very different responses to this proposal, depending on which end of the religious spectrum they stood at. Many religious liberals or progressives came to think the secularist proposal a reasonable one. By contrast, religious conservatives or traditionalists could not swallow it, and they still cannot swallow it to this day.[64]

---

[64] By "religious liberals or progressives" I mean those Christians who, in the interests of adapting Christianity to the cultural "advances" of the modern world, advocate a nondogmatic, or at least relatively nondogmatic, Christianity. In the nineteenth century, they were prompt in their acceptance of Darwinism and the higher criticism of the Bible. In the late twentieth century, they were prompt in their acceptance of unmarried cohabitation, abortion, and homosexuality. By "religious conservatives or traditionalists" I mean those who hold that Christianity is a strongly dogmatic religion. In the nineteenth and twentieth centuries, they were either very slow to accept Darwinism and the higher criticism, or they did not accept them at all; and in the early twenty-first century, they still show no signs of accepting cohabitation, abortion, or homosexuality. Liberals are mostly found in the "mainline" Protestant churches, although, in the last few decades, many of them have been found in the Catholic Church; conservatives

The Decline and Fall of the Catholic Church in America

The problem with the position taken by the religious conservatives is that they have had no viable alternative to offer to the PLP as a basis for moral consensus. What they propose is to return to the older consensus, the Judeo-Christian consensus. This is shown, for example, when they propose a constitutional amendment to permit prayer in public schools, thereby reversing the 1962 Supreme Court prayer decision.

But to return to the older consensus is impossible. For to return to this older state of affairs would be to exclude secularists from the nation's moral consensus, hence from full membership in the national community. It is far too late in the day for that — at least forty years too late. Secularists are numerous today, and they have a social and cultural importance that far exceeds their numbers. For better or worse, the national community *must* include secularists as first-class members; from which it follows that any moral consensus Americans arrive at will have to be acceptable to both religious believers and secularists.

The old moral consensus will never
work in a society that accepts secularists

This is something religious liberals clearly understand; hence their willingness to go a long way toward accepting the PLP and the conclusions derived from it. They want to find a moral common ground between Christians and secularists. Religious conservatives, by contrast, seem to feel that no common ground is possible. They reject the compromises made by religious liberals — e.g., a willingness to wink at cohabitation and abortion and a readiness to bless same-sex unions — regarding these compromises as nothing better than a betrayal of Christianity. Between themselves and the secularists, they feel, nothing is possible but a

are found in the Evangelical and Pentecostal churches, as well as in the Catholic Church.

fight to the finish. In the end, as they see it, either Christianity will win and the United States will return to being a Christian (or at least a Judeo-Christian) nation, or the enemies of Christianity will win and the United States will become a secularist or (what is, in their eyes, pretty close to the same thing) a religiously liberal nation. Hence the failure of religious conservatives to find any real common ground with secularists.

In saying this, I do not mean to imply that the moral ideas of religious conservatives — ideas such as biblical morality or natural law — are invalid in and of themselves. Not at all. Yet no matter how valid they may be in themselves, and no matter how much they may offer a true account of morality, these ideas will not serve as a basis for a consensus that includes secularists, just as the secularist PLP will not serve as a basis for a consensus that includes religious believers. Perhaps we can get all Catholics to agree on a natural-law basis for morality, and perhaps we can get all Christians to agree on a biblical basis for morality; but we cannot get all secularists to agree on either a natural-law or a biblical basis for morality. To have a moral consensus in America, we need something we can all agree on. Unfortunately for purposes of finding a national moral consensus, religious believers cannot accept the PLP, and secularists cannot accept either biblical or natural-law morality. Hence, at the moment, we have no moral consensus in the United States, and we have not had one since the early 1960s; and if we have no moral consensus, we have no national moral community.

But perhaps such a statement goes too far. It would be more correct to say that we now have an *exceedingly* thin moral consensus and hence an exceedingly thin national moral community. The only thing everybody agrees on is that it is wrong to engage in conduct that harms others; in other words, murder, rape, robbery, fraud, embezzlement, et cetera are wrong. But we do not agree on these prohibitions for the same reasons. Secularists embrace these

prohibitions on the grounds of the PLP, while religious conservatives embrace them on the grounds of the Bible or natural law. In
practice, this thin consensus represents a victory for secularists; for
this kind of moral consensus, a consensus compatible with the
PLP, is exactly what they want.

But in another sense, they have not won a victory; for although
they have effectively vetoed any consensus that goes beyond the
PLP, they have not persuaded religious conservatives to accept
this *de facto* PLP consensus as a *de jure* consensus. To return to our
"negotiations" metaphor, religious conservatives have rejected
the offer made to them by the secularist party; they have refused to
sign a contract. If they continue to cooperate with secularists in
the day-to-day life of society, this is not because they are satisfied
with the arrangement; far from it, they are radically dissatisfied.
And if they get a realistic opportunity to do away with the *de facto*
PLP consensus and establish something with more ample content,
they will not fail to seize this opportunity.

But religious conservatives are not the only people who are either unwilling or unable to arrive at a moral consensus, thereby preserving America's moral community. The same is true of secularists
and religious liberals. Both well understand the need for a moral
consensus that will be acceptable to all categories of Americans,
religious and nonreligious. What they cannot understand — or
refuse to understand — is that the PLP, since it is quite unacceptable to religious conservatives, who are no insignificant part of the
American public, can never serve as the basis for that consensus.
To ask conservatives to accept the PLP is, in effect, to ask them to
give up their moral-religious beliefs. And the standard answer secularists give ("You're free to hold those beliefs as private opinions")
will not wash. For how are religious conservatives to transmit to
their children the belief, say, that abortion is homicide or that homosexuality is an abomination in the eyes of the Lord, if the
American moral consensus — reinforced by the mass media and

by public-school teachers — says that abortion should be a woman's "choice" or that homosexuality is a perfectly acceptable option?

Secularists and religious liberals talk endlessly about the importance of pluralism and tolerance, as well they should; but asking religious conservatives to expose their beliefs and values to near-certain destruction is hardly a reasonable demand in the name of pluralism and tolerance. Instead of saying to themselves, "The PLP will never do as the basis for consensus, so we will have to go back to the drawing board and come up with some other basis," secularists have chosen to rail publicly at religious conservatives, calling them "bigoted" and "closed-minded" and "backward" and "unenlightened." Many secularists and religious liberals are very good at putting themselves, in imagination, in the shoes of hitherto marginalized people; for instance, racial minorities and homosexuals. But they are not very good at doing the same when it comes to religious conservatives. Most secularists simply lack the imagination required to look at the world the way a religious conservative looks at it.

The "culture war" issues cannot be simply overlooked or ignored

It might be argued that the American moral consensus covers so many issues that disagreement on the "culture war" issues is a minor matter. The Boston College sociologist Alan Wolfe makes an argument along these lines in his book *One Nation After All* (New York: Viking Penguin, 1998). But if abortion and homosexuality, for instance, are minor matters, why do they loom so large? Why do they play so important a role in American social and political life? They have become an important basis of division between the nation's two great political parties, the national Democratic Party now being married to the moral liberals and the national Republican Party to the moral conservatives. If these people are fighting over minor matters, they do not seem to know it.

But, of course, these are not minor matters. Perhaps Americans agree on twenty-five things for every one thing like abortion and homosexuality that they disagree on, but the same was almost certainly true on the eve of the Civil War. Northerners and Southerners agreed on most questions of value and morality, but the thing they disagreed on — slavery — was a really big thing, big enough to tear the nation apart. On this single thing hinged the entire Southern way of life, at least the way of life of the wealthy ruling class. And it is similar with abortion and homosexuality. From the point of view of traditional Christian believers, if abortion and homosexuality were to become universally accepted in America, Christianity would be pretty much finished here. And from the point of view of moral liberals, if abortion and homosexuality once again come to be rejected in America, as they were up until fairly recent times, then personal liberty will have been grievously diminished. For what remains of personal liberty if it does not include sexual freedom? And sexual freedom must include homosexual freedom; otherwise it is a halfway kind of thing; it is a bad joke. And sexual freedom, of course, requires the freedom to have abortions, for mistakes will sometimes be made, and abortion is necessary to clean up those mistakes.

The natural-law theory may explain why, as Alan Wolfe says, we Americans agree on so much. But it does little to explain why we disagree on certain very important things — abortion and homosexuality — that have already demonstrated a tremendous capacity for social disruption and may well demonstrate more in the future. Neither side is willing to make an offer that the other can accept. No wonder we have a "culture war" in the United States today.

A compromised Catholicism
cannot be authentic Catholicism

This culture war that has riven American society has also riven the Catholic Church in the United States, and as long as the

American culture war continues, it is likely that the Catholic culture war will continue as well. American Catholicism is not a separate thing from American society as a whole. In one sense, it is larger than American society, since it is an international religion. Yet in another sense, it is smaller than American society, a part of a larger whole. Thus, every battle the liberals win in the more general culture war will give heart to the liberals fighting in the Catholic culture war, just as every conservative victory in the general war will encourage conservatives fighting in the Catholic culture war. The American culture war is not something of insignificant concern to American Catholics. For better or worse, they stand in the midst of it.

One further word on this point. Although I am writing as a sociologist, not a theologian, I must note that liberal Catholicism is not *authentic* Catholicism. By this I do not mean to say that it is not authentic in the judgment of God — for *qua* sociologist I know nothing about the mind and judgment of God. No, I mean that it is not authentic when measured against the standard of Catholicism presented to us by nearly two millennia of history. Catholicism did not come into the world just the other day, and in the course of many centuries, it has acquired certain characteristics, among them a detestation of abortion and homosexuality, a largely celibate, all-male priesthood, a papacy that is close to being an absolute monarchy, an unambiguous rule against contraception, and so forth.

It can be argued that a church that is soft on abortion and approves of homosexual unions (and that allows married priests and female priests, et cetera) would be a better church than the Catholic Church has been for all these many centuries. In this book, I am not concerned with disputing that argument. I am only concerned with making the point — a *historical* point, not a *theological* point — that such a "new and improved" church would not be identical with the Catholic Church as it has existed for many centuries. This new religion would perhaps have the same name as Catholicism, and perhaps it would continue to hold ceremonies in the same old Catholic buildings, but it would not — could not — be the same thing.

Conclusion: the war goes on

The culture war has been going on for more than thirty years now, and it is hard to see how the two battling parties — religious moral conservatives and secularist moral liberals — can arrive at a peaceful settlement, since both sides have such high and apparently nonnegotiable demands. If the dispute were submitted for arbitration to an impartial judge from Mars, he might suggest that they compromise on an HAL basis. Abortion, for instance, might take place in an unrestricted manner for the first trimester of the pregnancy; but other than that, it would be strictly forbidden. And homosexual conduct might be completely legal, and no one would be allowed to discriminate against gays and lesbians in employment, schooling, housing, and the military; but there would be no same-sex marriage, and public schools would be strictly forbidden from condoning homosexual conduct in any way.

But this Martian solution, although it would give both parties part of what they want, would not work here on earth — at least not on the American portion of the earth. Moral liberals, for instance, would never accept a *limited* abortion license. These are the people, remember, who for years have been adamantly opposed to legislation to prohibit partial-birth abortions; and people who will defend the right to an abortion that is virtually indistinguishable from homicide are not likely to accept a three-month limit on abortions. Nor will moral conservatives accept a three-month license to abort. How could they do so if abortion is, as they contend, a kind of homicide? If it is gravely wrong to kill unborn babies at three months plus one week, how can it be okay to kill them at three months minus one week?

With regard to homosexuality, many conservatives would be willing, or at least *nearly* willing, to accept the proposed Martian compromise; for they have long since given up on the idea that gays and lesbians should be locked up in jail, and they have pretty much reconciled themselves to the idea that homosexuals should not be discriminated against — although they would have a hard time swallowing the principle that overt homosexuals may serve in the military. But moral liberals would not accept such a deal. For they sense that they are on the verge of a complete victory, "full victory" being defined as thoroughgoing social acceptance of the moral normality of homosexuality. This sense, which was strong already, was greatly strengthened by their United States Supreme Court victory of late June 2003, when, in *Lawrence v. Texas*, the Court ruled all American anti-sodomy laws to be unconstitutional. With victory so close, why would moral liberals give up on their push for same-sex marriage? Why would they agree to allow homosexuality to be treated as anything less than normal in our public schools?

While both sides would be reluctant to arrive at an HAL culture-war compromise, this reluctance would probably be much greater among liberals than among conservatives. When the conservatives refuse to compromise, they do so with the hope that this refusal will keep alive the chance of an ultimate victory for their side; but for the time being, of course, their refusal produces no victory. By contrast, when the liberals refuse to compromise, they are not just hoping to win an ultimate victory one of these days; rather, their refusal gives them, as I mentioned above, a kind of *de facto* victory right now. Absent a compromise in which they would agree to limit the abortion license, the nation has a virtually unrestricted abortion license. And absent a compromise in which they would agree to accept a kind of permanent second-class moral status for homosexuality, homosexuality already has at least a second-class status and seems to be on the verge of winning first-class status. So why should moral liberals compromise when they already have almost everything they want? The liberals will not be ready to compromise until the moral conservatives have grown so strong that they are in a position to re-stigmatize homosexuality and severely restrict, if not totally eliminate, abortion. But by that time (should it ever come, which it probably will not), we can be certain that the conservatives will be in no mood to compromise.

And so our hypothetical Martian arbitrator will have to return to his home planet, having failed in his assignment, and the culture war will go on and on, with little or no prospect of settlement.

Chapter 23

American Catholicism's
Key Battles in the Culture War

The division between the two parties, moral liberals and moral conservatives, has been most striking in matters having to do with sexual conduct. According to the pre-1962 moral consensus, the following things were morally wrong, some less seriously so, others more seriously: pornography, premarital sex (especially among teenagers), unmarried cohabitation, abortion, homosexuality, rape, and adultery. According to the PLP, most of these — with the exception of rape and the probable exception of adultery — ceased to be prohibited and became permissible. Rape continued to be wrong because it plainly causes harm to another; while adultery, at a minimum, runs the risk of causing harm to another.

Abortion is the vital issue

Over the last few decades, the most intense disagreements about these items have had to do with abortion. Here is the one case on the secularist approved list where it is plainly arguable that the action in question causes harm to another, namely, the fetus who is killed, and causes this harm, moreover, in a direct and tangible way. If the fetus is a human person, then abortion is wrong — even according to the PLP. In a culture that has gone a long way toward accepting the PLP, religious conservatives understand that they are far more likely to get a sympathetic hearing from the general public — especially that large portion of the general public which has no strong feelings one way or the other as to morality of the issues at stake in the culture war — for their objections to abortion than they are for their objections to, say, pornography or cohabitation.[65] Hence, they have hammered away at the abortion issue; and although they have done little, to date, to change America's exceedingly permissive abortion law, they have nonetheless succeeded in carrying a large part of public opinion with them.

Secularists and moral liberals, on the other hand, cannot afford to back down from their defense of abortion. Now, at first glance, it might seem logical that they should do so. After all, why should they invest lots of time, money, and energy in defending a position that is far from obviously justified by the PLP? Plainly the fetus is an entity in its own right, not just part of the woman who is carrying it; and it is very hard to prove that it is not a *human* entity, i.e., a human person; and if it is a human person, then is it not entitled to at least some human rights, most notably the right not to be

---

[65] A curious bit of common ground is shared by moral conservatives and a certain subclass of moral liberals — namely, those liberals, led by Andrea Dworkin and Catherine McKinney, who would like to impose legal restrictions on pornography because, they contend, pornography leads to male violence against women. But moral conservatives have a broader basis than Dworkin, McKinney, and company for their objection to pornography. They agree that pornography leads to antiwoman violence, but they object to pornography on other grounds as well. They consider indulgence in pornography to be intrinsically immoral, apart from its effects; and they consider one of its worst effects to be a corruption of the sexual morals of children and adolescents who are exposed to pornography. Moreover, very few liberals agree with the Dworkin-McKinney proposal that pornography should be legally restricted, feeling that whatever risk to women that may arise from pornography is a price worth paying for the sake of freedom of press and freedom of sexual expression.

killed? Why should moral liberals even bother to defend the right to abortion when it is so hard to give a rational defense for it? Why not just give up on abortion and stick to defending positions that are far more easily defended on a PLP basis — issues such as cohabitation, no-fault divorce, homosexuality, pornography, and sexual freedom in general?

But if abortion is prohibited, the rest of the sexual revolution will be diminished to the point of virtual nonexistence. A regime of great sexual freedom is bound to produce a considerable number of unintended and unwanted pregnancies, no matter how readily available contraception may be. There has to be a way of getting rid of these unwanted pregnancies; otherwise the risks of sexual freedom are too great.[66]

It follows that if abortion is directly banned, sexual freedom will be indirectly curtailed. Further, if sexual freedom between heterosexuals is curtailed, there will be no chance to develop genuine tolerance for homosexuality, since the ancient prejudice against homosexuality is far more intense than the prejudice against sexual freedom for heterosexuals. Unless we can destroy the latter taboo, we have no hope of destroying the former. Abortion, then, is essential to the entire sexual revolution. Lose the abortion fight, and the sexual counterrevolution will prevail. But if this happens, then we have no alternative but to return to something like the religion-based morality of the pre-1962 era. And this, from a secularist point of view, is absurd. Therefore, the right to abortion must be maintained at all costs.

---

[66] In the 1992 Supreme Court case *Planned Parenthood v. Casey*, Justice O'Connor wrote in the plurality opinion that the right to abortion could not be curtailed "without serious inequity to people who, for two decades of economic and social developments, have organized intimate relationships . . . in reliance on the availability of abortion in the event that contraception should fail."

This explains why otherwise intelligent people suddenly become remarkably irrational when arguing about abortion. For instance, moral liberals consistently refuse to respond to the central contention made by pro-life religious believers — namely, that the fetus is a human being. When confronted with this contention, they almost never give a pertinent answer. Instead, they change the subject, resorting to slogans (e.g., "a woman's right to choose," or "every child a wanted child") or calling pro-life people hypocrites (since, for example, they do not typically favor passing out condoms in schools, which, it is held by moral liberals, would lower the abortion rate). In logic textbooks, this tactic of evading the subject under discussion is called the *ignoratio elenchi* fallacy (or irrelevant conclusion). The truth is, the secularist party simply cannot afford to lose the abortion debate; and if they cannot win with good arguments, they will just have to win with bad.

An example of this irrationality can be seen in the resistance moral liberals have offered to partial-birth-abortion legislation. Here is a form of abortion (if it can even be called abortion) that is virtually indistinguishable from plain homicide. You would think moral liberals would say to themselves, "This is a battle not worth fighting. For how can we persuade the public that this is a victimless procedure, that no harm is done to a human being?" But that is not what they say. Instead, realizing that abortion is the lynchpin of the entire sexual revolution, again and again they have fought tooth and nail to block partial-birth-abortion legislation, both at federal and state levels. No matter that this fight increasingly gives them an image of being extremists. Since abortion is pivotal to the entire moral liberal agenda, it must be defended whatever the cost.

Incidentally, this also explains why moral liberals were, and remain to this day, rock-solid supporters of former President Bill Clinton. Clinton frequently disappointed his liberal supporters on many issues. He offended the unions with his support for NAFTA.

He offended blacks with his retreat on affirmative action ("Mend it, don't end it"). He offended advocates for the poor with his acceptance of Republican-initiated welfare reform. He offended teacher unions with his support for school uniforms. He offended homosexuals with his "Don't ask, don't tell" policy for the military. And he offended feminists by his sexual exploitation of a White House intern. But whatever else he did, he never offended supporters of abortion; they could always rely on him to be with them 100 percent. So moral liberals loved him. They forgave him everything else, they rushed to his defense during the Lewinsky scandal, and they expressed their deep outrage at his impeachment; for on the one thing needful — abortion — he was absolutely reliable.

In the great American abortion fight, which has been going on since the late 1960s, when the abortion-rights movement first appeared on the national scene, the Catholic Church in the United States has a mixed record. On the positive side, the national association of Catholic bishops (which used to be called the National Conference of Catholic Bishops and is now called the United States Conference of Catholic Bishops) has again and again issued statements on abortion, statements that have reasserted the traditional Catholic view, that have denounced abortion as immoral, that have cautioned Catholic voters and politicians that it would be wrong for them to do anything to support public policies favorable to abortion, et cetera. Many bishops have echoed these messages in their local dioceses. And many Catholic priests and laypersons have been active in the pro-life movement. In the years immediately following the 1973 *Roe v. Wade* ruling, conservative Protestants were not very engaged in the abortion struggle; and had it not been for the Catholic resistance, rather like Horatio at the bridge, it is likely that the abortion-rights movement would have swept all before it.

On the negative side, few bishops have done much in the way of action to follow up on the eloquent statements of the National

Conference of Catholic Bishops (NCCB) and the USCCB. Very few have organized an effective pro-life lobby to work at their state houses, and very few have mobilized wealthy Catholics to contribute big money to the pro-life cause and deny political contributions to pro-choice politicians.[67] Not enough parish priests have given frequent or effective sermons on abortion, and many have not given any sermons on the topic at all. And the participation of lay Catholics in the pro-life movement has been far weaker, at least after the first few years of the abortion battle, than that of lay Evangelical and Pentecostal Protestants.

Worse still, vast numbers of Catholics continue to vote, election after election, for pro-choice members of Congress, and many of the pro-choice politicians they vote for are themselves Catholic.[68] It is not too much to say that the political good fortune of the abortion movement has for several decades depended on an unholy alliance between atheists and Catholics. The atheists (i.e., the secularists) have provided the brains, while the Catholics have provided the muscle of the movement. That is, the secularists

[67] Some will remind me that the Catholic Church, as a tax-exempt corporation, cannot get involved in partisan politics. Granted; but a bishop, in addition to being the head of his diocese, is an American citizen and, as such, has as much right as anyone else to engage in political activity. Besides, he would not have to get deeply embroiled in politics. A wink and a nod and maybe a bit of a push to his rich Catholic friends would be enough to get something started. Yet how many bishops have troubled to do this?

[68] These Catholic politicians tend to be Democrats for the same reason Catholic voters tend to be: because of family and ethnic heritage. Rarely are they pro-choice out of deep philosophical conviction. Rather, they understand which way the political wind is blowing inside the Democratic Party, and a system of democratic government is, of course, structured to reward those politicians who respond successfully to political winds.

provided the leadership, while the Catholics provided the votes and many of the politicians.

The struggle over abortion is one of the great battlefields of the American culture war; hence, every victory for moral liberalism in the abortion battle is, however indirectly, a victory for liberal Catholicism in the in-house Catholic culture war. It follows that every time a Catholic, whether a bishop or a priest or a layman, aids the abortion-rights movement — either by doing little or nothing to resist it, or by voting for pro-choice politicians, or by *being* a pro-choice politician — he helps the liberal side in the intramural Catholic culture war. And since liberal Catholicism, as I mentioned earlier, is not *authentic* Catholicism, such a Catholic is, in fact, undermining his own religion.

Suicide and euthanasia are central points of dispute

As I have said again and again, ever since the breakdown of the old Judeo-Christian moral-religious consensus, Americans have been unable to arrive at a new moral consensus — secularists and religious liberals favoring a consensus based on the Personal Liberty Principle, religious conservatives trying to cling to the older Judeo-Christian consensus, along with some Catholics who would like to base it on natural law. This disagreement constitutes the culture war. "Negotiations" have failed. Open "warfare" is ongoing. But the controversy about abortion is not the only illustration of the failure to reach consensus; it is merely the most striking one. Let us look at a couple of others.

One of them is the dispute about the right to suicide, especially physician-assisted suicide. According to traditional moral-religious principles, suicide is a great sin; hence, assisting someone to commit suicide would be an equally great sin, perhaps even a greater one. But given the PLP, what objection can there be to suicide, provided it is committed by an adult who is not insane? None at all. After all, if a person commits suicide, it is his own body he is destroying, his own life. He is not inflicting direct harm on anyone else. And if there is no moral objection to committing suicide, how can there be any objection to assisting someone to commit it?

The physician-assisted-suicide law in effect in the state of Oregon — the only state that currently has such a law — permits a doctor to prescribe drugs that, in sufficient dosage, will kill the patient. But the law does not allow the doctor to do more than prescribe; he may not actually administer the drugs. Nor may anyone else administer the drugs except the patient himself. In other words, would-be suicides have to kill themselves.

But what about taking things a step beyond physician-assisted suicide — what about voluntary euthanasia? From the point of view of the PLP, what objection can there be to this? None, it seems. If it is morally permissible for a person to kill himself, since it does not hurt anyone but himself, how can there be any objection to killing someone else at his request? Let us say that A would like to kill himself, but he lacks the physical strength to administer the lethal dose or to give the lethal injection or to fire the lethal bullet. Given the PLP, it would seem there can be no objection if B, at A's request, helps out.

Involuntary euthanasia — that is, "mercy killing" in the absence of the victim's request or consent — is a somewhat different case. For the traditional religious believer, of course, it is a perfectly clear-cut matter: Mercy killing is a plain case of murder, hence grievously wicked. Many secularists oppose it, too. For them, its involuntary character distinguishes it from suicide, whether assisted or unassisted, and from voluntary euthanasia. If suicide and voluntary euthanasia are justified because they are the free choice of the person being killed, how can involuntary euthanasia possibly be justified? Despite this agreement between believers and many secularists, however, their grounds for agreeing are radically different. The former say it is wrong because it is *unwarranted* homicide; the latter say it is wrong because it is *involuntary* homicide, even though it might well be warranted if the person being killed had given his consent.

Other moral liberals, however, hold that involuntary euthanasia is morally permissible in some circumstances — for instance, when the person is near death and incapable of giving consent (because of a coma, maybe, or because of Alzheimer's disease). In such circumstances, if we have good reason to believe that the person *would* have given consent if capable of doing so, then it is morally permissible for us, acting as a proxy for the person, to consent to his or her euthanasia. Or to take it one step further, let us say we cannot be sure what the terminally ill but now incompetent person would have said; nonetheless, if assisted suicide would be the *reasonable* thing to do (what that familiar figure of law, the "reasonable man," would have done), then euthanasia is morally permissible according to the PLP.

At the present moment, secularists are divided on the question of involuntary euthanasia, but the momentum is with those who favor it, for two reasons. One is that it appears not to violate the PLP, which says I am free to do whatever I want, as long as I do not hurt others. Here is a case: I want to put my dearly beloved but now terminally ill grandmother to death. So the question becomes: Am I hurting her by doing so? No, it can be said, I am simply putting her out of her misery. Moreover, I am acting from a motive of compassion, not out of any ill will. So what is wrong with euthanasia in such a case? From the point of view of the PLP, secularism's ultimate Categorical Imperative, nothing.

The second reason momentum favors the pro-euthanasia party is that the main opposition to euthanasia comes from conservative religious believers. And since, as secularists see things, these believers are wrong on almost every other contentious issue of the day (abortion, homosexuality, sex education, censorship of pornography, prayer in schools, et cetera), is it not likely that they are wrong on this, too? Further, the secularist who happens to be opposed to involuntary euthanasia is bound to wonder if his opposition is not simply an old prejudice left over from the early years of his life, when, before he saw the light, he was being brought up as a religious believer. Or if he did not have a religious upbringing, could it be that he has unwittingly internalized a cultural residuum left over from the days when American culture had not yet been properly secularized? At all events, finding himself on the same side of this question with conservative religious believers, indeed with the dreaded "Religious Right," is more than enough to give him second thoughts.

Part VI

The Decline and Fall
of the
Catholic Church
in America

Chapter 24

The Probable Demise
of American Catholicism

Let us begin this chapter with a review of some of the main contentions of my argument so far.

Catholicism in the United States, I have said, has become a *de facto* denominational religion, on all fours with the Presbyterians, the Methodists, the Episcopalians, et cetera. This happened when Catholics became fully Americanized in the post–World War II era. The culturally dominant religion at that time was mainline Protestantism, the ecumenical Protestantism of the National Council of Churches of Christ; and mainline Protestantism was full of that spirit of genial tolerance which I have called the "denominational mentality" — the attitude that all religions, at least all Christian religions, are approximately as good as one another, as true as one another: an attitude that was perfectly expressed by President Dwight D. Eisenhower when he said, "Our government makes no sense unless it is founded in a deeply felt religious faith — and I don't care what it is."

It followed, then, that if Catholics were to be full-fledged Americans, they must either adopt the dominant religion or, if that was not a live option, at least adopt the denominational mentality that characterized the dominant religion. Catholics did the latter. By the later 1960s, their Americanism — seconded by the "spirit" of

Vatican II — drove them to the conclusion that their religion, while a very good thing, was not really any better than the religion of their Protestant neighbors. Naturally, Catholics had a preference for Catholicism, the religion of their childhood and of their parents and grandparents. But while this meant that Catholicism was better for them, it did not mean that it was better for everyone; Protestants, too, had childhoods and parents and grandparents.

The hierarchy of the Church, to be sure, has not officially embraced this denominational mentality; the bishops have not formally renounced the ancient claim that Catholicism is the one true Church of Christ. But for most practical purposes, they *have* embraced this mentality, or at least decided to put up with it with minimal protest. They do little or nothing to discourage the denominational mentality among their flocks, and rarely, if ever, do they publicly reiterate the Church's ancient claim to uniqueness. No longer can Catholic bishops be found making a remark like the one mentioned earlier: Cardinal Manning's remark to the Anglican bishop, "Yes, you serve God in your way, and I in His."

But we have also seen that Christian religions that adopt a denominational mentality thereby adopt a recipe for disintegration, for gradual ecclesial suicide. They set their feet on a slippery slope leading to skepticism. At first there is only a small amount of skepticism — just enough to justify their reluctance to claim a monopoly of truth for their own religion and their tolerance for other people's religions. Then the degree of skepticism increases as the need for tolerance increases, until finally the tolerance is nearly total and so is the skepticism. These religions become so tolerant that they are incapable of opposing unorthodox beliefs, even inside their own church walls. In the end, they are not even able to oppose outright agnosticism and atheism. Nor are they able to oppose practices that have always been condemned by Christianity: abortion, homosexuality, and suicide. They have no grounds for combating secularism.

This does not happen overnight, of course. It is a gradual process, faster in some churches, slower in others. But the tendency is all in one direction; it is hard to get off the slippery slope after stepping on it.

This process of tolerance/skepticism accelerated once the national moral community expanded to include non-theists. When the denominational mentality reached out to embrace — and to compromise with — downright nonbelievers, i.e., secularists, the loss of doctrinal content within churches, which had been a trickle, became a flood. The secularist agrees with *none* of the religious beliefs of the Christian; hence, everything the Christian believes becomes a matter of discomfort when fraternizing with the secularist; and this discomfort is compounded by the fact that the Christian, especially the liberal Christian, usually has a feeling of intellectual inferiority in the presence of an educated and up-to-date secularist. The easiest way of getting rid of this discomfort is either to discard these distinctively Christian beliefs or to soft-pedal them; and if this soft-pedal strategy is adopted over a long enough period, it becomes the practical equivalent of the discard strategy.

The bleak future of American Catholicism

If all this is correct, where do we go from here? What is likely to become of American Catholicism? It is, I think, likely to become a minor and relatively insignificant American religion.

This decline in doctrinal content, now an observable historical fact in American Protestant denominations, is currently in the process of being duplicated in American Catholicism. *It will be duplicated in its entirety if the latter is not able to liberate itself from the denominational mentality.* And, of course, a Catholicism with a doctrinal content that is either low or nonexistent is not really Catholicism at all; for it is of the essence of Catholicism to be a high-doctrine religion. Otherwise, why all the creeds, the councils, the catechisms? Why an infallible pope and an inerrant Bible?

To be sure, it is possible to *imagine* some future low-doctrine church calling itself "Catholic." Such Catholics of the future might believe little or nothing, but they would still use the Catholic label, and they would still attend occasional services at the old church buildings erected by their Catholic ancestors. Something very like this can be seen every Sunday in small New England towns, where people calling themselves Congregationalists attend services in lovely old church buildings erected in the eighteenth and nineteenth centuries by Congregationalists of the Calvinist persuasion. Between the old Congregationalists and the new, there is nothing in common except a name and a building.[69] The same thing could happen to the people who call themselves Catholic, but they would not really be Catholic anymore in any meaningful sense.

And will this actually happen? Will American Catholicism eventually be evacuated of all, or almost all, doctrinal content? Probably not. No matter how far most Catholics go in subscribing to the denominational mentality, no matter how much a secularist

---

[69] An example from my hometown of Newport, Rhode Island: In the late eighteenth century, there was a Congregational pastor here by the name of Samuel Hopkins, a thoroughgoing Calvinist and a loyal disciple of the greatest of American Calvinists, Jonathan Edwards, who had been the teacher of Hopkins in the latter's youth. Hopkins authored what became the standard textbook of New England Calvinism in the first half of the nineteenth century. There is still a Congregational church in Newport, its congregation directly descended from that of Hopkins. A few years ago, the pastor of that church was a woman who was an openly declared lesbian, in accordance with the very tolerant United Church of Christ (UCC) policy of ordaining gays and lesbians (most Congregational churches became part of the UCC a half-century ago). She was, as far as I know, a very nice woman; but whenever I have had occasion to be in that Congregational church in recent years, I have thought of poor Rev. Hopkins and of how, half a mile or so away, he must be spinning in his grave.

philosophy of life is adopted by ordinary Catholics, a traditionalist faction — a "saving remnant" of traditionalists — will always cling to orthodoxy. There are characteristics of Catholicism, essential elements in its makeup, that make it almost impossible for the Church to abandon its traditional dogmatic nature. These features make it likely that, in a showdown struggle between liberal Catholics and traditionalists, the traditionalists will win, even though the Church they are left with might be nothing more than a minor American denomination. Let us look at some of these characteristics.

• *Minimal lay influence.* If Catholicism had, like all Protestant churches, a democratic or semi-democratic ecclesial structure in which local congregations had the right to hire and fire pastors, or at least the right to veto pastoral appointments by the bishop; or if it had, like the Episcopal Church, election of bishops by diocesan priests and elected lay delegates; then ancient Christian doctrine, both metaphysical and moral, might be subject to change.

As a general rule, the greater the influence of the laity in the governance of a church, the less likelihood there is of doctrinal stability. Laypersons live more in the "world" than clerics; hence, they are more influenced by the fashions of the world, including its intellectual and moral fashions. Laypersons also have far less of a theological education than clerics, which means that they will be less well informed about the actual teachings of their church. This makes it easier to reject this or that doctrine, for one may not realize that it actually is a doctrine of the church, or one may not appreciate how closely this doctrine is tied in with others, so that its rejection will tend to create a domino effect. Thus, the layperson, more easily than the theologically trained cleric, can reject a doctrine and say, "What's the big deal? What difference does it make if we say Mary was not a virgin? What difference does it make if we bless homosexual unions?"

The Decline and Fall of the Catholic Church in America

But by being nondemocratic in structure — that is, by minimizing lay influence on Church governance — Catholicism avoids the bias toward doctrinal change that is almost inseparable from lay influence.

• *Bishops possessing strict authority over priests.* But laypersons are not the only ones with a capacity for drifting away from orthodoxy. Clerics can do it as well, including Catholic priests. Candidate priests study theology at seminaries and in universities, and there is no guarantee that their professors will feed them orthodox doctrine only. Nor is there any guarantee that, after ordination, they will remain free from contact with unorthodox ideas. Just the opposite, in fact. Living in a society that is religiously and philosophically and ethically pluralistic, how can an American Catholic priest — unless he is exceptionally stupid or devoid of curiosity, or both — be unaware that the world abounds with notions, many of them quite plausible, that contradict points of Catholic doctrine? Can anyone be surprised that many priests will now and again find at least some of these ideas attractive? And who can be surprised if a priest, finding this or that un-Catholic idea especially attractive, attempts to persuade himself that embracing it can be reconciled with his vocation and his profession of Catholicism? And so it is that a certain amount of doctrinal heterodoxy flourishes, in a more or less underground way, among the American Catholic priesthood.

Probably no one knows for sure how much of this priestly experimentation with heterodoxy there actually is; but there is certainly far more than there was in the old days of the Catholic "ghetto." For one thing, in the days before the great American cultural revolution of the 1960s and early '70s, the number of un-Christian and un-Catholic theories circulating in society was far smaller than it has been since that time. For another, priests of the pre-1960s era, living as they did inside the "walls" of the Catholic quasi-ghetto, had much less contact with whatever unorthodox theories were circulating in those days; and when they ran into those theories, they were much less likely to hear them presented by qualified exponents; more likely, instead, to hear of them from Catholic enemies of the theories. Learning about Marxism, for instance, by hearing a defense of it from a Marxist university professor was rather a different experience from learning about it by hearing Bishop Sheen denounce it on radio or television.

A very striking example of how priests can deviate from orthodoxy — in this case *moral* orthodoxy — was afforded by the birth-control crisis of the late 1960s: the Catholic crisis that followed publication of Pope Paul VI's encyclical *Humanae Vitae*, which reiterated the Church's ancient condemnation of artificial contraception. Beforehand, priests had, of course, been well aware that non-Catholics in the United States generally considered the use of contraceptives by married couples to be not only morally permissible, but even sometimes morally mandatory; nobody could live in America without being aware of that. And when the papal encyclical was issued, not only did non-Catholics treat it with scorn and ridicule, but so did many Catholics; a large group of Catholic theologians even published their dissent in a paid ad in the *New York Times*.

The typical parish priest was, of course, very aware of all this, and this awareness must have created at least a certain pressure on him to conform — to conform, that is, to the standard American view of contraception, which would be nonconformity to traditional Catholic teaching. What pressured him most of all in that direction, however, was the attitude of many of his parishioners: married couples who were practicing contraception. They were, as far as the priest could tell (and he knew them well; he heard their confessions), good persons, good Catholics, and they simply could not understand that there was anything wrong or sinful about the practice of contraception in certain circumstances. He had tried to explain the Church's view of contraception, and they seemed to understand what he was saying. Yet they could not buy it; they could not convince themselves that it was wrong.

What was the priest to do? How was he to advise such parishioners? He could not bring himself to condemn them. So he remembered the Catholic teaching on conscience, which is that one is obliged to follow his conscience even when the conscience is erroneous — provided, of course, that he has made every reasonable effort to form a correct conscience, and thus is not culpable for his conscience's error. He presumed that they had made such efforts, and he advised them to follow their conscience; that is to say, he told them they could practice contraception with a good conscience.

It seemed a harmless bit of pastoral advice to give. After all, it was only contraception. The priest was not telling anybody that a good conscience would absolve one from the guilt of theft or adultery or murder. If a parishioner had wanted to do something like that, something really harmful, the priest would not have been so accommodating; he would have insisted that the Church is right and the parishioner wrong. If he advised couples to continue practicing contraception with a good conscience, it was because he half-agreed with them, and perhaps more than half-agreed. Wonderful though the Church may be about so many things, in this case, the priest came to feel, perhaps it had made a mistake. Once upon a time, when everyone lived in an agrarian society and the childhood mortality rate was high, maybe then a ban on contraception made sense. But did it make sense in an advanced industrial society in the second half of the twentieth century?

For many a priest, this must have been the first step across the line of Catholic moral orthodoxy — the first time he had given his people a green light to do something he knew to be condemned by the Church, a green light to commit what the Church held to be mortal sin; the first time he himself had a serious doubt about the rightness of a Catholic moral doctrine. But crossing the line once makes it easier to cross it a second time and a third time. If the pope and the Church are wrong about contraception, maybe they are wrong about other moral questions as well, especially questions having to do with sex. And if they are wrong about moral questions, it was possible that they are wrong about other doctrinal matters as well. The Church, for such a priest, was no longer infallible, Church teaching is no longer immutable, and everything becomes, at least in principle, a debatable issue.

It is quite possible, then, for priests to stray from orthodoxy — and in the heady days of the American cultural revolution and the beginning of the post–Vatican II era, many of them did indeed stray. Many strayed so far that they decided they could no longer honestly remain within the priesthood; and so they left. But many others saw no incompatibility between holding unorthodox views and remaining a priest. Doctrine, it seemed to them, was not as important in this new era as it had been in the old; hence, a few deviations from doctrine did not really matter. Things were not as they had been, for instance, in the Church of England in Queen Victoria's time, when scrupulous clerics resigned from the church because they could no longer give inner assent to every one of the Thirty-Nine Articles. Many a priest must have felt that there was no need for such scrupulosity in the new age brought in by Vatican II — or in the new age in which Catholics had abandoned their old one-true-faith mentality and adopted instead (as I have put it) a denominational mentality.

But if unorthodox priests are a danger, the governing structure of the Catholic Church provides for containment of this danger. Priests work under the superintendence of bishops, who have the hiring and firing power. That is, bishops assign priests to this parish or that, and they can switch their assignments at will; and they are free to do this without consulting the preferences of the local parishioners. If a priest begins toying with unorthodox opinions, the bishop can call him on the carpet and order him to cease and desist. If the priest does not obey, the bishop can transfer him to another parish or deny him a parish altogether. And if a priest is punished by being transferred out of the parish in which he was uttering unorthodox views and sentiments, he is without recourse. There is almost never any effective way, for example, in which he could mobilize his parishioners to support him and block the bishop's decision; for Catholic laypersons, except for a very small minority of liberal Catholics, accept the right of bishops to assign parish priests; and rare is the parish in which there are enough of such liberals to amount to a critical mass.

But how does a bishop discover that one of his priests is propagating unorthodox views? After all, bishops are not elementary-school principals; they generally do not make unannounced visits to see how their charges are performing. So how do bishops find these things out? Often from an unhappy parishioner complaining about the priest. Now, these complaints are not always reliable; some of these complainers are, as the old saying has it, "more Catholic than the pope," and they often see heresy where none exists. But the complaints will not always be easily dismissible. Every so often, a parish priest really will cross the line, and the complainer really will have a valid point.

It is important for a bishop that he not lump these valid complaints in with all the others. And why? For two reasons. For one, bishops are normally thoroughly orthodox themselves (more on this in a moment), and they do not want their priests to be other than orthodox. For another, the complainers know that if they do not get satisfaction from their local bishop, they can go higher up. They can write to Cardinal Ratzinger, the head of the Vatican Congregation for the Doctrine of the Faith, the man often called the pope's doctrinal "enforcer." Or they can write to the pope himself, complaining about the bishop who did nothing about their valid complaint. Of course, every bishop runs the risk of having cranky complainers denounce him to Rome, but he would like to keep the number of such complainers at a minimum, and, above all, he would not want any of the complaints about him to be well-grounded. In the Vatican scorecard, one of the blackest possible marks against a bishop is that he could not control Father X, the priest in his diocese who is notoriously spreading un-Catholic opinions on matters of faith and morals.[70]

• *Only proven priests are made bishops.* Bishops are screened for orthodoxy and leadership quality, so the governing structure of the Catholic Church ensures that laypersons will have minimal influence on doctrine and that priests will be subject to the control of bishops, thereby limiting the capacity of priests to lead others into doctrinal deviance. But what about bishops themselves, those controllers of priests? What guarantees are there that *they* will not deviate, and therefore tolerate deviance further down the line? The answer is that they are appointed by the pope and recommended to the pope by senior Church figures having the pope's confidence, and that before they are named bishops, they will have established a track record of many years of service as a priest.

---

[70] An example of this can probably be found in the career of Cardinal Richard Cushing, Archbishop of Boston from 1944 until 1970. The man who gets appointed to the Boston archbishopric, one of the premier American sees, usually gets elevated soon thereafter to the rank of cardinal. But Cushing had to wait fourteen years to join the College of Cardinals. Why? I do not know whether anyone knows for sure, but very likely it was because he could not successfully silence the rebellious Jesuit priest Leonard Feeney, who very noisily insisted on giving a literal interpretation to the old Catholic teaching that "outside the Church, there is no salvation" — a literal interpretation that meant, contrary to the actual teaching of the modern Catholic Church, that all the good Protestants of Boston (and elsewhere) were doomed to Hell. Cushing's failure to control a priest who had crossed the line into un-Catholic teaching seems to have cost him a long delay in getting the red hat.

If they are not "safe men," their unreliability will very probably turn up before they get promoted to the episcopal level, and their lack of reliability will disqualify them for promotion.

Furthermore, before a man gets promoted to a very important episcopal or archiepiscopal see, he will have served time as a lower-ranking bishop, as an auxiliary bishop or as the bishop of a minor diocese. Before a man reaches a very important post, his reliability has been tested and scrutinized at various levels: in the seminary, as a diocesan priest, as an auxiliary bishop, and as the ordinary of a minor see. If he gives any indication at any of these levels that he is not "safe" on questions of faith and morals, it is very probable that he will not get promoted to the next level; and the scrutiny becomes more and more careful the higher he goes. The process is reminiscent of the process Plato contemplated for his ideal Republic, where no one was to get appointed to the highest rank, that of philosopher-ruler, until he had survived decades of testing and scrutiny.

By the time a man becomes an archbishop, or, even more, a cardinal, he has had to survive so many screenings that it is highly unlikely that he will be anything but perfectly safe when it comes to orthodoxy. He may be deficient in other ways — as amply illustrated during the great sex-abuse scandal that the Catholic Church in the United States has experienced in recent years. He may be a poor administrator, he may be a poor pastoral leader, he may even in some few cases be a bad man; but it is most unlikely that he will be anything but reliably orthodox. For it is understood by the people at the top — that is, the pope and others who effectively make these appointments and promotions — that the legitimacy of the episcopacy and the priesthood and the entire Church depends heavily on not making any departures from Catholic orthodoxy.

• *The system ensures an orthodox pope.* The key to the whole system, of course, is to have a pope who is reliably orthodox on matters of faith and morals, since, in the last analysis, it is the pope who guarantees the orthodoxy of bishops, who, in turn, guarantee the orthodoxy of priests. But what assurance is there that a man of doubtful orthodoxy will not be elected pope? It is a kind of circular assurance. Previous popes, along with the system in general, assure that the College of Cardinals is made up of nothing but (or almost nothing but) reliably orthodox men. And then these reliably orthodox men choose a new pope, always (at least for many centuries) one of their number; which is to say, a man they personally know. And why would they choose anyone but a man they can count on to be orthodox in the highest office? They understand that the legitimacy of the Catholic religion could be shattered if a man of dubious orthodoxy were to make it into the Chair of St. Peter.

Somebody may wish to argue that this does not always happen; that Pope John XXIII, for example, elected by his fellow cardinals in 1958, proved not to be a "safe" man, not a reliable man; and that if this can happen once, it can happen again. In fact, many liberal Catholics are counting on its happening again. They believe that the reign of John Paul II has been a reign of dark reaction in the Church. They look back with nostalgia on the days of John XXIII, and they look forward to a day, perhaps in the papacy immediately succeeding that of John Paul II, when another "unsafe" man will mount the papal throne and resume the progressive revolution that John XXIII initiated: a revolution which, this time, they hope, will lead to married priests, women priests, elected bishops, tolerance of contraception, the blessing of committed homosexual relationships, and a less narrow-minded attitude toward abortion.

The trouble with this theory is that John XXIII was definitely *not* a man of dubious orthodoxy; he was not a man who was anything but reliable when it came to matters of faith and morals. Certainly he was not "safe" from the point of view of those ecclesiastical archconservatives who wanted to keep the fortress mentality of the Tridentine era in place. But that is a question of policy, not of doctrine; it is quite a different thing from being of doubtful orthodoxy. John XXIII was liberal on Church policy, not on Church doctrine.

Liberal Catholics saw that the Church under his leadership was moving in a liberal direction, and they imagined what would happen if the Church continued to move further and further along that liberal line. This is something like imagining what will happen if a brick, dropped from the top of the Washington Monument, kept following its downward path. It would, of course, travel all the way to China, and for those who like the idea of bricks getting to China, this is an exhilarating thought. But of course it will *not* travel all the way to China; it will stop when it hits a significant barrier — namely, the ground at the foot of the monument. Nor would the liberalism of John XXIII and the Second Vatican Council travel all the way to enactment of the liberal Catholic agenda; it would stop when it hit a significant barrier — namely, Catholic doctrine and ancient Tradition.

• *Traditionalists have more stamina for the fight.* In a showdown struggle between Catholic liberals and Catholic traditionalists for control of the Catholic Church in the United States, much depends on which party is more likely to be the first to tire and give up the struggle. It is clear, I think, that the liberals would be first to tire and quit the field.

The traditionalists are solidly convinced that the Catholic Church is the true church of Christ. So how could they possibly give up the fight? How could they despair of Catholicism and switch to another religion? Or roll over and passively accept liberal control of their Church? The answer, of course, is that they could not. To do so would be a kind of psychological impossibility. They would fight to the bitter end. They would even fight *beyond* the bitter end. If — very unlikely though it is — the Catholic Church in the United States were to abandon orthodoxy, ordain women, give its blessings to same-sex unions, et cetera, there is no reason to believe that the traditionalists would accept it passively. They would keep on going, rather like the "Old Believers" in Russia, who never accommodated to the reforms of the Russian Orthodox Church instituted by Peter the Great. And they would be better situated than the Old Believers; for, although a minority among American Catholics, they would be part of a worldwide majority, linked to a universal network of traditional Catholics, including the great traditionalist presiding over the see of Peter in Rome.

By contrast, the liberals, because of the very nature of their liberalism, have a more shallow commitment and attachment to the Church. They are far less persuaded than the traditionalists that the Catholic Church is the true church of Christ. For them, Catholicism is only one division of the Church of Christ, and a very imperfect division at that; hence the need for lots of liberal or progressive "improvements." Since liberals would like the Catholic religion to adopt many of the features of today's liberal Protestant churches, above all the Episcopal Church — married priests, female priests, semi-democratic election of bishops, a diminution of papal power, approval of contraception, greater tolerance for divorce and nonmarital sexuality (including homosexuality) — it is hard to see how the liberal can claim that Catholicism is in any way superior to these other religions. And if it is not superior, why would anyone bother fighting to the bitter end for control of such a church? Would it not be easier simply to give up an apparently unwinnable fight against traditionalists and their traditionalist popes and bishops, and instead join a congenial liberal Protestant church?

Many Catholic liberals have, of course, done precisely that. They can now be found on Sundays in the pews of a more or less liberal Protestant church, often an Episcopal church. Yet many other liberals have stuck with their Catholic identity, refusing to switch, despite an unending series of disappointments with the pope and the bishops. How can this be explained if, as I argued above, the logic of liberalism makes it far less likely that they will continue, come what may, to adhere to Catholicism?

To this question I offer a twofold answer. First, although many liberals have retained their adherence to Catholicism, their rate of continued adherence is far lower than the rate of continued adherence among traditionalists. Traditionalists have nowhere else to go; hence, there is almost never a defection from Catholicism among their ranks — although, on rare occasions, a traditionalist who feels that the Catholic Church has accommodated too much to modern ways will join a traditionalist schismatic group or perhaps the Orthodox church. Defections from the liberal ranks, on the other hand, are everyday occurrences.

Second, although many liberals of the older generation (i.e., the generation of Catholics who grew up in the days before Vatican II) continue to adhere to Catholicism and will, it seems, remain Catholic until their deaths, it is unlikely that their stubborn attachment to the Church will be duplicated by younger generations of liberal Catholics. Catholics who received their religious education in the pre–Vatican II era, that is, in an age when liberal Catholicism was virtually nonexistent, were taught that the Church is an end in itself, an intrinsically valuable thing, an object worthy of love and devotion for its own sake. Quite naturally, persons who had this kind of education developed a very strong attachment to the Church, an attachment that has often remained ineradicable, no matter how many times these persons have been disappointed by the "unprogressive" policies of popes and bishops.

But their children and grandchildren have received a very different kind of education in Catholicism, a more liberal education. For them, the Church is an instrument, a means to an end. The

Church can help the individual to live in hope and charity, and it can help bring justice to the world by fighting against poverty and racism and sexism and war. But if the Church does not deliver on these things, if it proves to be ineffective at promoting these many good things, then it is a defective instrument, and it can be discarded. For the "old" Catholic, the Church did not have to prove itself by its performance. For the "new" Catholic, the Church *does* have to prove itself. Catholics of this newer type do not have a "till death do us part" relationship with the Church. Defections from Catholicism among liberal Catholics, which have been fairly common among the older generation of liberals, will be far more common among the younger generations.

The eventual victory of traditionalists
in the American Church may be pyrrhic

In conclusion, then, because of the peculiar makeup and structure of the Catholic Church and because of the tenacity of its traditional believers, we may be confident that, in a showdown fight for control of American Catholicism, the traditionalists will win. But what will their victory leave them with?

An American Catholic Church reduced to a "saving remnant" of traditionalists will be a very poor thing. (I concede that it will perhaps not be a poor thing in the eyes of God, who has worked with apparently unpromising saving remnants in the past. But it will be a poor thing from a sociopolitical point of view.) It will certainly be small, since it will have lost all its liberals, and it will have lost many "moderates," who, although not outright liberals, will feel uneasy in a Church that has reverted to traditional beliefs and values and practices. Among those last liberals and moderates are sure to be some of its most talented and best-educated members.

In sum, it will be forced to retreat to a new Catholic quasi-ghetto. But unlike the old Catholic ghetto — which was optimistic, building up its strength, looking forward to the day when its people would be first-class Americans — this new ghetto will be pessimistic, carrying a memory of failure, realizing that true Catholics will never have an important role to play in what will, by that point, be America's thoroughly secularized dominant culture. This saving remnant will have little or no influence on the larger American society, almost as little as the Amish or the Hasidic Jews have.

Chapter 25

Losing the Catholic Voice
Will Harm American Culture

If American Catholicism fails and its defeated remnant retreats into a new quasi-ghetto, and hence, into social and cultural irrelevancy as far as the larger society is concerned, it is not just the Church that will suffer. American society and culture as a whole will suffer from the absence of an effective Catholic contribution. In fact, it is already suffering from this absence. For while Catholics are contributing in important ways to American life (in science and scholarship, in education, in their professions, in the arts, in the military, in politics, et cetera), they are contributing *qua* secularized Americans, not *qua* Catholics. Yet in the Western world, Catholicism is the normal custodian of certain civilizational treasures, both intellectual and moral — treasures that American society desperately needs. If American Catholics are incapable of offering these cultural values to their fellow Americans, it is highly unlikely that anyone else will offer them.

The devastating loss of
Catholic intellectual contributions

In his *Timaeus*, Plato says that Solon the Athenian was once told by an Egyptian priest, "You Greeks are children" — meaning that the Greeks, when compared with the Egyptians, had only a brief history, hence, only a brief memory. It might also be said that we Americans are children, having a history that goes back less than four hundred years, a history as a republic that goes back only a little over two hundred years, and a history as a unified nation that goes back only to the late nineteenth century (the unification that resulted from the Civil War). The Catholic Church, by contrast, has a history and memory that reaches back to the golden days of the Roman Empire. Now, there is something to be said for the short historical memory that most Americans have: it liberates us from the burdens of the past and readies us for ventures into the future. But a future-oriented mentality can, like all good things, be overdone. It needs to be balanced by a memory of what has gone before, and Catholicism, whatever its other merits or shortcomings, has a long memory.

One of the consequences of the American forgetfulness of the past is that we fail to appropriate the classical culture of the ancient world to which we are the legitimate heirs. There is, for one, the philosophical heritage: how few, even among well-educated Americans, have given careful study to Plato or Aristotle or the Stoics or Cicero? And then there is the literary heritage: very few educated Americans have an intimate knowledge, even in translation, of the epic poets Homer and Virgil; or of the great dramatists Aeschylus, Sophocles, and Euripides; or of the great historians Herodotus, Thucydides, Polybius, Plutarch, and Tacitus.

And if we Americans fail to appropriate the classical culture of the ancient world, we fail even more completely to appropriate the culture of the great Christian civilization of the Middle Ages. In the popular mind, the medieval age still, to a great degree, stands under the condemnation passed upon it by the anti-Christian writers of the Enlightenment, a condemnation aided and abetted by the anti-Catholicism that used to flourish among Protestants who held that mankind had lived in something like utter darkness for many centuries until Luther and Calvin flooded the world with light.[71] And thus, there is a great underappreciation of even the most important writers and thinkers of the Christian centuries — Augustine, Aquinas, and Dante — not to mention the scores of lesser poets and theologians and mystics.[72]

If American society appreciated its own inherited cultural wealth, these ancient and medieval writings would be our intellectual meat and potatoes. Catholicism, born in an age when the classical philosophers, poets, and historians were cultural staples, has assimilated these ancient treasures; and Catholicism itself gave birth to the creative minds of the Middle Ages. A Catholicism that played its proper role in American life would serve as a cultural transmission belt, conveying the philosophical and literary treasures of the ancient and medieval worlds into modern American society, just as it has done in other lands in other ages. In the early Middle Ages, it was Catholic monasteries that preserved, through monk-copyists, the treasures of Latin literature. In the high Middle Ages, it was Catholic universities that recovered Aristotle. In the fifteenth century, it was the Catholic Renaissance that restored Plato to Western Europe. In the sixteenth and seventeenth centuries, the colleges operated by the Jesuits made sure that the higher classes in much of Europe became acquainted with the literature of Greece and Rome. A similar service, I contend, should be provided by American Catholicism today. If

---

[71] It is interesting to note that Luther and Calvin, although they detested the Church of Rome, did not hold the Middle Ages in contempt. How could they? They were virtually medieval figures themselves, relying heavily on theologians of the Middle Ages.

[72] For both the ancient and the medieval world, it must be conceded, we are far better acquainted with the visual arts — sculpture, architecture, and (in the case of the Middle Ages) painting — than we are with literature and philosophy. Credit for this must be given to museums rather than to any generalized American appreciation of the ancient or medieval worlds.

The Decline and Fall of the Catholic Church in America

Catholicism does not instruct the people of the United States in the thought and literature of the ancient and medieval worlds, who will?

At this point, the following objection might be raised. It may be said: If Catholicism has so much to offer American intellectual life, how come it did not offer it in the days when the Church was stronger, in the days before Vatican II, when Catholics were still largely uninfected by secularism?

The answer, of course, is that Catholicism was not part of the American cultural mainstream in those days; it was still living in its quasi-ghetto. Further, American Catholicism was not intellectually mature at that time. Before Catholics could transmit the treasures of classical culture to their fellow citizens, they first had to appropriate these treasures themselves. But Catholics were still emerging from their immigrant and lower-class status. With hardly any exceptions, their colleges were third-rate. And although these colleges taught Thomism — a magnificent synthesis of Christian theology with Aristotle, Stoicism, and Neoplatonism — it was, with very few exceptions, merely a "textbook Thomism": an uninspired collection of correct answers that you could write down on your final exam. Very few educated Catholics, although they might be familiar with many of the classical names, had any genuine feel for classical culture. They had more of a feel for medieval culture, but it was the degenerate medievalism typical of their Thomistic textbooks.

This is not to say that Americans, lacking Catholic help, never had any effectual acquaintance with classical culture. Not at all. From the very beginnings of British America, educated Protestants, especially in New England, were readers of Latin and familiar with Latin literature. (Knowledge of Greek was more rare.) By the early twentieth century, however, the educated Protestant of this type was becoming more and more rare, even among the ministry. As accessibility to secondary and higher education expanded in the decades following the Civil War, public-school policy-makers cared less and less for Latin and Greek and more and more for either scientific education for the college-bound or vocational training for the workplace-bound. At the same time, a great split was taking place within the world of American Protestantism: a split between the modernists and the fundamentalists. The modernists, being "modern," had no great affection for dead languages and dead literature; while the fundamentalists tended to care for no literature except the Bible, which, of course, they did not think of as "literature." And so the classical languages gradually disappeared from the curriculum, and the literature that these languages gave access to faded from the American consciousness.

What happened to American Catholicism in the 1960s was nothing less than a tragedy in the history of American culture, especially "high" culture. Just at the moment when American Catholicism was nearing intellectual maturity, when it was on the verge of being able to appropriate its own cultural treasures and pass them on to other Americans — at precisely this moment, it began a process of disintegration. Instead of appropriating these treasures and passing them on, Catholic intellectuals, newly released from their quasi-ghetto, decided they had much to learn from secular culture but nothing to teach it.

Further, what happened at the individual level was duplicated at the institutional level. Catholic colleges and universities upgraded their academic quality, some evolving into genuine first-rate institutions. But instead of becoming a means of transmitting Catholicism's rich philosophical and artistic heritage, they tended to transform themselves into institutions that were barely distinguishable, apart from a superficial Catholic veneer, from thoroughly secular colleges and universities. The intellectual benefits that Catholicism, after more than a century of preparation, might finally have delivered to American society were never delivered. And the United States is the poorer for this.

The Decline and Fall of the Catholic Church in America

America will lose Catholicism's communitarian spirit

In addition to its intellectual treasures, Catholicism has some distinctive moral treasures to offer. I am thinking of three of these especially: its sense of the common good, its belief in the intrinsic value of chastity, and its religious and political rhetoric of order.

Deep down, Protestantism has always stood for the principle of individualism in religion. Having rejected the pope and the official church, Protestantism made the Bible the ultimate religious authority. But who was to be the authority when it came to interpreting the Bible? Answer: The *private* judgment of the individual, inspired (it was hoped) by the Holy Spirit. To be sure, this individualistic tendency was countered by strongly communitarian tendencies found in early Lutheranism, Calvinism, and Anglicanism. But the individualism was never killed off, for it could not be, since it was of the very essence of Protestantism. In fact, it grew stronger with time, until, at least in the United States, Protestantism splintered into innumerable sects and a kind of religious anarchy.

Now the United States, historically speaking, is a Protestant country. Indeed, in many ways, it is the most Protestant of all countries. From its colonial beginnings, it has been home to what Burke called "the dissidence of Dissent, the Protestantism of the Protestant religion." And when, in the second half of the twentieth century, Protestantism (more particularly, liberal Protestantism) went into decline in the United States, individualism and the right of private judgment did not die out; instead, they took a secularistic form (the Personal Liberty Principle). In that form, they continue to thrive today. In fact, now they thrive more than ever, since communitarian countervailing forces are now weaker than ever.

What is more, Protestant religious individualism prepared the ground for economic individualism — in other words, the capitalist or free-enterprise business system. Economic individualism soon took on a vibrant life of its own, becoming a central element of American society and culture.

Deep down in the personality of the typical American, then, is to be found these dual forms of individualism: the right to determine one's own beliefs and the right to pursue one's economic interests in the way one sees fit.

Catholicism, by contrast, is far more communitarian in its outlook, far more concerned with the common good. From the Catholic point of view, a community is not simply a collection of individuals, nor is the common good merely a collection of individual interests. The community is a whole greater than the sum of its parts, and the common good is something to which the interests of the individual will often have to be sacrificed. When Emile Durkheim wrote his sociological classic, *Suicide*, he explained the fact that Catholics had lower suicide rates than Protestants in terms of community versus individuality: Protestants are more individualistic, hence more independent, while Catholics have stronger community attachments; and stronger attachments mean a lower rate of suicide.

In the seventeenth and eighteenth centuries, and for the first two-thirds of the nineteenth, the individualistic tendencies of Protestantism and capitalism were counterbalanced by communitarian tendencies that Protestantism had inherited from the early Reformers, who had, in turn, inherited these tendencies from the older world of medieval Catholicism. But in the post–Civil War decades, when the United States went through an explosive process of industrialization and urbanization, individualism, especially economic individualism, got the upper hand, and it largely retained this upper hand until the coming of Franklin Roosevelt and the New Deal in the 1930s. The New Deal swung the pendulum of social values back to the communitarian side, something it could not have done without the help of Catholic voters, who strongly backed FDR and his programs. This support, in addition to its economic and ethnic motives, was in large measure the result of anti-individualistic inclinations that were second nature to Catholics. But it was also partly the result of social encyclicals by modern popes, especially *Rerum Novarum* (Leo XIII) and *Quadragesimo Anno* (Pius XI). It is not that Catholic voters had personally studied these encyclicals; very few had. But the contents of the papal pronouncements were well known to bishops, priests, and teachers in Catholic schools; thus, the ideas and values contained in them were indirectly transmitted to rank-and-file Catholics; they "trickled down" from the clergy and the academics.

In the mid to late 1960s, American Catholicism was beginning to disintegrate, and Catholics, abandoning the communitarianism that had long been second nature to them, were entering the mainstream of American life and becoming almost as individualistic as their fellow Americans. A process of circular causality was at work. The sudden expansion of a culture of individualism weakened the Catholic Church in the United States, and the weakened Church permitted an even greater flourishing of individualism. The same circular process was at work, incidentally, in another hitherto strongly communitarian set of institutions: labor unions. Unions can flourish only in a culture that places a high value on community, and they, in turn, strengthen that communitarian culture. In the 1960s, labor unions, like the Catholic Church, went into decline. The dominant American culture had become too individualistic to allow them to thrive, and their decline accelerated the growth of individualism. It is more than a mere coincidence that Catholics have always been represented in labor unions in numbers disproportionate to their share of the general population; at least this has been true since the rise of the CIO in the 1930s.

With this weakening of communitarian values among Catholics, individualism found that it had a clear field in front of it. Taking advantage of the weakness of communitarian elements in American culture, individualism has had things pretty much its own way for the past thirty or thirty-five years. To be sure, there have been in-house disputes among individualists, who (to use the terminology of Robert Bellah,[73] come in two varieties, expressive and utilitarian. The "expressive" individualists (who favor things like abortion rights and gay rights) have become a dominant force in the national Democratic Party, while the "utilitarian" individualists (who favor things like tax cuts and government deregulation of business) are running the national Republican Party.

Although it is very probable that the United States will always be a strongly individualistic society, this individualism, if it is to avoid getting carried to dangerous extremes, needs a communitarian counterbalance. Yet, absent a large body of Catholics who adhere to the traditional Catholic system of values, this balancing force is not likely to have any significant strength. There is, to be sure, an intellectual movement in support of communitarianism, its leading spokesman being the sociologist Amitai Etzioni.[74] But for ideas to prevail, especially in a democratic society, these ideas have to be internalized by large numbers of people. A few decades ago, the Catholic Church, along with the labor unions (heavily populated by Catholics), ensured this necessary mass internalization of the idea of community. But neither the Church nor the unions perform this function very well anymore, with the result that individualism — in both its expressive and utilitarian forms — has been allowed to run wild in America.

The Catholic vision of chastity will be drowned out by sexual prudence

It is hard to say a good word for chastity nowadays, since, from the dominant secularist or moral liberalism point of view, few

---

[73] *Habits of the Heart.*

[74] See, for example, his book *The New Golden Rule: Community and Morality in a Democratic Society* (1993).

things are more ridiculous than this quaint old notion. It is not that moral liberals champion promiscuity (although, being tolerant, they do not disapprove of it for those who like that kind of thing). No, the moral liberal/secularist believes in a certain amount of sexual restraint, thus, there are certain "commandments" that you should heed. For instance, you should avoid rape and child molestation; you should avoid disease; you should avoid unwanted pregnancies. You should make sure that your sexual life does not impact unpleasantly on other significant aspects of your life, e.g., your education, your marriage, your job, and your emotional well-being. You should normally abstain from adultery. If you get sexually involved with a coworker, make sure this relationship is not one that will get either one of you fired. The very young should usually abstain from sex, since they lack the emotional maturity and good judgment needed to handle it with minimal good sense (but people mature at different rates, so there is no agreed-upon definition of "very young"). Further, apart from the pregnancy caution, all these rules apply just as much to homosexual as to heterosexual sex.

So the secularists are not without their own code of sexual rules. But these are rules of *prudence*, not chastity. That is to say, these rules view sexual restraint as an instrumental good (a means to an end), not an intrinsic good (an end in itself). Abstinence is a strictly negative thing, not a positive thing; a way of avoiding pain and suffering. It is not a form of moral goodness; it is not a way to live in conformity with an unwritten moral law; and it is certainly not a way of earning merit in the eyes of God.[75]

The traditional Catholic view is just the opposite. It sees chastity as a positive thing, an intrinsic good. It sees consecrated

[75] For two examples of secularist organizations promoting a "prudential" approach to sexuality, see the websites of SIECUS, the Sexuality Information and Education Council of the U.S. (www.siecus.org) and of the Planned Parenthood Federation of America (www.plannedparenthood.org).

virginity as a very high intrinsic good. It sees acts of unchastity — even such apparently harmless acts as sexual relations between two unmarried adults — as a misuse of sexual powers and a deviation from God's plan for those powers. Even within marriage, couples must regard sex, not as an end in itself, but as a means for uniting them in love and begetting children — the true ends of marriage. Thus, Catholicism holds that even marital contraception is immoral.

From a secularist point of view, of course, all this sounds nothing less than idiotic. Small wonder, then, that secularism tends to concentrate its anti-Christian fire on the surviving remnants of the ancient Catholic sexual morality still found in America today. Contemporary secularism/moral liberalism rejects almost all of traditional Christian sexual morality. It tries to sweep it away, sometimes by criticizing it, sometimes by laughing at it, always by endorsing practices contrary to it. Secularists generally disapprove of adultery or any other form of sexual infidelity (except, of course, in cases in which one partner has consented to the other partner's "infidelity"), but their disapproval is mild when compared with the traditional Christian disapproval of adultery.

Christianity has always disapproved of adultery for at least two reasons: it is the breaking of a solemn promise, and it is an act of unchastity. The secularist, by contrast, has only one reason for objecting: infidelity is an instance of promise-breaking; its relationship to chastity or its opposite is nothing to the point, for chastity is a pointless thing. Secularists generally do not like promiscuity, but it is an aesthetic, more than a moral, objection; they find it in bad taste. Secularists have no objection to some Christian virtues, e.g., love of neighbor. But chastity — when it is anything more than prudential abstinence in certain risky circumstances — is from the secularist point of view an absurdity, clear evidence of the irrationality of old-fashioned Christianity.

Now, one does not have to be a great fan of the Catholic ideal of chastity to realize that the secularist ideal of prudent unchastity has not worked terribly well in American society in the last few decades. The fact is, people have not been as prudent as the secularist ideal calls on them to be; and perhaps, given the sexual side of human nature, they never will be. Thus, in the past thirty years or so, we have had skyrocketing rates of sexually transmitted diseases (including AIDS); we have had an epidemic of out-of-wedlock births; we have had phenomenally high divorce rates; we have had millions of children growing up in impoverished single-parent households; we have had tens of millions of abortions; and we have had a pornography explosion in print and film (compounded by an even larger secondary explosion of Internet pornography) — and all this with no end in sight. Admonitions to prudence are apparently not enough.

The Catholic ideal of chastity, even if not widely adopted, could have served as a counterforce to the sexual madness that seems to have infected much of American society. And for a long time, up until the early 1960s, it did serve as a counterforce, functioning as a check on the first stage of the sexual revolution, the stage that began in the "roaring Twenties." But the Catholic love affair with chastity collapsed in the mid to late 1960s, just at the moment when the second stage of the sexual revolution was breaking out. There was no longer any adequate counterforce. Henceforward it would be prudence or nothing. And to a great degree, it has been nothing.

The Church will no longer offer a rhetoric of order

Ever since at least the eighteenth century, if not earlier, America has had two parallel and complementary traditions of public rhetoric. One, the political tradition, has been a rhetoric of freedom or liberty. The other, a religious tradition, has been a rhetoric of order and restraint.

When American politicians, even conservative politicians, get into an oratorical frame of mind, they find it difficult to speak of anything other than freedom, the mainstay of American political rhetoric. Take for example the current president, George W. Bush, very much a conservative. Bush defended his 2003 war in Iraq as a war for freedom; in fact, the campaign was officially named "Operation Iraqi Freedom." In many ways, of course, it was an accurate name, for it brought to an end several decades of an unfree regime presided over by a brutal tyrant at the head of a thoroughly antidemocratic political party.

So, yes, it was indeed a war for freedom — but it was at least equally, if not more, a war for order. During the last half-century or so, few, if any, regions in the world have been as lacking in good order as the Middle East, and by going to war in Iraq, the Bush administration hoped to encourage social and political order in the region. For if order and stability can be restored — or rather, created for the first time since the collapse of the Ottoman Empire, more than eighty years ago — then many benefits for the United States and the world might follow: for example, security for Israel, prosperity for the Arabs, a decline in terrorism, and a sure supply of petroleum for the world's industrialized nations.

And yet, despite the importance of order and stability, President Bush was unable to appeal to these values when he tried to rally popular support for the war. Foreign-policy experts can speak of order and stability when they have their small but important meetings. But politicians cannot speak this way to the public. Why? Because a rhetoric of "order" and "stability" is simply not available to American politicians.

It is not curious, of course, that Americans should be moved by appeals to freedom and liberty. After all, the founding event of the nation, the American Revolution, was based on a demand for freedom — freedom from overseas rule, from what the Founding Fathers perceived to be an incipient tyranny. And the nation's refounding event, the Civil War, was also a war about freedom, in this case, freedom from slavery.

The Decline and Fall of the Catholic Church in America

Our economic system, the most prosperous in the history of the world, is a system of "free enterprise." World War I was sold to the public as a war "to make the world safe for democracy" (of which liberty is an essential ingredient) and World War II as a fight for the "four freedoms." The Cold War was a struggle of "the free world" against Communism. And in the culture war of the last thirty years or so, moral liberals have been doing battle for personal "autonomy," for "sexual freedom," and for "freedom of choice" (with regard to abortion). After more than two centuries of hearing *freedom* shouted from the rooftops, it is not surprising that Americans have grown used to this kind of talk.

And yet it *is* curious in some ways that our political rhetoric is *monopolized* by talk of freedom, that we do not also have a political rhetoric of order. After all, the American Revolution (a freedom event) was quickly followed by the adoption of the United States Constitution (an order event). And the Civil War (a freedom event) established the principle that no state could secede from the Union (a principle of order). World War II (a freedom event) was soon followed by the establishment of the United Nations and the founding of NATO (both order events). And our economic system, although it grants great freedom to individual businesses, takes place within a framework of law and order, and is operated by individuals who, for the most part, are willing to abide by the requirements of law.

Our lack of a rhetoric of order and stability can be explained by a number of factors. For one, the freedom events — the Revolution, the Civil War, the World Wars, the Cold War — have been much more dramatic than the order events; they have had a more striking impact on the national imagination. (Everybody knows about Civil War reenactments, but has anybody ever heard of a Constitutional Convention reenactment?)

Second, most of the news that the general public hears about the United States Constitution stresses the Constitution's function as a guarantor of freedom — freedom of press, of speech, of assembly, of religion, of contraception, of abortion, et cetera. Guaranteeing freedom, however, is an important but secondary function of the Constitution. Its first function is to establish a national government that will guarantee order and stability. Yet this primary function is so well performed that it does not attract great public attention; it rarely makes the headlines. This has left the public with the incorrect impression that the Constitution is primarily a freedom document, not primarily an order document.

Finally, it has been less necessary to develop a political rhetoric of order, since American religion has taken care of that. The politicians can talk about freedom and nothing but freedom because churchmen have talked about order.

Or at least they *used* to talk about order. Of course, it was not order as an abstract concept that they talked about, and the word *order* itself probably worked its way into no more than a small percentage of all sermons. But they talked about sin (this was especially true of Calvinist and semi-Calvinist preachers, who constituted the majority of Protestant preachers until into the twentieth century). And this naturally led them to talk about the opposite of sin — namely, holy and virtuous conduct, which, whatever else it may be, is orderly conduct. They denounced drunkenness, they denounced adultery and other sexual sins, they denounced laziness and dishonesty, they denounced gambling, and they denounced luxurious living. They praised sobriety, chastity, honesty, industry, thrift, and simplicity of life. In other words, they denounced things that made for personal and social disorder, and they praised things that made for personal and social order.

The Catholic idea of sin was somewhat different from the Calvinist idea, and the Catholic list of virtues was not identical with the standard Protestant list. (Catholics worried less about drinking and gambling, while worrying more about sexual sins.) But Catholic priests and nuns also talked about sin and virtue; they also insisted that their charges must live clean and upright lives. They reminded their people of the same thing that the Protestant preacher reminded his people — namely, that if they failed to live upright lives, they would spend eternity in Hell.

This was a rhetoric of order, a socially necessary counterweight to the political rhetoric of freedom. But in the second half of the twentieth century, it went into decline. Of the three great divisions of contemporary American Christianity — Catholicism, liberal Protestantism, and conservative Protestantism — only the third preserves the old-fashioned Christian rhetoric, the emphasis on sin and a list of specific virtues and vices, not to mention the emphasis on Hell as a punishment for sin. Popular Catholicism (which has become a branch of generic Christianity), in disregard of official Catholicism and nearly twenty centuries of orthodox Christianity, tends to reduce the virtues to a single virtue, love of neighbor; it tends to ignore the concept of sin (except to make an occasional *pro forma* acknowledgment that we are all sinners); and while not repudiating the idea that certain sexual conduct is sinful, it would rather not mention it; and certainly it would not dream of suggesting that God is such a narrow-minded puritan as to condemn anyone to an eternity of punishment.

Liberal Protestantism is pretty much the same, except that it has gone a step further: it tends, for example, to approve openly of things such as cohabitation and of nonpromiscuous homosexuality. Only Evangelical and Pentecostal Protestants are keeping vividly alive the idea that we are all terrible sinners, that we lack the power to save ourselves from sin, and that we therefore need a Redeemer to save us. This is old-fashioned Christianity, the kind of Christianity that official Catholicism still holds and that popular Catholicism used to teach.

A society that stresses order and restraint to the exclusion of freedom (and there have been many such societies in the world's history) is an unfortunate society. For that way lies tyranny. But equally unfortunate — although its misfortune lies in the opposite direction — is a society that stresses freedom to the exclusion of order and restraint. For that way lies anarchy. And American culture has started to move in that direction. For a long time, we had a balance between talk of freedom (political talk) and talk of order (religious talk). But this balance has been upset, as the religious talk of order — that is, talk of sin and specific virtues and vices — has gone into decline. We still have a vigorous rhetoric of freedom, but we no longer have an equally vigorous rhetoric of order.

A vigorous and orthodox Catholicism would contribute to the badly needed American rhetoric of order, just as it once did contribute for more than a century. But a popular Catholicism in decline, a Catholicism that has become little more than generic Christianity, cannot make that contribution. Here is another price that American society as a whole has paid, and will continue to pay, for the decline of Catholicism.

Chapter 26

The Church Faces
a Crisis of Leadership

In September 1938, the two great western European powers —
Britain and France — still failed to recognize Hitler as a dangerous
enemy. The evidence was certainly there. He had destroyed German democracy, throwing political opponents into concentration
camps. He had murdered dissidents in his own party and made
himself the sole fount of legality in Germany. He had enacted the
anti-Semitic Nuremberg laws and sanctioned a nationwide series
of anti-Semitic pogroms. In defiance of the Treaty of Versailles, he
had rearmed Germany and sent troops into the Rhineland. In
March 1938, he had taken over Austria and incorporated it into
the German Reich (the *Anschluss*), and now, six months later, he
was threatening to invade Czechoslovakia, on the pretext that it
contained a German-speaking region, the Sudetenland.

One would think that such a record of belligerence and law-
lessness and violence would have persuaded Europe's leaders that
Hitler was too dangerous a man to have in the neighborhood, a
man not to be trusted. But it had not. Chamberlain and Daladier,
operating out of either profound political ignorance or the wish-
fullest of wishful thinking, presumed that Herr Hitler was a gentleman they could make a deal with. And so at Munich they allowed
Hitler, without firing a shot, to annex the Sudetenland.

The Decline and Fall of the Catholic Church in America

A few months later, they discovered, to their astonishment, that the German chancellor was not a man of his word, for now he appropriated the remainder of Czechoslovakia. He shocked them still further in August, when he made a deal with Stalin, and on September 1, 1939, he shocked them one last time by invading Poland, thereby forcing them to abandon all illusions. Herr Hitler was no gentleman.

Munich is a classic historical case of the failure of leaders to recognize a dangerous enemy. Something like it has happened to the Catholic Church in the United States during the last thirty or forty years. Most of its leadership — bishops and priests and religious — and most of its rank-and-file members have given little evidence of being aware that they live in an extremely hostile secularist culture, or that the Church is today increasingly populated with nominal Christians who are, in fact, indifferent to Christianity, not to mention liberal Christians who have embraced the values of anti-Christian secularism.

The emergence of secularist anti-Christianity

Of course, in every century since its birth, vast numbers of people have been indifferent to Christianity. Yet for many centuries, this very considerable indifference did little or nothing to impair the legitimacy of Christianity. For although these people did not care for the religion and its moral requirements, they had nothing to put in its place; they had no rival system of belief and conduct to offer the world. As individuals, they wished to shake off the burden of Christianity. But they did not form a party or send out missionaries to preach an anti-gospel.

There had been competing versions of Christianity, of course — versions that differed from the official Catholic Faith. There were Albigensians and Waldensians and Lollards and Hussites, and, later, Lutherans and Calvinists and others; and all of these *did* form parties, and they *did* send out missionaries. But these groups were products of in-house quarrels, disagreements among people who sincerely and earnestly professed to be Christian. It may be plausibly argued that these rebellions of dissenting Christians against Catholicism opened the door to an eventual secularist rebellion against Christianity itself. True enough. Nonetheless these dissenters were not secularists; far from it; and they would have been as shocked by modern secularism as would, say, Pope Innocent III.

Rationalism and Romanticism

In the eighteenth century, an alternative to Christianity finally arose in western Europe: the great cultural movement known as the Enlightenment. This had an organized party ("the party of humanity," as the historian Peter Gay has termed it), and it produced propaganda, and it sent missionaries into the field. Some men of the Enlightenment were deists (Voltaire), some were skeptics (Hume), and some were outright atheists (Diderot); but they all agreed in rejecting Christianity, as indeed they rejected any religion that claimed to be based on divine revelation. They rejected belief in miracles, including the miracle of divine grace. They held that man, by virtue of his faculty of reason, was sufficient unto himself.

In the later years of the eighteenth century, a reaction to the Enlightenment set in — namely, the Romantic movement. The Romantics were dissatisfied with the overly rational conception of human nature favored by the Enlightenment. By contrast, they held that men and women are creatures of *feeling* even more than of intellect. And the feelings they spoke of were not mere emotions: they are forms of cognition as well, instruments of knowledge. We are able to "think with our blood" (the phrase of a twentieth-century Romantic, D. H. Lawrence). For the Romantics, the knowledge given to us via emotion was deeper and truer than the knowledge given to us by reason. This was especially true of moral knowledge. As one of the greatest of the Romantics, William Wordsworth, put it:

> One impulse from a vernal wood
> Tells us more of man,
> Of moral evil and of good,
> Than all the sages can.

The intellect, by contrast, "murders to dissect."

Unlike the men of the Enlightenment, the Romantics were not uniformly anti-Christian. Some of them were (Shelley, Victor Hugo, and the father of Romanticism, Jean-Jacques Rousseau), but some were pro-Christian (Friedrich Schlegel, Chateaubriand, and Wordsworth).

The French Revolution emerged as the issue of a strange marriage between the Enlightenment and the anti-Christian wing of the Romantic movement. Not until the coming of the Revolution, with its very open persecution of the Catholic Church, did it fully dawn upon Catholics that the Enlightenment had been its enemy all along. Only after the near-destruction of the Church in France did Catholics come to understand the dire situation their religion was in; only then did they rally and produce the great revival of Catholicism that marked France in the first fifty years or so of the nineteenth century.

Socialism, nationalism, and radicalism

In the nineteenth century, there were three great anti-Christian political movements: socialism, nationalism, and radicalism. (This last may also be called liberalism of the secularist variety. The adjective *secularist* is important here, since there was also a liberalism of the Christian variety, best typified in the career of William Gladstone.)

Socialism was explicitly anti-Christian, except in Britain, where it did not arrive on the scene until late in the century, and where it contained a mixture of Christian and anti-Christian elements. On the Continent, however, to become a socialist was tantamount to renouncing Christianity. The most influential socialist theorist of the century was the German Karl Marx, who had said that religion is "the opiate of the people." To be sure, he had said that in the years before he became a socialist, but it continued to represent his views even in his mature years. The ideal socialist (or communist) society would be classless and propertyless; it would also be religionless. Christianity was an element of the bourgeois ideology, useful for maintaining the capitalist status quo. God was a fiction that would not be needed when the human race came of age.

Nationalism was not explicitly anti-Christian; in fact, it often clothed itself in the language of Christianity, claiming that God had especially blessed the nation. But it was often anti-Christian in practice — especially in France and Germany, where it tended to elevate the community of the nation above the community of the Church, and where it demanded that one's ultimate loyalty be to the nation rather than to God. The most interesting theoretical example of this demand can be found in the theory of religion propounded by the great French sociologist, Emile Durkheim, in his work *The Elementary Forms of the Religious Life*. In this work, Durkheim, a religious nonbeliever, even though he had been reared as a pious Alsatian Jew, argued that God has never been anything more than a symbol of the community, of the community's great value for its members and its absolute moral authority over them. When we worship God, then, we are really worshiping the community in a disguised form. Well, then, why not throw off the disguise and worship the community directly? Let France be our God. Let the service of France be our religion.

One very striking example of *radicalism* was Benthamism, or Utilitarianism, which flourished in Britain, supported by the affluent business classes. The Benthamites had little use for religion in general or Christianity in particular, but they were exceedingly discreet in their repudiation of it. For instance, one can read almost everything John Stuart Mill published during his lifetime without realizing that he was not a Christian, that he was not even a believer in God. Frequently he speaks with great respect of Christianity and of its contribution to the moral improvement of the human race. Only in his posthumously published works, his *Autobiography* and his *Three Essays on Religion*, does his irreligion become clear. The reason for this discretion was partly, no doubt, a matter of English courtesy; it would be rude to irritate believers by pronouncing blasphemies in their hearing. Mostly, however, it was a matter of political prudence. For the Benthamites, although abounding in ideas for the reform of society, were relatively few in number. To translate their ideas into practice, they had to form alliances with liberals of a Christian type, e.g., with Nonconformist Protestants of the middle classes, and with that very pious and theologically very learned Anglican, Mr. Gladstone.

In France, nineteenth-century radicalism had no such reticence about its irreligion. It was very frankly and very aggressively anticlerical — that is to say, anti-Catholic. The Church, from the point of view of the radicals or anticlericals, had too much power: too much influence on social life, too much influence in government, and, above all, too much influence on education. The Church was an antiprogressive force, and it used its control over education to instill antiprogressive ideas into the minds of the young, thereby slowing France's movement toward modernity. If France was to become a truly modern nation — that is, a liberal nation, characterized by freedom of religion, freedom of thought, and freedom of trade — the power of the Church would have to be broken or at least sharply reduced.

This breaking or reduction was accomplished in some measure by the founding (in 1871) of the Third Republic in the aftermath of the disastrous Franco-Prussian War, a republic created by anticlericals. And it was accomplished even more decisively as a result of the Dreyfus Affair (late 1890s and early 1900s). The anticlericals took the right side in this struggle — namely, the pro-Dreyfus side, the side of the innocent Jewish army captain who was being framed for treason; whereas the Catholics took the wrong side, the anti-Semitic side. This brought tremendous discredit upon Catholicism, and the radicals quickly followed up on their advantage, taking control of public education completely out of the hands of the Church and expelling all religious orders from the country.

Nazism, Communism, and moral liberalism

In the twentieth century, two of the great anti-Christian movements manifested a ferocity that anti-Christianity had not shown since the early years of the French Revolution, indeed a ferocity that far surpassed anything seen in the 1790s. One of these movements was Nazism, the lineal — albeit extreme — descendent of nineteenth-century nationalism. The other was Communism, a similarly extreme descendent of nineteenth-century socialism.

Of the two, Communism was far more open in its enmity of Christianity, just as socialism had been more open in its enmity than nationalism. In the Soviet Union and, to a lesser degree, in other eastern European countries that came under Communist control in the aftermath of World War II, the old socialist hostility was aggravated a hundredfold. On a vast scale, churches, monasteries, and convents were closed, and priests, monks, and nuns were murdered. The practice of religion became close to impossible, and it became illegal for the Church to teach religion to the young. Atheism was openly taught in government schools.

Hitler, who later was to fool Chamberlain and Daladier, fooled many leaders of Christian churches as well. He had them convinced that Nazism and Christianity were not incompatible, just as, in the nineteenth century, his ardent nationalist predecessors had convinced many Christians that nationalism was not incompatible with Christianity. Some Protestant leaders were so far deceived (or self-deceiving) as to create a German national church, thereby institutionalizing the weird union between Nazism and Christianity. Other Protestants, recognizing the fundamental incompatibility between the two, would have nothing to do with such a scheme. They constituted the "Confessing Church," which defied Hitler. The Catholic leadership fell, for the most part, between these two Protestant extremes. The bishops and archbishops and cardinals were not about to fall for the crazy idea that Christianity and Nazism are compatible; but at the same time, they hoped, and more than half-believed, that Hitler was a man one could do business with.

In 1933, Hitler's first year in office, the Vatican signed a concordat with the new regime, intended to guarantee the full freedom of the Church in Germany. The attitude of Church leaders — both in Rome and in Germany — seemed to be that, no matter how wicked and foolish the German leadership might be, Catholics would at least be free to practice their religion and to pass it on to their children: an arrangement far better than anything that could be hoped for in a Communist country. A few years of experience would show that Hitler was not prepared to respect the terms of the concordat[76] and that he had dire things in mind, very dire things indeed, for both Catholicism and Protestantism.

Today Nazism is dead, and Communism is dying. They once were grave threats to Christianity, not only because they persecuted Christians, but, even more, because they provided a non-Christian alternative philosophy of life that was attractive to millions of people. They are grave threats no longer. Their day (with the significant exception, as of this writing, of Communist China) has come and gone. Christianity, and, in particular, Catholicism,

---

[76] See the anti-Nazi encyclical of Pope Pius XI, *Mit Brennender Sorge*, issued on March 14, 1937.

has managed to outlast one more rival, just as it has outlasted so many rivals, both secular and religious, in the course of its long history.

But these two were not the only great anti-Christian movements in the twentieth century. There was a third movement, and this is a movement that is still going strong today: *moral liberalism.* As Communism was the lineal descendent of nineteenth-century socialism, and as Nazism was the lineal descendent of nineteenth-century nationalism, so moral liberalism is the descendent of nineteenth-century radicalism. And like that older radicalism, the social base of moral liberalism is the affluent classes of society. This is the movement and philosophy I have discussed at length in earlier chapters of the book. Its fundamental tenet, as I have said, is the Personal Liberty Principle, and it is thoroughly incompatible with the morality of traditional Christianity. And since Christian morality is an essential element of Christianity, to embrace the morality of moral liberalism is to reject, not only Christian morality, but Christianity itself; and to attack Christian morality is to attack Christianity itself.

The Church historically has
overlooked subtle, shifting enemies

American Catholicism might be better off if the moral liberalist enemies of Christianity were to shoot a few priests and bishops, or burn down a few convents. Perhaps *this* would persuade Catholic clergy and laity that their religion is facing a serious enemy in contemporary America, and it might lead them to mobilize against the enemy. For some reason, it seems that Catholics need to witness such extreme and transparent enmity before they can recognize an enemy for what it is. Thus, it was easy for Catholics to be anti-Communist, because Communists, by shooting priests and nuns and by conducting show trials of bishops (e.g., the 1949 trial of Cardinal Mindszenty in Hungary), removed all doubts as to their hostility toward Christianity in general and Catholicism in particular. By contrast, it was not at all easy for German Catholics to be anti-Nazi, since Hitler, who openly proclaimed himself to be anti-Communist and anti-Jewish, did not openly proclaim himself to be anti-Catholic or anti-Christian. Thus, Catholics found it easy (as did Chamberlain and Daladier) to convince themselves, despite an enormous mass of evidence to the contrary, that Hitler and Nazism were not enemies of their religion.

Is there something about Catholicism — some sociological if not theological fact — that renders Catholics incapable of recognizing any but the most overt of enemies? Who knows? At all events, for the past thirty or forty years, American Catholics have done a very poor job of recognizing the danger that moral liberalism poses to their religion. For moral liberals do not shoot priests and nuns; they do not burn down convents and monasteries. That is not their style, for they are believers in tolerance. They rarely even go so far as to denounce Christianity, and when they do, it is usually because they perceive Christianity as promoting that worst of all sins, intolerance — a sin that, if not nipped in the bud, could eventually lead to mass murder.[77] Moral liberalism's attack on Christianity is not done by way of violent persecution, but done by way of seduction and ridicule and a certain amount of righteous indignation. Coercion and violence might be effective methods of destroying Christianity in a dictatorial or totalitarian society, but in a liberal democracy, seduction and ridicule and indignation work much better. And over the last few decades, such methods have worked very well indeed.

It has, of course, occurred to some Catholics that their religion is under serious attack in the United States; and some have tried

---

[77] For instance, among moral liberals, it is something like a doctrine of faith that the 1998 Laramie, Wyoming, murder of Matthew Shepard, a young homosexual man, was a by-product of the Christian teaching that homosexuality is sinful.

to fight back. But such Catholics have been relatively rare. This is not the case with conservative Protestantism.[78] Generally speaking, they have a high level of awareness that their Christian faith and its moral values are endangered in contemporary America. They are also the ones organizing and mobilizing to defend it. If old-fashioned Christians are fighting back in the culture war, and doing so in a fairly effective manner, it is more likely to be the work of conservative Protestants than of Catholics.

But why should there be this discrepancy? Why have conservative Protestants been so quick to understand and respond to the secularist attack on Christianity while Catholics, broadly speaking, have been so slow? Two explanations suggest themselves.

Conservative Protestantism's
sectarian mentality keeps it on guard

For one, conservative Protestants, for the most part, belong to religions that have, sociologically speaking, *sectarian* roots and traditions. It is in the very nature of a sect to draw a sharp line of distinction — a wall of separation, so to speak — between itself and the outside world. When sectarians speak of "the world," this is usually a pejorative term: the "world" is a realm of sin as opposed to holiness, of darkness as opposed to light, of moral danger as opposed to virtuous security. Hence, it is relatively easy for people with a sectarian mentality, and even people with no more than traces of a sectarian mentality, to be suspicious that outsiders are enemies; and when outsiders *really* are enemies — as secularists

---

[78] I have especially in mind such groups as Southern Baptists and other Evangelicals, Pentecostalists, Missouri Synod Lutherans, and the (quasi-Protestant) Mormons, although many conservative Protestants can also be found even in more or less liberal Protestant denominations, e.g., the Episcopal Church, the United Methodist Church, the Presbyterian Church USA, and the Evangelical Lutheran Church of America.

and moral liberals really are — it is easy for people with a sectarian or semi-sectarian mentality to detect their enmity. They are not easily fooled when it comes to anti-Christian hostility.

Recall that Catholicism, by contrast, is not a sectarian religion; sociologically speaking, it is a *churchly* religion. This means that it has an openness to the world that the sect lacks. It does not erect a wall of separation between itself and the secular world; instead, it communicates with the world, attempting to influence it and, in turn, allowing itself to be influenced by it. It is true that, prior to the 1960s, during the era of the so-called "Catholic ghetto," American Catholicism had erected something of a wall of separation between itself and the larger society. But that was a temporary aberration necessitated by the special historical circumstances American Catholics found themselves in; they were socially inferior immigrants (or children and grandchildren of immigrants) living in an overwhelmingly Protestant society. In its normal state, Catholicism builds no walls — or only the very lowest of walls, walls easy to step over — between itself and the outer world. Hence, Catholics lack the suspicion of the world that is habitual with conservative Protestants; hence, too, they are far less ready than conservative Protestants to identify and guard against worldly enemies of Christianity — unless, of course, the enemy, like the Communists, is considerate enough to remove all doubt by resorting to open violence.

A global religion, Catholicism does not overly concern itself with one country

For another, Catholicism is a worldwide religion, and the American section of that religion is only a small part of the whole: smaller than the European part or the Latin American part or the African part. And the headquarters of the religion is in Rome; it is not in New York or Washington or Dallas or Salt Lake City. If Catholicism collapses in the United States, this will not mean that it collapses altogether. It has collapsed in this place or that place in the past without collapsing altogether. In the centuries following the Arab conquests, it gradually collapsed in Western Asia and North Africa, while at the same time surviving in Europe. In the sixteenth century, it collapsed very suddenly in much of Northern Europe, but it survived in Southern Europe, in Poland, in Ireland, and in Latin America; it even showed some promise (a promise that eventually fizzled out) of expanding into East Asia. Today it shows great promise in Africa. Catholics are aware of this. They know that their Church can afford to lose a province here and there — even so magnificent a province as the United States, and nonetheless go on living and even thriving. People with an attitude like this are not likely to fight very hard to protect their religion.

The attitude of conservative Protestants, by contrast, is just the opposite. The United States is the homeland of Evangelical and Pentecostal Protestantism; it is also the homeland of Mormonism. All three of these have spread widely in much of the rest of the world; nonetheless, the center for each is in the United States. Here, for the most part, missionaries are trained; here Bibles are translated and published; here funds are raised to make the worldwide missionary effort possible. If their forms of Christianity collapse in America, the ripple effect — or rather, the tidal-wave effect — will be felt worldwide. For Evangelicals and Pentecostals and Mormons, the United States is no mere province, not some dispensable part of the whole. It is at the very heart of the matter. People who believe this are ready to fight for the faith in their country.

The great failure of episcopal leadership

But there is one more reason, equally important, for the Catholic failure to recognize the secularist enemy and to mount an effective resistance: *an appallingly poor level of episcopal leadership in the past generation*. Now, Catholics are normally reluctant to find fault with their bishops, especially to find fault with them in a public way. And there is good reason for this reluctance. The local bishop is the leader of the local Church and its official teacher of Christianity. This has been recognized since the time of St. Ignatius of Antioch, who, in the early second century, wrote a number of letters in which he stressed that Christians must trust their bishops and be unswervingly loyal to them. Or rather, it has been recognized since *before* the time of St. Ignatius, since his letters treat the eminence and authority of bishops, not as novel propositions, but as long-established facts.

Catholicism is of its essence an episcopal religion. Bishops stand to their people as fathers to their children. (This ideal of paternalism is hard to swallow in a democratic age, but Catholicism is an ancient religion, and lots of its elements are hard to swallow in the modern world; which explains why persons with a thoroughly modern mentality either reject Catholicism or wish to modernize it.) One is expected not to criticize one's father, above all not in such a way that the neighbors can hear. And so Catholics — except, of course, for liberal or "progressive" Catholics, who care little or nothing for the admonitions of such an obscure and antiquated figure as Ignatius of Antioch — have, over the years, been reluctant to criticize their bishops, even as they watched the Church in America go downhill.[79] But filial regard, fine thing though it may be, has its limits, and those limits were reached and surpassed in the year 2002, the year of the Great Sex-Abuse Scandal.

The scandal was not simply that some priests were sexual abusers of young persons, mostly adolescent boys; Catholics had known that for at least ten or fifteen years prior. What Catholics learned in 2002 were three things:

[79] I should note that this is a reluctance shared by the writer of this book.

• *The abuse was far, far more widespread than they had previously believed.* True enough, only a minority of all priests were abusers, but it was not, as previously believed, a *miniscule* minority.

• *A substantial number of American priests are homosexual* — still probably a minority, but a very substantial minority.[80] Almost all of the known abusers were homosexual — unlike with true pedophiles, their victims were rarely prepubescent children, but rather almost always adolescent boys. And if the Catholic priesthood contains a significant number of criminal homosexuals, it stands to reason that it must have an equally great or perhaps even greater number of noncriminal homosexuals, i.e., men who limit their sexual contacts to adult men. And surely there must be some, perhaps many, homosexually oriented priests who strictly observe their vows of chastity. Add together the criminal homosexuals, the active homosexuals, and the chaste homosexuals, and you have to conclude that for the past thirty years or so, the American Catholic priesthood has had lots of priests with a homosexual orientation. How many? Who knows for sure? Estimates have ranged all over the place, from as low as ten percent of all priests to as high as fifty percent. Whatever the actual number, it has been so large that insiders could not have failed to notice the phenomenon. It is very hard to see how bishops could not have known that many of

[80] I realize that some Catholics will argue that there is no reason the Church should not open its doors to priests having a homosexual orientation, provided, of course, that these priests are faithful to their vows of chastity. I agree that no harm is done if a small number, a very small number, of celibate homosexuals find their way into the priesthood. But I believe that it is obvious — so obvious that the point hardly needs arguing — that an open-door policy welcoming homosexuals into the priesthood is an invitation to catastrophe. Yet something like this open-door policy seems to have been followed by many American dioceses during much of the last third of the twentieth century.

their priests were homosexual. It is even harder to see how they could not have known that many of them were homosexual in a criminal way, i.e., they were abusers of young boys.

* *The highest Church authorities — bishops and their most important advisors — had done far too little to root out and put a stop to pedophilic abuse and the homosexual abuse of teenage boys.* It is not simply that bishops often gave an inadequate response to cases reported to them: sometimes accepting the dishonest denials offered by accused priests; sometimes sending the accused priest off for "treatment" and then accepting the judgment of the treatment facility that the abuser had been "cured" of his perverse propensities; and sometimes buying the silence of the parents of the abused child or boy. No, worse still was the fact that all too few bishops recognized reports of abuse for what they were — namely, the tip of an iceberg. If three or four complaints crossed a bishop's desk, he should have realized that these were symptoms of a much larger problem; they were an indication that there were probably thirty or forty or more cases out there, the great majority unreported. The bishop should have been proactive instead of merely reactive. He should have investigated, and investigated very vigorously. He should have found out how many of his priests were homosexual, how many were actively homosexual, and how many were guilty of abusing underage boys.

Would this have been a "witch hunt"? Not at all, for (*pace* the Wiccans) there are no such things as witches; but there *are* such things as homosexual priests, a good number of whom have been criminal abusers of teenage boys, and an even larger number of whom have violated their priestly vow of chastity.

The buck stops with the bishop

In defense of the ineffective bishops, some people have said: "What would you have done in their place? They listened to their advisors; they listened to the psychologists and psychiatrists; they listened to the denials coming from the accused priests. They were concerned, and legitimately so, with the well-being of the Church. They felt it was important to avoid scandal, as indeed it is. By blaming them for their failures, you are holding them to a far higher standard than you would hold anyone else to. You are asking them to be superhuman. That's unfair."

To which I reply: Yes, we are indeed holding them to a higher standard, but it is not a superhuman standard; it is a *leadership* standard. Bishops are supposed to be *leaders,* possessing exceptional talents and character; they are not supposed to be ordinary people. As Harry Truman famously said about the role of the president in American government, "The buck stops here." It is never a valid excuse for a leader to say, "I am only human," for that is equivalent to saying, "I am not qualified, and never was qualified, to be a leader." Many American Catholic dioceses experienced catastrophic failure on the matter of sexual abuse. And in a Catholic diocese, the buck stops with the bishop.

This tremendous failure of leadership on the issues of homosexuality and sexual abuse helps to explain the American Church's failure to recognize and respond to the attacks on Christianity made by secularism and moral liberalism during the past forty years or so. If the bishops were too incompetent to recognize and respond to a great and obvious sexual crisis taking place in their own house — taking place under their own noses, so to speak — how much more likely must it have been that they would also be too incompetent to recognize and respond to the relatively subtle attack on their religion taking place in the larger society! The bishops who were paralyzed when it came to homosexuality and criminal sexual abuse among the priests of their dioceses were the same bishops who did not know what to make of the rapid rise of secularism and moral liberalism in American society; who were unable to insist that their parish priests sermonize frequently and earnestly about the sexual sins of cohabitation, contraception, and homosexuality, and about the homicidal sins of abortion and euthanasia; who were unable to do anything much in the way of mobilizing their Catholic people to put up a political resistance to the abortion movement, the homosexual movement, and the euthanasia movement (the "unholy trinity" of American moral liberalism); who were unable to take any significant action against Catholic elected officials who strongly supported legal abortion.

Two reasons Catholic bishops, especially, must be good leaders

No organization can afford the luxury of incompetent leaders. But this is even truer for the Catholic Church than for most organizations, and this for two reasons. First, the bishop is a kind of absolute monarch who is above criticism. He does not share his power with a legislative or judicial branch of Church government. In his diocese, he holds all three governmental powers — executive, legislative, and judicial — in his own hands. He may, of course, delegate those powers to subordinate officials, but this is no more than a matter of delegation; by right, the powers belong to him. And by ancient Catholic tradition (remember the letters of Ignatius of Antioch), it is considered extremely discourteous, if not downright disloyal, for Catholics publicly to find fault with their bishop. Hence, the bishop is deprived of the constant stream of criticism to which presidents and governors and mayors and legislators are subject, criticism that often helps them improve the quality of their practical judgments.

Second, the people whose well-being the bishop is supposed to look out for cannot fire him if he does a bad job. Voters can cashier incompetent elected officials; boards of directors can fire incompetent CEOs; and the owners of baseball teams can sack incompetent managers; but only the pope can relieve a bishop of his position — and this is something popes are extremely reluctant to do. In practice, once a diocese gets a poor bishop, it may expect to keep him until the mandatory retirement age of seventy-five.

A system of this kind, a system of lifetime appointments with no accountability to the "flock," can work, indeed it can work very well — but only if the men appointed to the office of bishop are men of exceptional courage and good judgment. Ordinary courage will not do, nor will ordinary good judgment. A good bishop has to have both virtues, and has to have them in spades. This is true at all times, but it is especially true at times when the Church is in a crisis situation, as it has been ever since the time of Vatican II. It has been an era in which the Church in the United States needed bishops whose leadership qualities would remind us of George Washington and Abraham Lincoln and Franklin Roosevelt. Instead it got bishops reminding us of James Buchanan and Herbert Hoover — men unsuited for high leadership during dark and dangerous times.

Part VII

Can the Fall Be Prevented?

Chapter 27

Three Small Steps That
Must Be Taken Immediately

I prefer not to end on a pessimistic note. Indeed, my analysis has
taken me someplace I would rather not go, to a conclusion I would
rather not have to accept — namely, that the Catholic Church in
the United States is doomed to be a relatively small church, having little impact on the larger American society and culture. Is the
conclusion unavoidable? Can I envision a way the Church can
avert its fall?

One consoling thought is that with God all things are possible.
Humanly speaking, the situation may look dark, but who knows
what surprises Divine Providence may have in store for us?

A second rosy thought is that there is no such thing as a science of the human future. Thus, my prediction of the bleak future
of American Catholicism, no matter how plausible it might seem
at the moment, may be mistaken. Early in this book, I said that the
Church in the United States went into decline because of an unlucky convergence of events: Vatican II, the full Americanization
of United States Catholics, and the great cultural revolution of
the 1960s and '70s. Not all these events were predictable. The full
Americanization of Catholics may have been more or less predictable, but Vatican II came as a great surprise, and so did the cultural
revolution of the 1960s; above all, the convergence of the three

events was unpredictable. Further surprises may be in store for us tomorrow or the day after tomorrow. In fact, they are almost certainly in store for us; if there is anything we can safely predict about the future, it is that, in the future, many unpredicted and unpredictable things will happen. My pessimistic conclusions in this book are based on the assumption that certain current social and cultural trends will continue. But maybe they will not. Maybe a future *good-luck* combination of unpredictable events will converge and revitalize the American Church.

The third rosy thought is that my pessimistic prediction is conditional, not categorical. That is, it is not a prediction that a Catholic demise will happen regardless of other circumstances; rather, it is a prediction that this demise will occur *if* things continue to move along the present path. It is like the prophecy given to Scrooge by the Ghost of Christmas Future: "Such and such will happen, Ebenezer, *if* you do not amend your life." Likewise, I am saying that Catholicism will fail in America, or will at least be reduced to little more than a culturally irrelevant remnant, if the American Church does not amend its life. This book is a warning from the Ghost of the Catholic Future.

But what is the likelihood that American Catholicism will amend its life, will renounce its denominational mentality and its consequent tendency toward secularism? Not terribly great, I fear. Amending its institutional life will be far more of a challenge than it was for Scrooge to amend his individual life. For one thing, individuals amend their lives in the literal sense, whereas institutions amend theirs only in a metaphorical sense. For it is individual human beings, individual members of the institution, who must amend the life of an institution if it is to be amended at all. And there is always the danger that individuals who are responsible for an institution will think that terrible thought: "It will last my time" — and hence, will fail to act as they should act. For another, amending a life, whether individual or institutional, is not always just a matter of will; it is also a matter of knowledge. My desire to amend my life may be the strongest thing in the world, but if I have no idea *how* to amend it, it will not get amended. For Scrooge, the knowledge part was easy. Once he developed the will to change, he knew what he had to do: accept his nephew's invitation to Christmas dinner, be generous with Bob Crachit and his family, adopt a cheerful demeanor, et cetera. But even supposing that American Catholics decide they would like to amend their institutional life, what steps will they then have to take to transform this intention into reality? It is not easy to say.

But let me suggest a few steps that must be taken to stay or reverse the Church's American decline.

• *End the denominational mentality.* American Catholics will have to get rid of the denominational mentality. This means they will have to return to believing what their parents and grandparents used to believe — that, far from all religions being essentially equal in worth, Catholicism is a uniquely privileged religion, the one true Church of God. This does not mean that they have to regard other religions as totally false and improper. No, Catholics can concede that other religions are partially true and partially proper, while at the same time holding that the fullness of religious truth and propriety are to be found only in Catholicism. They can even concede that there is a certain amount of truth to be found in secularist philosophies. Claiming that Catholicism is the most perfect religion and the most perfect custodian of religious truth is not incompatible with recognizing that everybody, even the hardcore secularist, has a partially true perception of metaphysical and moral truth.

In this connection, it would be useful for Catholics to utilize a distinction the once-famous French Catholic philosopher Jacques Maritain employed habitually — the distinction between the intuitive grasp of a truth and the conceptual formulation of this intuition.[81] It is quite possible, in fact it is quite common, for someone to have a genuine insight into an important truth while failing to express this insight adequately when putting it into words. The way we verbally formulate our insights depends largely on our theoretical preconceptions; and when these preconceptions are erroneous, as they often are, sound insights get distorted as they pass through the filter of theory. The task of those having a better theory (Catholicism, for instance) is not simply to criticize the inadequate conceptual formulations of others, although that is certainly an important part of their task. The other part, equally important, is to "rescue" the valid intuitions that lie at the heart of these inadequate formulations. Thus, those who have the best religious theory, if they will take the trouble to understand those who differ from them, will be able to appropriate the sound insights of the latter; more, they will be able to preserve these insights better than the discoverers themselves could.

Of course, such an "appreciative" or "affirmative" critique will be a lot of trouble, requiring great intelligence, great learning, great open-mindedness, great diligence, and great diplomatic tact. This kind of tolerance is hard work, not at all like the "easy" tolerance that comes from indifferentism and the denominational mentality. But if Catholicism wishes to hold on to its claim of religious superiority, and hold on to it in a society that demands we get along with everybody who disagrees with us, there is no other way. Mere tolerance leads to the denominational mentality and the demise of Catholicism, while a merely "negative" critique leads to the social-cultural marginalization of Catholicism.

• *Re-Catholicize Catholic colleges.* Catholic colleges and universities will have to be truly Catholic (not just nominally so), while

---

[81] See, for example, Maritain's essay, "Philosophical Cooperation and Intellectual Justice," in his book *The Range of Reason* (New York: Scribner's, 1952).

at the same time maintaining high academic quality. In the last thirty years or so, their academic quality has greatly improved, so that many of these Catholic institutions now compare very favorably with secular colleges and universities; but their Catholic quotient has declined. This decline can be attributed perhaps to the dramatic drop in the percentage of priests and nuns on the faculties (which, in turn, is the result of overall retention and recruitment problems found among priests and nuns), and to the hiring of faculty members purely on the basis of academic credentials, regardless of whether they are believing Catholics. But the deeper cause is the weakening of a determined will to remain unequivocally Catholic. This weakening of will was only to be expected as the denominational mentality gained strength among those in leadership positions in these institutions of higher education.

In restoring a Catholic identity, these colleges and universities will have to attend to two aspects of this identity, one exterior, the other interior. By the *exterior aspect*, I mean things having to do with extracurricular matters. Physically, the campus should have a "Catholic" look: a large and handsome chapel, along with religious images (statues, icons, crucifixes) on the grounds and in the buildings. Masses and other religious services, prayer groups and Bible studies, should be plentifully available to students and faculty. The student body should be predominantly Catholic, and so should the faculty and administration.

By the *interior aspect*, I mean things having to do with the academic and scholarly life of the institution. Students should be required to study philosophy and theology (not just "religious studies") — the philosophy having a Catholic angle, the theology being unquestionably orthodox. A Catholic flavor should permeate other sections of the curriculum, e.g., literature, history, and sociology. In research universities, a significant percentage of the faculty should be working on topics having to do with religion in general or Catholicism in particular. Concerts of sacred music, exhibits of religious art, and lectures on Catholic topics should be offered, not only to the university community, but to the general public.

But more will be needed on the interior side of things. For a long time now in the American academic world, a conventional "wall of separation" has stood between religious faith and scholarly or scientific knowledge. Each side has agreed not to meddle with the other. Scientists and scholars stipulate that religious belief is beyond their competence *qua* scientists and scholars, and believers stipulate that the findings of science and scholarship are beyond their competence *qua* believers. Hence, both parties are able to live in peace with one another. And if certain individuals happen to belong to both parties at the same time, they simply move back and forth from one category to the other, not letting their convictions in one category influence their convictions in the other. They wear their religious hat here and their scholarly or scientific hat there.

From the point of view of a nondogmatic conception of religion, the terms of this division of labor — this "peace treaty" — are satisfactory. If religion were a purely ethical thing, or if its statements about the objective world referred, not to the world itself, but to the way we *feel* about the world, then it would make sense for religion and science to leave one another alone. Religion will say nothing about reality; science will say nothing about religion — that is, about ethics and religious feelings.

But from a Catholic point of view, the terms of this peace treaty are far from satisfactory. Catholicism is a dogmatic religion. It makes assertions about the nature of reality, and it claims that these assertions are *true*; they are not merely expressions of how Catholics should *feel* about reality.

Moreover, these assertions are not confined to statements about God as he exists in himself, statements about God entirely cut off from the world of nature. On the contrary, Catholicism has always taught that God routinely interacts with nature, including human nature. For one thing, he created the world of nature. Second, he ordains and governs its ordinary operations. Third, from time to time, he interrupts these ordinary operations to produce miracles. Fourth, he provides us humans with a moral law according to which we should live our lives. Fifth, he supplies us with the grace needed to comply with this law, a compliance that would otherwise be impossible. Sixth, he punishes noncompliance (sin), and at least in some cases, these punishments are inflicted in the course of this earthly life. Given these teachings, it follows that the orthodox Christian student of nature, especially of human nature, will be guided by somewhat different heuristic principles than those that guide the "pure" scientist or scholar.

A distinctively Christian approach would be most evident in the human sciences, i.e., in psychology, sociology, economics, and history. Catholic sociologists, for instance, would be especially interested, for example, in the harmful social consequences of widespread unchastity. They would not be surprised to find that a society that tolerates, and even recommends, sexual immorality will have to pay a heavy price: in millions of fatherless children, in poverty, in crime and drugs and poor education, in AIDS, et cetera.

And there is no reason the Christian approach should be entirely absent in the natural sciences. The approaches that Kepler and Newton took to physics was strongly influenced by their Christian belief system, by their conviction that the universe which they studied was created and governed by a power that is all-powerful and thoroughly rational. Pre-Darwinian biology was largely shaped by the Christian conviction that God had designed the world of living things, from which it seemed to follow that all organs had utility and that all organisms fit their environment. Darwin seemed to explode this idea; yet even today Christian evolutionists will take a different approach to living things than will "pure" evolutionists.[82]

I realize, of course, that, with only a small number of exceptions, today's Catholic social and natural scientists are no different from their non-theistic colleagues. Almost all Catholic scientists accept the conventional division of labor between science and religion. But this only proves that Catholic scientists do not realize the scientific implications of their religious belief system. Or rather, it proves that contemporary Catholicism does not realize the implications of its beliefs. For if it did, it would have pointed out these implications to Catholic scientists.

• *Get the Catholic census right*. The Catholic Church in the United States will have to get over its habit of grossly overestimating the actual number of American Catholics. Routinely this number is placed near 70 million, about 25 percent of the American population. But this is absurdly high. Maybe there are 70 million Americans who were baptized in a Catholic church; and from a strictly theological point of view, it may be true that once a person is baptized Catholic, he remains so, or at least remains so until he or she makes a formal act of apostasy. But when we do a census, we are not doing theology; we are providing sociological data. And sociologically speaking, Catholics — *real* Catholics, that is — probably make up much less than 10 percent of the American population.

What do I mean by *real* Catholics? I *do not* mean to make a theological distinction between the true faithful and the pretenders, between the sacrosanct saved and the reprobate damned. But for sociological purposes, we need to make a distinction between those Catholics who are regular churchgoers and those who are not. On any particular Sunday, the most optimistic reports say that

---

[82] See, for example, Michael J. Behe's book, *Darwin's Black Box* (New York: The Free Press, 1996).

between 40 and 45 percent of all Catholics attend Mass; more pessimistic reports put the number in the 25-to-35-percent range;[83] and, as we saw in the *Boston Globe* report cited in the introduction of this book, in Boston the percentage may be less than 15 percent. That means that 55 to 60 percent of Catholics do not attend on a weekly basis; or perhaps 65 to 75 percent; or perhaps as many as 85 percent. Let us call these two groups, respectively, practicing and nonpracticing Catholics. The majority of American Catholics, as we see, are nonpracticing.

Let us make a further distinction among those who are nonpracticing. On the one hand, there are those who are lost to the Church for good. Catholicism means nothing to them, and with only the rarest exceptions they will not return to the Church in their later years. They will live and die outside the Faith. Let us call them "merely nominal" Catholics. On the other hand, there are those who, although living outside the Faith for the time being, may return later on. These are people whose Catholic identity still matters to them, even though they may find day-to-day Catholicism boring or irrelevant or offensive. Among those who were raised Catholic, many young unmarried people fall into this category. They are passing through an anti-Catholic "phase" in their lives; but when they settle down, marry, and have children, they will shift from the nonpracticing to the practicing side of the ledger. Let us call them "recoverable" Catholics.

Yet another distinction needs to be made among currently practicing Catholics (i.e., those regularly found in church each week). First, there are those who are thoroughly orthodox, or at least very nearly so. They subscribe to the official Catholic creed, not dropping those articles that are embarrassing or unfashionable in "liberal" Christian circles, e.g., the Virgin Birth and the Resurrection and the Real Presence. Further, they subscribe to official

---

[83] See Appendix 1.

The Decline and Fall of the Catholic Church in America

Catholic moral teaching, even if, being sinners, they do not always live up to it. And here, too, they are undeterred by liberal fashions. They hold, for instance, that abortion, homosexuality, suicide, fornication, and even contraception are sinful. Finally, they hold that the Catholic Church is the true Church of God. Let us call them "real" or "authentic" Catholics.

Second come those who may be called "generic Christians." By this name, I refer to Catholics who, in their minds and hearts, soft-pedal specifically Catholic beliefs while emphasizing those beliefs common to all American Christians. But since, nowadays, very few beliefs are held in common by all Americans who count themselves Christian, the Catholic who is a generic Christian will emphasize very few beliefs. Many self-described Christians doubt or deny the divinity of Christ, the Virgin Birth, the Resurrection, the Real Presence, and life after death (not to mention the authority of the pope); hence, Catholics of the generic-Christian type will soft-pedal all these beliefs. Further, many Christians find fornication, cohabitation, homosexuality, and abortion morally unobjectionable; hence, the generic Christian Catholic will soft-pedal the Catholic objection to these. In practice, the Catholic of the generic-Christian school will have a very short creed, consisting of the following articles: (1) God loves us regardless of race, religion, gender, or sexual orientation; (2) Jesus was a fine fellow, an example we should all aspire to follow; and (3) love of neighbor (which often means tolerance of neighbors who are "different") is the sum of all virtue.

So we have four categories of Catholics:
- Authentic Catholics
- Generic Christians
- Recoverable Catholics
- Merely nominal Catholics

What is the point of making these distinctions? If the leadership of the American Church, i.e., bishops and priests, is to be effective, it has to have a realistic understanding of the nature and composition of its rank and file.

The Church must focus its efforts
on the authentic Catholics first

If I were not afraid of the harshness of the expression, I would say that merely nominal Catholics should be written off as a waste of time and energy. But I will say something milder instead: the leadership of the Church must realize that the future health of the Church in the United States depends, above all, on those I have called real or authentic Catholics, to a lesser degree on the generic Christians, to a lesser degree still on the recoverable Catholics, and virtually not at all on the merely nominal Catholics.

Merely nominal Catholics frequently indicate their displeasure with the Church and its teachings. When criticizing the Church, in public or in private, their criticism sounds ever so much more plausible when they preface it with, "Speaking as a Catholic . . ." or "Speaking as one raised in the Catholic Faith . . ." Bishops and priests should learn not to worry about such criticism — the way smart politicians have learned not to worry about criticism coming from hardcore members of the opposite party. Critics of this type are just not on your team; they are on an enemy team, and no matter how much you try to win them over by amending your conduct, they will not — barring some semi-miraculous change in their personality — be won over.

What this means, in practice, is that the leaders of the Church, i.e., the bishops and priests, should accustom themselves to the idea that they lead a much smaller Church than they had hitherto imagined — a Church whose membership is nowhere near the 65 or 70 million usually claimed for it. Now, it may seem harsh to say that Church leadership should disregard tens of millions of baptized although now inactive Catholics. But, in the long run, probably the best service the leaders can render these nominal

The Decline and Fall of the Catholic Church in America

Catholics is to "forget" them for a generation or so and build up the rest of the Church. After the Church is greatly strengthened, there will be more hope of recapturing these lost Catholics.

Recoverable Catholics are a different story. They are likely to return to the fold in their mature years if they were strongly attached to the Church while growing up. Hence, it is imperative to make sure Catholic children and teens develop a strong attachment to the Church, while realizing that many of them will temporarily leave the Church sometime between the ages of sixteen and forty. This requires a strong Catholic socialization process. Catholic parents must be encouraged to impress the Faith strongly on their growing children; and the system of Catholic schools must be revitalized and expanded.

Of the four groups, generic Christians are the most difficult to deal with. They have a certain amount of loyalty to the Church, although not a terribly strong loyalty, since they do not consider the Catholic Church "the true Church" — at least not any truer than a dozen other Christian denominations. As they see it, generic Christianity is the "true faith," and all these rival denominations believe in generic Christianity. They come to church on Sunday, and they contribute money and volunteer work, often a lot of both. If you are a priest or bishop, you do not want to offend these people. But you might offend them if you preach full-blooded Catholic dogma and morality. So you are tempted to water things down; you are tempted to preach nothing more than generic Christianity.

And it is generic Christianity, not Catholicism that one hears preached in many Catholic dioceses and parishes all over America. The trouble with this strategy for dealing with Catholics of this type — quite apart from the fact that it is a kind of treason to the Faith — is that it confirms them in their generic Christianity. If they never hear anything but generic Christianity preached from the pulpit, will they not conclude that their interpretation of

Catholicism is sound? One of the most pressing needs of the American Catholic Church is for its leadership to develop a strategy for re-Catholicizing these generic Christians.

Finally, it is essential for the leadership to identify and cultivate the real Catholics, the hardcore of orthodox believers. If Catholicism is to be saved in America, it will have to be saved, humanly speaking, by these people. They are the true believers; they are the bearers of the Catholic Faith. They are the "faithful" that Cardinal Newman had in mind when he wrote his work recommending consultation with the faithful on matters of doctrine.

Nowadays the faithful are a minority among American Catholics. The clerical leadership of the Church should show these people a greater degree of respect than they have typically received since Vatican II. To revert to the political analogy I used above: Smart politicians know that they must "tend to their base"; that is, they must keep their hardcore supporters happy. These hardcore supporters are rarely more than a small minority of the electorate, and so they are incapable, all by themselves, of enabling the politician to win an election. But all by themselves they are fully capable of causing him to *lose* an election. For if they desert him (as, for example, many hardcore Republicans did the elder George Bush in the 1992 presidential election, after he had violated his "Read my lips: no new taxes" pledge), he will be in big trouble. In the last thirty or forty years, the clerical leadership of the Catholic Church in the United States has not tended to its base of hardcore or authentic Catholics.

Quite the contrary: Church leaders have disappointed these Catholics on many fronts. They have failed to preach sermons denouncing abortion and homosexuality and fornication, or sermons enunciating distinctively Catholic doctrine (as opposed to generic Christianity). They have failed to prevent the substantial contraction of the Catholic school system, and failed to prevent many Catholic colleges and universities from de-Catholicizing themselves. They have failed to communicate effectively the message that Catholic voters have no business voting for "Catholic" politicians who support such grievously un-Catholic practices as abortion and same-sex marriage. They have failed, along with their catechetical and ministerial collaborators, to produce a doctrinally literate and assenting faithful.

And, of course, they have failed to prevent or even effectively contain the enormous sex-abuse scandals of the last thirty years or so. Bishops and fellow clergy tolerated a great number of homosexuals in the priesthood: not simply priests who happened to have a homosexual orientation but were practicing strict celibacy, but priests who were actively homosexual. Bishops failed to take proactive measures to isolate and discipline known abusers. Small wonder that a Church leadership that will tolerate widespread homosexuality, even widespread pedophilic and homosexual child abuse, in the priesthood will also tolerate that less shocking thing, generic Christianity.

And it is not simply that the leadership of the Church has paid insufficient attention to the base of hardcore Catholics. At the same time, they have paid considerable attention — too much attention, the base would say — to more liberal elements in the Church. The clerical leadership has responded to radical and semi-radical feminists in the Church, for example, by soft-pedaling the Church's opposition to abortion and lesbianism, while feeling vaguely ashamed at being part of a patriarchal Church. Bishops are forbidden to ordain women to the priesthood, so many of them, in their embarrassment, have appointed women (often the same would-be women priests) to relatively high levels of nonordained Church leadership — a kind of ecclesiastical affirmative action. Many priests unofficially rewrite canonical language to avoid giving offense to feminists in the pews: saying in the Creed, for instance, that Christ "became one of us" instead of that he "became man." And when the cycle of readings brings us around to the Sunday when we must hear, to the embarrassment of some priests, the text from Ephesians that tells wives to be subject to their husbands, the offending scriptural sentence is often simply eliminated.

Another example of the great attention Catholic leaders pay to liberal elements in the Church could be found in the controversy surrounding Pope John Paul II's statement about Catholic higher education, *Ex Corde Ecclesiae*. The Vatican demanded that any theologian teaching at a Catholic institution of higher education must get a *mandatum* from the local Catholic bishop, certifying that the theologian teaches authentic Catholic doctrine. Among Catholic college and university presidents, there was widespread resistance to this Vatican demand; they claimed that it was an infringement on academic freedom. At first, the bishops — that is, the National Conference of Catholic Bishops — caved in to the resistance, and agreed to a compromise that omitted the *mandatum*. The Vatican rejected the compromise and told the American bishops to go back and do it again, this time with the *mandatum* included. And so they did, but in substance, the final agreement seems to be in effect no different from the earlier one; the *mandatum* seems to have become little more than a *pro forma* thing, a dead letter. What the Vatican envisioned — that the bishops should police the Catholic orthodoxy of the theology departments of Catholic colleges and universities — seems to have come to nothing.

Of course "real" Catholics will not desert their clerical leaders as quickly or as readily as hardcore Republicans deserted George Bush the elder in 1992. But their patience is not infinite. Despite their loyalty, their enthusiasm for the Church can wane; their energy can be exhausted; their hands can grow less eager to reach into their pockets for money to give to the Church. These are real dangers. Only a foolish politician would neglect his base the way the Church's clerical leadership has neglected *its* base for the last thirty years or more. Perhaps this is because bishops are not as politically astute as they were in the heyday of the American Catholic Church. Today's bishops are academically more sophisticated than their predecessors of generations past; they have issued some fine collective pastoral letters; but they seem to lack that almost instinctive feel for political realities that their intellectually less-polished forebears once had.

Chapter 28

The Church Must
Identify Its Enemies

But the most important step of all, if American Catholicism is to recover and revive, is to designate contemporary secularism as the "official enemy" of contemporary Catholicism.

Organizations are defined negatively as well as positively. That is to say, they are defined in terms of what they are *against* as well as in terms of what they are *for*. They are defined in terms of what they *are not* as well as in terms of what they *are*. This is true almost by definition, since you cannot very well be for something unless you are against something else. For instance, if you are a physician, you are for health and against illness. If you are a judge, you are for justice and against injustice. If you are a teacher, you are for learning and against ignorance. And so forth.

Of course, there are degrees of being against a thing. You may be opposed to X in a merely *pro forma* way, opposed to Y with a moderate degree of intensity, and opposed to Z as if your very life depended upon it. Further, something that is a life-and-death struggle at one moment may evolve into a *pro forma* differentiation at some later date, or vice versa. During the Counter-Reformation, for instance, Catholicism was locked in a life-and-death struggle with Protestantism; but over the centuries, the danger from Protestantism abated, and so did the degree of Catholic opposition, until finally, with the coming of Vatican II, this opposition be-came what it is today, little more than *pro forma*.

A thing can have a multitude of negative identities, indeed virtually an infinity of them. A dog, for instance, is a non-fox and a non-wolf; but it is also a non-cat, a non-elephant, and a non-cup-of-tea. The Catholic Church is non-Protestant, but it is also non-Jewish, non-Muslim, non-Hindu, non-Buddhist, and so on through the entire catalog of the religions of the world. Further, it is non-Communist, non-Nazi, non-agnostic, non-atheist, and so on through the entire list of secular philosophies and ideologies. There is no end to this kind of thing.

But not all negative identities are equal in importance. While it is true that a dog is not a cup of tea, there is no likelihood that anyone will confuse the two; so there is no need to stress this par-ticular negative identity. On the other hand, there is a real possi-bility that children, for instance, will confuse dogs with foxes or wolves; hence, there is a real need to emphasize that dogs differ from foxes and wolves. For centuries, the great threat to Catholi-cism came, not from Judaism, Islam, Buddhism, or Hinduism, but from Protestantism. Thus, for a number of centuries — from the Counter-Reformation until Vatican II — Catholicism quite nat-urally stressed its non-Protestant negative identity, paying scant attention to all its other negative identities. Of course, there were local variations on this theme. In India, for instance, Hinduism was at least as great a threat as Protestantism. Thus, Indian Ca-tholicism, unlike European and American Catholicism, paid particular attention to the line that separated Catholicism from Hinduism.

Picture a land-locked country surrounded by many potential enemies. This country would probably not be attacked by all its enemies at the same time, but from one or two enemies at the most. Hence, the defense of the country will be particularly con-centrated at those points where it is exposed to attack from those one or two enemies, leaving only a light defense force to guard against all other potential enemies. So it has always been with the Church. It has concentrated its defenses at those points at which it was endangered by its religious and philosophical enemies. In other words, it has stressed those negative identities that were important for defensive purposes.

Catholicism has always defined itself in opposition to its enemies

In the early centuries of the Church, there were many heresies to deal with. To make clear what it stood for, the Church had to denounce these various heresies; to clarify its positive identity, it had to stress a series of negative identities. Thus, the endless repetition of the Trinitarian formula ("In the name of the Father, and of the Son, and of the Holy Spirit") was a way of saying, "We are not Arians." And the great devotion to Mary as *Theotokos* ("God-Bearer," Mother of God) was a way of saying, "We are not Nestorians."

During the Middle Ages, there were only two non-Christian religious groups that the average Christian was aware of — one inside and the other outside Christendom: the Jews and the Muslims. Islam was a real political and military danger to Christianity, and wherever Islam conquered (except in Spain), Christians eventually defected from the Faith in great numbers. Judaism was no military and political threat, but it was a danger in another way; for it was a constant reminder that the life, death, and Resurrection of Jesus had failed to persuade the majority of his ancient coreligionists.

So the Church stressed its non-Islamic, non-Judaic identities, emphasizing those doctrines that clearly differentiated it from both rival religions: the Trinity, the Incarnation, the Resurrection, Mary as Mother of God. All this was a way of saying, "We are not Muslims; we are not Jews." This emphatic contrast encouraged

Christians when they made war on Muslims, first in the Spanish *Reconquista*, and later in the Crusades.

It also led to some absurd anti-Muslim prejudices. For instance, in the great folk epic *The Song of Roland*, Islam is represented as a kind of devil-worship: Muslims are said to worship Mohammed (named *Mahound* in the poem), who is identified as a devil from Hell.

Inside the boundaries of Christendom, Jews were routinely held in great contempt, they were deprived of civil liberties, they were expected to live a ghettoized existence, and from time to time (most notoriously, at the beginning of the Crusades), they were subjected to mob violence. In principle at least, Jews had no objection to living in ghettos — although no doubt they would have preferred more comfortable ghettos than the ones they actually had — since they, too, had an important negative identity. Negatively, they defined themselves as non-Christians; so why would they want to mix freely with the enemy? Both groups, Jews and Christians, wanted to live apart from the other, while at the same time, they wanted to be able to point to the other and say, "We are not those people; we are not those enemies of God."

With the coming of Protestantism in the sixteenth century, the danger from Islam and Judaism suddenly seemed a relatively minor thing. This new kind of Christianity — or rather, these new kinds (in the plural), for Protestantism soon proved to be a multifarious thing — was a tremendous threat to the Church, the greatest intra-Christian threat since Arianism in the fourth century. All the defense forces had to be rushed to that side of the Church where Protestantism was attacking. The Church had to define a new negative identity for itself, a non-Protestant identity, indeed an anti-Protestant identity. One of the great achievements of the Counter-Reformation was that the Church succeeded in framing for itself, out of old Catholic materials, a new non-Protestant identity.

The Church Must Identify Its Enemies

In constructing this non-Protestant (or anti-Protestant) Catholic identity, the ruling principle was this: every feature of Catholicism that Protestants find objectionable should be emphasized. Do Protestants object to the pope? Very well, then, let us be more papist than ever. Do they object to the veneration paid to the Virgin Mary and the saints? Fine, let us multiply the number of devotions to Mary and the saints. Do they object to the doctrine of transubstantiation? Then let us make adoration of the Blessed Sacrament one of our central devotions. Do the more puritanical Protestants object to ornate church buildings? Let us make them more ornate than ever. And so on.

It is a simple and very effective formula. By emphasizing precisely those points that the enemy finds offensive, you accomplish several things: you draw a bright line between yourself and the foe; you show the enemy that you have no intention of giving up the fight, no matter how long he continues the assault; and you get your own people to renew their commitment to your side by repudiating the enemy. This is not, it should be noted, a formula whose utility is confined to religion. For instance, in its Cold War struggle against the Soviet Union, the United States gloried in precisely those values and institutions that Communism denounced: capitalism, "bourgeois democracy," free speech, et cetera.

At all events, this was the defensive strategy adopted by Catholicism at the time of the Counter-Reformation. Insofar as the object of the strategy was to preserve the Catholic Church at a moment in history when it was being battered by a nearly lethal assault, the strategy was phenomenally successful. True enough, many individual Catholics, from the sixteenth to the twentieth centuries, would complain about this strategy because of the pains it inflicted upon them, pains of intellectual and moral constriction. But whatever the price paid by some individuals, the institution itself was saved from mortal danger. This Catholic rally was one of history's great institutional comebacks.

The absence of a new identified
enemy has created an identity crisis

But if, as a result of Vatican II, Protestantism was no longer an enemy, what then? Who was to be the new enemy? What was to be Catholicism's new negative identity?

Seen from this point of view, the trouble with post–Vatican II Catholicism, not only in the United States, but in much of the rest of the world as well, especially in Western Europe, is that it did not replace the old Protestant enemy with a new enemy. Oh, there were plenty of nominal enemies; even Protestantism remained something of an enemy; but these were no longer regarded as *serious* enemies. The Church had survived all its enemies of recent centuries — not just its great religious rival, Protestantism, but its secular rivals as well: anticlericism, Communism, Nazism. The first two of these were still on stage in the 1960s, when the Church entered its new era; but it seemed that they were no longer lethal threats. Catholicism had not only survived; it had triumphed. There was no longer, it seemed, a need for a posture of defense. The time had come for the Church to spread its benefits about, to shower the great world of half-believers and nonbelievers with the treasures of truth and goodness stored up in the Church. Instead of fighting Protestantism, the time had come to fight ignorance, poverty, disease, and the many forms of social injustice. Moreover, this new, more positive attitude seemed, at least to many — both Catholic and non-Catholic — much more genuinely Christian than the old attitude. Christianity, after all, is a religion of love, not a religion of hostility and belligerence.

If someone argued that the Church truly had enemies and that it was permitted even to Christians to defend against enemies, the post–Vatican II answer was given along the following lines: "Yes, but not all things permitted are wise. If the enemy poses a threat that is clear, present, and grave, go ahead and defend yourself; you have scant choice. But if the threat is little more than trivial, if the attacks are no more than pinpricks, why go into a defensive mode? When you do so, you distort your soul, you constrict your spirit of Christian love. Besides, when your enemy is weak, magnanimity and kindness are more likely to defeat him than counterattacks. They will defeat him by removing his motive for hostility and perhaps even by winning him over."

Is the lack of enemies actually evidence of progress?

Indeed the objection may well be raised: "Is it not un-Christian to designate certain parties as enemies?" And one might add: "Is it not also un-American? Should we not encourage people to get along with one another? Should we not promote universal brotherhood and sisterhood? Does the long and bloody history of religious warfare and persecution not give us fair warning not to travel down the road you are proposing?"

Let me deal with the "un-American" part of the objection first. Intergroup antagonism is as American as apple pie. In saying this, I do not have in mind violent and hate-filled intergroup conflict, e.g., what the nation experienced in the Civil War and during the long era of racial segregation. Rather, I have in mind intergroup antagonisms that we consider, because they are kept within legal and nonviolent boundaries, morally legitimate: competition among businesses, among professional firms, among dueling lawyers in a courtroom, among nonprofit organizations, among cities, among states, among colleges and universities, among newspapers and radio and TV stations, among sports teams, and between the two great political parties, Democrats and Republicans. Underlying all this intergroup antagonism is a kind of universal competition among individuals; for it may be said that the United States is a land in which everybody is in competition with everybody else. There is nothing un-American about this; on the contrary, it is the most American thing in the world.

The Decline and Fall of the Catholic Church in America

On the whole, this universal competition works rather well. People play by the rules most of the time, and they accept defeat more or less gracefully, often promising themselves that they will get back into the competition at a later date. No doubt this is a social arrangement that could not have been introduced overnight; it took centuries of social and cultural preparation before a great nation could combine social peace with universal competition. And in societies in which this social-cultural preparation has been lacking, the sudden introduction of widespread competition has produced corruption and violence and despair; witness Russia today or many Third World countries.

Now, if the United States is a society permeated by a spirit of universal but controlled competition, how could there be anything "un-American" about my proposal? Why should Catholics not enter into a frank competition with their opponents? If the Republicans and the Democrats have one another as "official enemies," and if this competition is not "un-American," why should Catholicism not be allowed to have its official enemy?

At this point, somebody will object: "Yes, but there is a crucial difference here. History shows that religious competition has often led to bloodshed. Look at the sixteenth and seventeenth centuries in Europe. Look at Northern Ireland in the twentieth century. The Republicans and Democrats, by contrast, do not come to blows over their differences."

But go back and look at the late seventeenth-century English predecessors of America's Republicans and Democrats — namely, the Tories and the Whigs; they frequently came to blows. Not content with winning election victories, they chopped one another's heads off from time to time. Or go back earlier in that century and look at the predecessors of the Whigs and Tories — namely, the Roundheads and Cavaliers, antagonists in England's great Civil War of the 1640s. Further, it should be remembered that Republicans and certain Democrats, those from the South, did indeed come to literal blows once — in the American Civil War of the 1860s.

The fact that political struggle has a bloody history is no reason for believing that American political struggle today must be bloody. Likewise, the bloody history of religious conflict is no reason for believing that American religious struggle must be bloody today.

And if it is "un-Christian" for Catholicism to have an official enemy today, then Christianity has always been un-Christian, since it has been engaged in battles with enemies from the very beginning. The New Testament, especially in the Acts of the Apostles and the letters of St. Paul, makes it abundantly clear that early Christianity was engaged in battle against enemies, especially Jews and Judaizing Christians. Jesus himself is represented in the Gospels as struggling against Pharisees and Sadducees. As the centuries passed, new enemies cropped up: polytheists, Docetists, Marcionites and other gnostics, Arians, semi-Arians, Nestorians, Monophysites, Manicheans, Pelagians, Muslims, Waldensians, Albigensians, Lollards, Hussites, and so forth. In some cases, this struggle led to persecution and even warfare; but for the most part, it was conducted with the nonviolent weapons of propaganda and persuasion and excommunication. And struggles of this kind did not end with the coming of Protestantism. Besides the great Protestant-versus-Catholic struggles, there were scores of conflicts among various Protestant groups.

The simple fact is that Christianity, as long as it claims to be the custodian of a God-revealed system of truth, is bound to engage in struggle against "enemies." For there will always be those who reject this truth-claim and attack its assertions as untrue.

And how is Christianity to regard those who do this except as enemies, enemies of the truth? To regard such attackers as anything other than enemies is tantamount to renouncing the truth-claim. It is only during the last two centuries, and only among liberal Christians, that these attackers have *not* been regarded as enemies; and it is no mere coincidence that this very tolerant attitude is found precisely among those Christians who are unwilling to insist that Christianity is the custodian of a God-revealed system of truth.

Catholicism's mid-century
strength led to overconfidence

In addition to making peace with its former primary enemy, Vatican II, in its self-confidence, seriously underestimated the strength of what, during the preceding era, had been counted as secondary foes.

It has often been said that Vatican II rejected what has been called "triumphalism" — meant to describe the attitude of those traditional Catholics who were so confident of the superiority of their Faith that they felt Catholicism had little or nothing to learn from the outside world. These triumphalists often rejected as something hardly worth the trouble of examination the ideas typical of modern thought.

But there was another kind of Catholic triumphalism at the time of the Second Vatican Council — not the kind that closes itself off from the outer world, but the kind that is so confident of Catholicism's superiority that it *opens* itself to secular modernity with no adequate sense of the danger the latter poses for Catholicism. It feels so sure of the superiority of the Faith that it drops its defenses; it fears no evil. The Church prior to the council had been so successful in building a wall of separation between itself and modern secularist culture that many Catholics, including many bishops who attended Vatican II, had no real notion of the power and attractiveness of modern secularism. Besides, the Church had so gotten into the habit of identifying Protestantism as the chief enemy that the bishops were likely to underestimate the far more serious danger emanating from another source:

modern secularism.[84] Of these two kinds, let us call the first "cautious triumphalists" and the second "incautious triumphalists." The latter were probably the more sincere of the two. The caution of the former suggests that they did not fully believe their own rhetoric. They spoke of the great superiority of Catholicism, true enough; yet they were unwilling to put their confidence to the test by permitting it to have wide-open contact with the culture of modernity. At some level of consciousness (or perhaps unconsciousness), they doubted the real superiority of Catholicism. The incautious triumphalists, by contrast, had been so persuaded by the propaganda of triumphalism that they were eager for contact between Catholicism and modernity, confident that the Faith would carry the day.

Vatican II was dominated by the incautious triumphalists. In the last analysis, it was they who wrote the documents of the council. Hence, the virtual absence, in those documents, of that denunciatory style which had characterized solemn Vatican documents for centuries. To be sure, false teaching was still declared to be false; no attempt was made to compromise traditional Catholic doctrine. But instead of denouncing those who propagated false doctrine, the council extended them an olive branch, the hand of brotherhood. At its most negative, it did not denounce them;

---

[84] Even Pope John XXIII himself seems to have fallen into this overconfidence trap. In his message convoking the council, *"Humanae Salutis"* (delivered Christmas Day, 1961), the pope spoke of how the world stood in need of the teachings of the Church; yet he did not speak of the Church standing in need of the teachings of the world; and above all, he did not note that the Church may be endangered by the teachings of the world. Consistent with this view, he drew a striking contrast between the contemporary world and the Church, speaking of "this twofold spectacle — a world which reveals a grave state of spiritual poverty and the Church of Christ, which is still so vibrant with vitality" (Walter M. Abbott, S.J., ed., *The Documents of Vatican II* [New Century Publishers, 1966], 705).

rather, it pitied them for being trapped in falsehood. Instead of warning Catholics to shun these false teachers, the council noted that they were commonly persons of goodwill and that, in their false teachings, elements of truth were often admixed.

The bishops who dominated the council may have been incautious triumphalists, but Catholic intellectuals, both clerical and lay, who especially cheered the results of the council were not triumphalists at all. They were quite the opposite. Instead of being convinced of the superiority of Catholicism, they were convinced that it was inferior in many respects. Rather than feeling that the Church had an important message to deliver to the contemporary world, they felt that the world had important messages to deliver to the Church. Their aim was not to Christianize modernity, but to modernize the Church.

The result was a strange and accidental coalition between the most extreme triumphalists (the dominant bishops at Vatican II) and the most extreme modernizers. The former produced conciliar documents intended to lead to the Christianizing of the modern world, while the latter applauded these documents for providing an opening for achieving exactly the opposite — namely, modernizing the Church. That the documents would not bear this modernistic interpretation was no more than a minor inconvenience, which the modernizers got around by making their appeal, not to the letter of the documents, but to some nonliteral "spirit of the Council." Besides, hardly one Catholic in ten thousand read the official documents of the council, they were so lengthy, so technical, so tedious in style. (Faced with a long and difficult book, it is always more pleasant to cut to the "spirit" of the book than to read the whole thing.) Thus, very few were in a position to challenge the modernizers when they professed to be carrying out the mandate of the council.

So the great change produced by Vatican II left the Church with a sense that Catholicism no longer had any significant enemies. This produced two disastrous consequences. First, there was a rapid decline in Catholic in-group solidarity, ordinarily kept at a high level by opposition to a common enemy. Second, with defenses now down, the Church was exposed to the influence of those hostile to it, but not yet recognized as such.

Chapter 29

The Secularist Agenda
Is Enemy Number One

All right, then, let us agree that the Church needs a new enemy to replace the old enemy, Protestantism. But who is the new enemy to be? Keep in mind that the new enemy has to be a *real* enemy and has to be the single *most* threatening enemy.

Secularism: a generic name for a recurring modern foe

We need a generic name that will cover all forms of anti-Christianity, both rationalistic and romantic. Let me suggest *secularism*. Granted, it is not an ideal name, since it is so similar to the word *secular*, which carries no anti-Christian connotations. To say that the supermarket and movie theater, for instance, are secular institutions is not at all to suggest that they are secularist or anti-Christian institutions. It is to say, rather, that they are nonreligious; but to be nonreligious is quite a different thing from being antireligious. A cheeseburger is nonreligious, but it is not anti-religious. Yet *secularism* is a word with a long history, dating back more than a century now; and throughout that time, it has always carried an antireligious signification, more particularly an anti-Christian signification. Therefore, it will have to do.

I nominate *secularism*, then, as Catholicism's new "official" enemy.

The Decline and Fall of the Catholic Church in America

By way of objection to this nomination, it might be pointed out that the two most spectacular forms of secularism, Communism and Nazism, are no longer serious dangers. Nazism is dead (except for handfuls of nitwit neo-Nazis here and there), while Communism is either dead or dying. Can it not be argued, then, that the secularist project has failed? And if it has failed, what point is there in designating it as Catholicism's principal enemy? After all, we have agreed that only a genuine and serious enemy will do.

But secularism — which is nothing but a generic name for modern anti-Christian and antireligious worldviews — can take many different forms, Nazism and Communism being only two of them. Two particular forms of secularism may have failed, true enough, but the secularist project as a whole is far from having failed.

Secularism also comes in a more civilized form — what may be called a *liberal* form. That is the form it takes today in the United States, indeed in much of the industrialized world. I hasten to add that, in saying this, I do not mean to assert that all liberalism is secularist. Not at all; as a matter of historical fact, most liberals have been Christians of one type or another: think of William Gladstone; think of Franklin Roosevelt. But there is a species of contemporary liberalism that is secularist, i.e., antireligious in general and anti-Christian in particular. This species has existed in the United States from the earliest days of the republic: Jefferson was very near to being a liberal of this kind, and Tom Paine was definitely of this type.[85] Throughout most of its history, however, secularist liberalism has been of only marginal cultural and political importance in the United States. In this respect, American history has been very different from that of countries like France, where secularist liberalism — usually called laicism or

---

[85] See Paine's anti-Christian diatribe, *The Age of Reason*.

anticlericism — has played a major cultural and political role for more than two centuries.

Not until the cultural revolution of the 1960s and '70s did secularist liberalism become a major force in American life. Prior to that era, it led a marginal and often underground existence, largely confined to circles made up of respectable intellectuals and not-so-respectable bohemians. But about three or four decades ago, it broke out into the open, becoming for the first time a mass phenomenon. Since then, it has done much to transform the intellectual, artistic, and moral life of the nation — especially its moral life. Politically, it is now one of the key sections of the contemporary Democratic Party coalition.

I do not mean to suggest that secularist liberalism expressly publishes its antagonism to Christianity. You will never (at least almost never) find contemporary American secularists who openly say anything along the lines of "Down with religion; down with Christianity." No, their anti-Christianity is of the *de facto*, not the *de jure*, kind. That is, although they promote a moral and political agenda that is flatly incompatible with Christianity, an agenda that, if it succeeds, will have the effect of destroying Christianity, nonetheless the destruction of Christianity is not their direct aim; it is only a by-product — an inevitable by-product — of their direct aims.

Nor do I mean to suggest that all secularist liberals are conscious of the anti-Christian consequences of their agenda. Some of them are, and they are happy to strike blows against a religion that, for any number of reasons, they dislike; but people of this type make up only a small fraction of all secularist liberals. By contrast, the general run of secularists would disclaim any intention of destroying Christianity, and would deny, if faced with the charge, that their agenda tends toward the destruction of Christianity. They are aware of a personal lack of sympathy with Christianity, yes, even perhaps of some personal hostility toward it. But this is merely a personal preference; they have no wish to impose this preference on others; if others prefer to live Christian lives, that, they would say, is fine with them.

Nonetheless, and despite the sincere goodwill of these "pluralistic" folks, I contend that the agenda of secularist liberalism, if successfully implemented, will tend to destroy Christianity in the United States. At least it will do so with all forms of traditional or old-fashioned Christianity, whether Catholic, Orthodox, or Protestant. Liberal Christianity is another story. By increasingly incorporating secularist beliefs and values while retaining the music and poetry of religion, liberal Christianity progressively empties itself of all genuine Christian content, until finally it becomes nothing but an empty shell and collapses upon itself.

The Church must take a tip from the Counter-Reformers

To combat secularism successfully, Catholicism must return to its Counter-Reformation tactic of stressing precisely those elements in its makeup that are most offensive to its opponent. Whatever Protestant reformers objected to, Catholicism deliberately gloried in, embracing those elements of the Faith with redoubled emphasis and vigor: the seven sacraments (not just the two that Protestants recognized), the Virgin Mary, the veneration of saints, the authority of the pope, Purgatory, the Real Presence, et cetera. These could not be abandoned without abandoning the Faith itself, and, by stressing them, the Church drew a bright line between Catholicism and Protestantism, leaving no room for those who would prefer straddling a hazy borderland between the two. By getting rid of this hazy borderland, by making it clear that Protestantism was a quite different thing from Catholicism, the Church intensified its in-group solidarity, its *esprit de corps*.

This, I suggest, is the principle to be followed in the struggle against secularism. Identify the essential elements of Catholicism that secularism finds most objectionable; then embrace these elements with redoubled emphasis and zeal. The result will be an antisecularist Catholicism, just as the Catholicism of the centuries between Trent and Vatican II was an anti-Protestant Catholicism.

Nowadays the secularist agenda is essentially a moral agenda, not a directly theological (or antitheological) one — although its moral aims have theological and philosophical implications, as I will point out later. Its general aim is to replace the old Christian morality, which claims to be based on God-given commandments, with a new morality based on human autonomy and choice. More specifically, its aims are as follows:

• Make the production of *pornography* (other than child pornography) legal, and make its consumption both legally and morally acceptable.

• Make *nonmarital cohabitation* morally acceptable and provide it with legal protections and privileges. Prohibit housing discrimination against cohabiting couples. Provide employee benefits for "domestic partners" (in this case, heterosexual). Encourage the idea that cohabitation is a normal stage in the personal and sexual maturation process, either leading up to marriage or as an alternative to marriage.

• Make *divorce* legally easy and morally acceptable. Legalize no-fault divorce (which is, in effect, unilateral divorce).

• Make *nonmarital teenage sex* morally acceptable. Promote the idea that it is almost inevitable that kids will have sex. Promote sex-education courses in school that are based on the premise that kids will almost surely be having sex, courses that encourage "safe sex." Provide contraceptives free of charge to teenagers.

• Make *out-of-wedlock childbearing* morally and legally acceptable. Do not stigmatize such mothers. Provide them with welfare benefits and public housing on a nondiscriminatory basis. When the mothers are of school age, supply them with support groups and special programs in public schools.

• Make *homosexuality* legally and morally acceptable. Condemn all opposition to homosexuality (even — or especially — that which is religiously motivated) as bigotry and "homophobia." Outlaw all discrimination against homosexuals. Create public-school support groups for teenage homosexuals (gay-straight alliances). Provide employee benefits for homosexual "domestic partners." Permit adoption by homosexual couples. Legalize same-sex marriage or at least "civil unions" (same-sex marriage by another name). Promote the idea that sexual orientation is an inborn thing, something we have no control over; hence, that homosexuality is perfectly normal and natural for certain individuals.

• Make *abortion* legally and morally acceptable, a matter to be left to the free choice of the woman (or girl) having the abortion. In the case of poor women, provide public funds to pay for abortion services. In the event that national health care becomes a reality, make sure abortion is included under standard health-insurance coverage. Require medical schools to train doctors in abortion techniques. Require hospitals to provide abortion services (with no opt-out "conscience clause").

• Make *physician-assisted suicide* legally and morally acceptable, at least for the aged and the terminally ill. Promote the idea that each of us is sovereign over his or her life and is therefore free to do away with this life. Argue that restrictions on suicide (and assisted suicide) are inhumane ways of forcing people to endure intolerable pain and indignity.

• Once assisted suicide has become legally and morally acceptable on a widespread basis, make *euthanasia* legally and morally acceptable. Start with voluntary euthanasia, which is hardly distinguishable from assisted suicide: in the latter, the physician can provide the lethal drugs, but not administer them; in the former, the physician can actually perform the lethal act, but only at the request of the person who will be killed. Eventually move on to involuntary euthanasia (as they have done in the Netherlands), providing a gentle death to incompetents who, if they were still competent, would choose to die.

The "self-regarding conduct" canard

The more circumspect defenders of the secularist moral revolution respond to the foregoing account of their "agenda" by saying that they are not trying to *impose* sexual freedom, divorce, abortion, homosexuality, and so forth on anyone. Christians and others, they say, are perfectly free to abstain from such conduct if they wish, but at the same time, Christians must respect the freedom of those who wish to engage in this conduct. The point of our moral revolution, these circumspect secularists say, is not to encourage certain kinds of conduct, but to encourage tolerance for all conduct — provided it falls within the sphere of the *private* and the *personal*. We do not want people to be tolerant of murder and bank robbery, of course; these are public offenses, not private preferences. But nonmarital sex, consumption of pornography, divorce, abortion, homosexuality, suicide, et cetera — these are all matters of private, personal morality. They are nobody's business but the individuals directly involved. (This is the Personal Liberty Principle spoken of at length in an earlier chapter.)

This is pretty much the line taken by John Stuart Mill in his classic, *On Liberty*, where he makes a distinction between two kinds of conduct: that which is "other-regarding" and that which is "self-regarding." The former has an impact on others; the latter has an impact on no one but the person engaged in the conduct. When other-regarding conduct is likely to hurt others, society has a right to make rules against it and to punish those who violate the rules — punish them both by legal sanction and by public-opinion censure. But when conduct is merely self-regarding, even when it hurts the person engaged in such conduct (provided the person is sane and adult), public opinion and government should keep their noses out of it. In the self-regarding sphere, we should be free to do whatever we wish, even when what we wish is immoral, stupid, and self-destructive.

Today's secularists have "improved" somewhat on Mill by substituting "private" for "self-regarding." This allows them to avoid the question of whether certain forms of conduct — abortion and unilateral divorce, for instance — are truly self-regarding. For it can be argued by critics that such kinds of conduct are other-regarding, that they have a profoundly negative impact on innocent parties. No matter; we need not worry about such arguments once we define abortion and divorce as "private" issues and adopt the rule that private issues are the business of no one but the private parties concerned.

The secularist defense is attractive at the level of pure abstraction, but when brought in touch with concrete reality, it falls to pieces.

For one thing, Mill's distinction between self-regarding and other-regarding conduct is vacuous. Since individuals are part of society, it follows that anything individuals do to themselves is bound to have an impact on society at large, and when they harm themselves, they harm society. If I choose to be a drunkard or a drug addict, for instance, I do not hurt myself alone; I also hurt my family, my friends, my employer, and society at large. Thus, the fundamental premise of Mill's famous and vastly influential book is fatally flawed.

Nor can the situation be saved by substituting "private" for "self-regarding." Certain conduct is private in the sense that it normally takes place in private places. For instance, it is customary for people to have sexual relations in private, and (except for those who jump off bridges and tall buildings) suicides tend to occur in private. But from the fact that something is private in its setting it does not follow that it is private in its consequences. Sexual conduct, for instance, abounds in public consequences, some of them not very fortunate. On the positive side, it often leads to happy marriages and well-raised children. On the negative side, it can lead to sexually transmitted diseases, out-of-wedlock births, and broken families. Only an ideologue (unfortunately America today abounds in them) would deny that the public has a legitimate interest in encouraging certain kinds of sexual behavior (the kinds that tend to have good public effects) and discouraging certain other kinds (those that tend to have bad public effects).

It is an amusing and curious fact that many of those who insist most strongly on the importance of sexual freedom are opposed to the freedom to smoke cigarettes. The latter freedom, they argue, hurts others through what science has shown to be the effects of "second-hand smoke," and therefore it is a freedom that can legitimately be curtailed. Granting the validity of these scientific conclusions, the prohibition they ask for is reasonable enough. But why do they fail to apply the same rule to sexual conduct? Why do they not say, in a spirit of logical consistency, that the freedom of sexual conduct can be legitimately curtailed because of the harmful effects it often has on others, e.g., the production of out-of-wedlock children, the spread of sexually transmitted diseases, and so on?

The answer, I submit, is that Christianity has always condemned sexual license, while it has almost never (except in the case of a few Protestant sects) condemned smoking. If one's aim is to undermine Christianity and Christian morality, one can do this by promoting sexual freedom, but not by promoting tobacco freedom. And so, however illogical it may be on the point of consistency, it makes perfect sense that secularists, given their fundamental anti-Christianity principle, should champion fornication and homosexuality while restricting smoking.

The Decline and Fall of the Catholic Church in America

Further, while the secularist party line is that they are not trying to promote divorce, abortion, homosexuality, suicide, et cetera, and that the only things they are trying to promote are freedom and tolerance, this is not entirely honest. The fact is that for many secularists, probably most, this party line is no more than a convenient rhetorical alibi. In truth, they find abortion, homosexuality, suicide, and so forth to be morally quite unobjectionable. They want such conduct to be tolerated, not because it is private, but because they regard it as morally right.

During the slavery debates in the decades preceding the Civil War, the original line of Southern defense was that slavery was a necessary evil (this was the circumspect defense). Although no doubt a bad thing, it should be allowed; for if we abolish it, even worse consequences would follow. The Southern defense was revolutionized when Senator John C. Calhoun of South Carolina rejected the "necessary evil" defense and declared slavery to be a "positive good." This new line of defense widened the gap between abolitionist sentiment and slaveholder interests, making secession and civil war virtually inevitable. But at least it had the merit of honesty and forthrightness. Calhoun was saying what slaveholders had for a long time really believed, even though few or none of them had previously had the courage to say so in public.

Not many secularists have advanced to the stage of Calhoun-like honesty. In their heart of hearts, they believe that abortion, suicide, condoms in schools, et cetera, are "positive goods," not merely "necessary evils," yet they are, by and large, unwilling to say so out loud. They do not want to reveal how great is the abyss that separates them from religious traditionalists, at least not while these traditionalists remain a powerful force in American life. Above all, they do not want to lose the rhetorical advantage that comes from styling themselves as defenders of "tolerance," a virtue acknowledged by all Americans.

Secularist morality breeds secularist doctrine

Secularism aims at substituting a secularist moral code for the traditional Christian code. Christian morality is at least one-third of Christianity — the other two-thirds being doctrine and ritual. And in practice, morality is more than a mere one-third. Matthew Arnold was probably correct when he used to say that conduct was "three-fourths of life." Even if its role were smaller, it would remain an essential element of Christianity. The heart is but a small fraction of the total body mass; but remove it, and the body will die. Likewise, destroy the moral element of Christianity, and you will have dealt a fatal blow to Christianity as a whole. To reject Christianity's values as unsound is, by implication, to reject the beliefs as untrue.

Neither is the morality of secularism a free-standing thing. It too, like Christian morality, rests on a worldview, on a number of epistemological and metaphysical premises. Secularism rejects all forms of supernaturalism, preferring naturalistic explanations of reality. The only knowledge-claims it is willing to entertain are empirical claims, i.e., scientific and nonscientific claims that are ultimately based on sense experience. It is at least agnostic, if not fully atheistic, about the existence of God, and this agnosticism often amounts to *de facto* atheism. It rejects belief in Providence, both general and particular. It rejects belief in miracles, including such miracles as divine grace and divine revelation. And, of course, it is exceedingly skeptical that there is life after death.

If we accept the secularist moral code, it is difficult not to accept the secularist worldview. Even though acceptance of the former may not, logically speaking, entail the latter, still there is a close affinity between the two. If we are secularists in morality, we will sooner or later seek a worldview justification for this morality; and there is no better justification available — indeed there may be no *other* justification available — than that provided by naturalism, agnosticism, skepticism, et cetera. Secularism, in short, is a package, having moral, metaphysical, and epistemological elements. If we accept part of the package, it will be difficult not to accept the whole thing.

Oh, perhaps we can resist for a short while. Having been reared Catholic, having embraced a Catholic identity early in life, we may, in our young adult years, abandon the Christian moral code in favor of secularist morality, while still believing in God, still attending a Catholic church, still saying our daily prayers, still hoping for life after death, and so forth. In fact, there are plenty of people like this in the United States today (and not just in the United States): Catholics in religion, secularists in morality. But this is too illogical a synthesis to keep up over the long run. Maybe it can be sustained during the lifetime of an individual (although even that is doubtful). But it cannot be kept up for two or three or four generations. In other words, it cannot be a normal and enduring Catholic attitude. Sooner or later, cognitive dissonance will set in, and we will have to become logically consistent in one direction or the other: either we become thoroughgoing secularists, rejecting the Catholic doctrinal system, or we become thoroughgoing Catholics, rejecting the secularist moral ideal. In the long run, we cannot have it both ways.

Plenty of empirical evidence for this conclusion is available, since certain American Protestants have already tried the experiment. In the course of the twentieth century, as we saw earlier, American Protestantism has increasingly been divided into two great camps, the liberals and the conservatives. Liberal Protestantism has attempted a synthesis between secularism and Christianity, while conservative Protestantism has rejected secularism root and branch.

The result? Sociologically speaking, the denominations infected with liberal Protestantism — e.g., the Episcopalians, the Presbyterians, the Methodists, and, above all, the United Church of Christ — have declined in numbers and strength in the second half of the century, while conservative Protestantism — e.g., the Southern Baptists and Assemblies of God — have grown in both. Morally and doctrinally, liberal Protestantism has drifted further and further from its traditional Christian moorings, while conservative Protestantism has remained pretty much loyal to the original Protestant version of the Christian tradition. Catholics have only to examine the history of liberal Protestantism if they wish to discover what happens to churches that attempt to combine secularism and Christianity.[86]

[86] I hope it is unnecessary to note (yet I will note it anyway, just to make sure) that, in saying it is impossible to effect a synthesis between Christianity and secularism, I am not contending that it is impossible to effect a synthesis between Christianity and certain modern beliefs and values. Far from it. Many essential modern beliefs and values — the natural sciences, science-based technology, capitalism, democracy, the rights of man, and so forth — are fully reconcilable with Christianity. In many cases indeed, they are the offspring of Christianity, in the sense that they are the kinds of thing that could never have emerged except in a Christianized civilization. Thus, secularism must not be confused with modernity; the two are not the same thing, not by a long shot.

Chapter 30

What a Vigorous, Surviving Church Will Look Like

Catholicism, just like any religion, is composed of three essential elements: doctrine, ritual, and morals. In the case of Catholicism — and more so here than in almost any other religion — a fourth element is also of great importance: church polity or government. An antisecularist Catholicism, then, will have to be antisecularist in all four dimensions: doctrine, ritual, morals, and polity.

It would be convenient at this stage in my argument to be able to draw a picture of what, in all four dimensions, this antisecularist Catholicism would look like. The trouble is that no one knows how to draw accurate pictures of the human future. It is hard enough to predict tomorrow's weather, never mind predicting what vast numbers of human beings will do over the next century or two.

If American Catholicism is to take on an antisecularist form, this form will have to be *discovered* on an experimental basis over an extended period. Things will have to be tried out, retained if they work, discarded if they do not, until American Catholicism finally achieves a viable antisecularist form. It will not be the work of a summer's day. Above all, it will not be the work of an architect who lays down *a priori* plans.

The Decline and Fall of the Catholic Church in America

What a surviving Church will *not* look like

Granting the above, let us nonetheless speculate (this is *only* a speculation) as to the shape of a future Catholic Church in the United States. It is clear that a viable Catholic Church in America will necessarily have to be like something we have never seen. For one thing, it will have to be a religion of a "fifth way," neither a church nor a denomination nor a sect nor a quasi-ghetto.

• It cannot be a *church*, because a church (in the sociological sense of the term) embraces virtually the entire population of a society, and there is no likelihood that Catholicism will come to embrace anything like the entirety of the American population. Right now, Catholicism includes no more than 25 percent of the population, and we get to 25 percent only by counting millions of indifferent and merely nominal Catholics. If we restrict the count to "real" Catholics (defining them as those who attend church on a weekly basis), we would talk of a number closer to 10 percent of the American population. This percentage can, of course, grow in the future (and it can shrink as well), but there is no chance that Catholicism will become the dominant, near-monopolistic religion in the United States.

• It cannot be a *denomination* (in the sense in which the word has been used in this book, i.e., as signifying a religion that considers all other religions to be approximately as good and as true as itself) — at least not if it means to thrive. Today, of course, it is, in fact, a denomination, and has been such since the late 1960s. But denominations, as I explained earlier, lack vitality; in the long term, they go into decline. This has been the history of Protestant denominations in the United States, and for the last 30 years, it has been the history of American Catholicism. If Catholics do not mind belonging to a religion that grows weaker and weaker, smaller and smaller, then they can continue to be a denomination. The premise of the present discussion, however, is that American

Catholicism wants to flourish; and if this is its wish, it cannot afford to remain a denomination.

• It cannot be a *sect*. Historically speaking, no religion has been less sectarian than Catholicism. True enough, during the long era of the Catholic "ghetto" in the United States, American Catholicism took on a few sectarian characteristics, e.g., sharp boundaries dividing it from the non-Catholic world, a suspicion of outsiders, a high degree of in-group solidarity, and a high average level of religious intensity. But these were not enough to turn it into a full-fledged sect, and it is impossible to imagine how the Church can turn into a sect without ceasing to be Catholicism.

• Nor can American Catholicism return to the *form it took during the "ghetto" era*. But wait a minute: Was that quasi-ghetto not a successful way of being a religion — neither church nor denomination nor sect? Yes, in a way, it was; and perhaps this is why so many Catholics of traditional bent have a nostalgic desire to return to those "good old days." They sense that Catholicism has no future in the United States as church or denomination or sect; so they yearn to return to a form that worked well once upon a time. But this earlier way of so-called "ghetto Catholicism" was a temporary expedient only. To succeed, it needed a peculiar and unrepeatable set of social-historical circumstances: an immigrant population that was poor, uneducated, and economically ambitious; a more-than-ample supply of priests and nuns from the old country; and an old-stock American Protestant public that looked on Catholics as socially and morally inferior beings. All that has changed utterly. There is no going back to that way.

If Catholicism, then, is to thrive in the United States in the twenty-first century, it will have to find a new way of being a religion, a fifth way, neither church nor denomination nor sect nor quasi-ghetto. But this fifth way is not something that can be prescribed ahead of time — by, for instance, somebody (like me) writing a book. It will have to be, as I have said, *discovered* experimentally, by a process of trial and error, a process that will involve the entire Catholic population and will take, at a minimum, many decades to complete.

The positive characteristics
of an antisecularist church

One thing that can be said, however, is that it will have to be an antisecularist Catholicism, for secularism, as we have seen, will have to be regarded as the new "official enemy" of the Catholic religion. That being the case, this new thing, this fifth way, will almost certainly have to stress certain key propositions:

Pertaining to knowledge

• *The cognitive value of faith.* Since secularism insists that religious faith is nothing more than a man-made construct grounded in a combination of emotion and imagination, having no cognitive value, Catholics will have to affirm the contrary, that faith *does* have cognitive value, that it is a genuine form of knowledge. They will have to insist that the person of faith, other things being equal, *knows* more about reality than does the unbeliever; that he, in other words, is more of a realist.

One of the great advantages that came from dropping Protestantism as the official enemy of Catholicism is that Catholics, ever since Vatican II, no longer have their old rationale for avoiding the Bible. And one of the great advantages of adopting secularism as the new official enemy is that Catholics will now have a strong motive for studying the Bible; for Bible-reading will be one of the marks that distinguishes Catholics (and other Christians) from secularists, who have no use for the Bible except, on rare occasions, as an anthology of what they usually consider to be second-rate ancient literature.

It must be acknowledged, of course, that increased Catholic Bible-reading will have a downside. Many Catholic readers will, in fact, do what in the past was so often feared — namely, they will interpret Scripture in ways that are incompatible with Catholic doctrine. But this is a price well worth paying. When millions or tens of millions are being lost to the Faith because of the seductive lure of secularism and moral liberalism, the thousands or tens of thousands who may be lost to Protestantism because of a somewhat erratic reading of the Bible hardly weigh in the balance.

• *The cognitive value of religious experience, especially mystical experience.* Catholicism (along with Orthodox Christianity and most forms of Protestantism) has always held that prayer is a two-way street. It is not just we who communicate with God in prayer, but God communicates with us as well. This is especially true in mystical experience, the highest and most intense form of prayer, in which (the mystics tell us) the soul of the mystic enters into a kind of union with God, such that the distinctive personality of the mystic momentarily vanishes and the mystic becomes, in a sense, one with God. This union with the divine is a union of love, but it is also a union of knowledge. The mystic comes away from the experience with more wisdom than he had when going into it; the mystic has acquired a personal and intimate knowledge of God that the rest of us lack.

This is a largely incommunicable knowledge, in that the mystic, after the event, cannot find words that come even close to describing the experience. Nonetheless, the mystic insists, it is genuine knowledge he has acquired. And what is true of mysticism is true, to a lesser degree, of other forms of religious experience — namely, that they involve a communication from God, that the religious person comes away from this experience knowing something about God, and indirectly about God's creation, that he did not know beforehand.

The secularist does not deny (or at least does not need to deny) that these experiences take place in the lives of many individuals. What he denies is that the experiences have any objective validity, that they give knowledge of some reality outside the mind of the person undergoing the experience. Instead they are purely *subjective* experiences. They are nothing more than feelings and attitudes on the part of the religious person, feelings and attitudes that have no objective correlate. Sure enough, the person who undergoes one of these religious experiences *feels* that all is well, that all is exceedingly well; and feels that all creation rests in the hands of a loving God. But this is a mere psychological state. It may have beneficial effects in the life of the individual, but it proves nothing about the nature of reality; it gives no evidence for the existence or nature of God. In certain mental institutions, there are people who sincerely *feel* they are Napoleon, after all, but this is no evidence that they really *are* Napoleon.

Catholicism has never held that every claim to a mystical religious experience is valid. It can freely admit that some of these claims are innocent mistakes, others are self-delusions, and others downright frauds. Thus it can go a long way with the secularist in his dismissal of certain claims. But it cannot go all the way, for that would be tantamount to denying that God has the power to communicate with individuals if he wishes; or at least it would be tantamount to affirming that God, notwithstanding his capacities, has a strict policy of noncommunication. But either of these propositions would be absurd from the point of view of the Catholic Faith. Hence, Catholicism holds that God *can* communicate with individuals in a religious experience; and furthermore, that from time to time, God *does* communicate with individuals. The Church has even gone so far as to canonize as saints individuals who claimed to have received such communications (most notably, the two great Spaniards who have written at length about their own mystical experiences, Teresa of Avila and John of the Cross).

• *The reality of moral knowledge.* Secularism teaches that moral codes and values are, in the last analysis, no more than cultural constructs or personal choices or preferences. Catholics, therefore, heirs to the natural-law theory of the ancient Stoics, will have to insist that there is such a thing as moral knowledge; that ethical propositions are either true or false; and that the human mind is capable of recognizing an objective moral law.

• *The reality of intellectual knowledge.* Contemporary American secularism has a powerful bias toward skepticism, not just religious and moral skepticism, but skepticism of a more generalized kind; this is commonly called "postmodernism." As heir to the great schools of classical philosophy (Plato and Aristotle), Catholicism will have to insist that the human intellect is proportioned to the objective world, capable of grasping reality. Catholicism, which has often been charged by its enemies with being the enemy of modern scientific knowledge (e.g., the case of Galileo, which is endlessly thrown in the face of the Church), will now have to defend scientific knowledge against the skeptics.

Pertaining to metaphysical reality

• *The existence of God.* Secularism is either atheistic or agnostic; that is, it either denies or doubts the existence of God; moreover, this agnosticism is usually a *de facto* atheism. Therefore, Catholics will have to stress their belief in God. In the long anti-Protestant era, from Trent until Vatican II, there was no need for this fundamental belief (the most fundamental of all beliefs) to be stressed. Since it was not a point of disagreement between Catholics and Protestants, it could be taken for granted. But in the new antisecularist era, this is the principal point of differentiation between Catholics and their rivals. Thus, no matter how hard it is to imagine new ways of stressing belief in God, Catholics must discover and invent new ways of emphasizing precisely this difference.

The Decline and Fall of the Catholic Church in America

Such an emphasis will produce two incidental benefits. First, it will highlight what Catholicism has in common with other religions, especially other Christian faiths (Protestantism and the Eastern churches), thus making it easier to join these other Christian faiths in a great Christian alliance against secularism, and even to join non-Christian faiths (especially Judaism and Islam) in a great monotheistic alliance. Second, more attention to the idea of God will lead to a deeper understanding of that idea, not just at the level of theology and philosophy, but, perhaps more importantly, at the level of popular belief.

• *Life after death*. From a secularist point of view, belief in life after death makes little or no sense. Thus, Catholics, in order to draw a very sharp line of division between themselves and secularists, must stress this belief. All the considerations just mentioned with regard to belief in the existence of God apply here as well.

• *The reality of grace and free will*. Secularism has embraced psychology and sociology, both in their scholarly and "pop" versions; and according to the usual understanding of these social sciences, human behavior is totally explainable, at least in principle, in naturalistic terms. Explanations of human behavior in terms of supernatural forces — the grace of God — are ruled out of court; and often explanations in terms of free will are ruled out as well (for free will, if not exactly a supernatural force, is not a "natural" force either). As against secularism, Catholicism will have to stress that grace and free will play important roles in human conduct. This will be a very ticklish undertaking, since, while asserting the reality of grace, Catholicism will have to refrain from rejecting psychology and sociology wholesale, although it will, of course, have to reject the naturalistic and deterministic framework that typically lies in the deep background of these social sciences. This probably means that Catholic social scientists and philosophers (in cooperation, of course, with Protestant social scientists and philosophers) will have to develop specifically Christian versions of psychology and sociology.

Pertaining to morality

• *The objectivity of moral law.* Secularists hold that the rules of morality are purely man-made things, either societal and cultural products or the creation of individuals. Hence, Catholicism will have to emphasize the diametric opposite, that there is a moral law that is not man-made, a God-made — or at least a God-*based* — law.[87] Under "the cognitive value of faith," I argued for the need to affirm the *knowledge* of natural law; here I am arguing for the need to affirm the *reality* of natural law.

• *The sanctity of human life.* For a long time, secularism has found nothing morally objectionable in abortion; for the most part, it finds nothing morally objectionable in suicide; and increasingly it finds nothing morally objectionable in euthanasia, especially voluntary euthanasia, but even involuntary euthanasia

---

[87] To speak of the moral law as "God-made," while acceptable at the level of popular discourse, especially discourse involving children and poorly educated adults, is philosophically misleading, for it suggests that the moral law is the product of God's arbitrary will; from which it would follow that lying, cheating, stealing, adultery, murder, et cetera, while wrong today, would be right tomorrow if God were to change his mind and declare them right. Although this is what some Catholic theologians (e.g., the fourteenth-century English philosopher-theologian William of Occam) have had in mind when they spoke of the moral law, this is not what the main current of Catholic theology has held (as represented, notably, by St. Thomas Aquinas). Aquinas and others have held that the moral law is ultimately based on God, as all creation is based on God, but not on God's will so much as on his reason; and more immediately, the moral law is based on the rational nature of the human person. See Aquinas, *Summa Theologica*, I-II, Q. 90.

in cases in which the victim would be "better off" dead, but lacks the capacity to make this decision. Catholicism, therefore, must emphasize its opposition to abortion, suicide, and euthanasia.

• *The importance of chastity.* Secularism has a highly permissive attitude toward sexual conduct. Such conduct, it allows, ought to be regulated by considerations of health, prudence, and nonviolence; but once these considerations are attended to, sex is pretty much a morally indifferent matter. Thus, secularism has no principled objection to fornication, cohabitation, homosexuality, or even adultery (provided the adultery is successfully concealed from the spouse whose feelings would be hurt if the adultery were detected). From the secularist point of view, chastity is not a virtue; indeed, the notion of chastity as a virtue is downright laughable. Thus, Catholicism must reassert its ancient emphasis on chastity as a virtue, indeed as a very important virtue. This reassertion will not be easy, of course, since vast numbers of American Catholics more or less subscribe to the dominant cultural attitude of sexual permissiveness.

• *The immorality of homosexuality.* Secularism is particularly aggressive in its contention that homosexuality is morally permissible, and that those who disagree are motivated by bigotry — not by reason or by honest religious conviction; or if they are motivated by honest religious conviction, then the religion that supplies such motivation is itself bigoted. Say the secularists: If anti-gay people were true Christians (as they pretend to be) and not hypocrites (as they really are), they would, in a spirit of compassion, give their blessing to same-sex relationships. Catholicism, if it wishes to draw a bright line of division between itself and its secularist foes, has no choice but to reassert its traditional teaching on this topic: that homosexual conduct is immoral, that it is a perversion of nature and that it is especially abominable in the eyes of God.

This will not be easy to do; far from it. For to the secularist and the semi-secularist (the liberal Christian), strong moral disapproval of homosexuality is quite shocking. It is perceived as nothing less than bigotry, as "homophobia." Hence, it takes a courageous Christian to utter his disapproval of homosexuality in the company of secularists and semi-secularists. Nor will many of today's Christians, even very orthodox Catholics, feel the shock and disgust at homosexuality and homosexuals that Christians once routinely felt. Now, there is nothing in Catholic moral doctrine that says homosexuals should be treated like dirt. (On the contrary, precisely because they are compelled toward a vice that the Bible regards as an abomination, they merit special compassion.) Yet Catholics will nonetheless have to affirm the grievous wrongness of homosexual conduct (as well as recognize the possible effects that the ethos of homosexual conduct, freed from cultural taboos, might have on marriage, the family, and societal sexual morality in general), even while they love and respect the homosexual person. At least they will have to do so if Catholicism is to hold secularism to be its official enemy.

Pertaining to devotion

A religion is not simply a matter of beliefs and moral code. Above all, it is a matter of ritual, of devotion. Catholicism has always been a ritualistically rich religion: more so than those that have belonged to the "churchly" wing of Protestantism (e.g., Anglicans and Lutherans) and far more so than the churches that have emerged from the sectarian wing (e.g., the Baptists). The most important Catholic ritual is, of course, the Mass. But there have been dozens, perhaps even hundreds, of lesser devotions, some of them public, some private.

In creating and sanctioning these lesser devotions, the Church has often had in mind the official enemy of the time. Take, for instance, private and public recitation of the Rosary, for centuries now the most famous of Marian devotions. If Protestantism was the official enemy, and if Protestants objected to the Catholic veneration of Mary, then it was important for Catholics to practice Marian devotions; it was a way of drawing a very bright line between Catholics and their official enemy. The same with the devotion known as adoration of the Blessed Sacrament. Protestants — even those who considered the Eucharist to be more than a mere symbol of Christ, who considered that Christ was in some sense truly present in the Eucharist at the moment of Communion — rejected the Catholic theory that Christ is present in the Eucharist by way of transubstantiation. In other words, they denied the Catholic notion that Christ is substantially present — not just spiritually present — in the bread and wine from the moment these elements are consecrated at the altar by the priest, and that consequently Christ remains present after the Communion service is finished.

From the Catholic theory, it follows logically that the consecrated bread (that is, the body of Christ) deserves to be worshiped in much the same way that Christ in human form would deserve to be worshiped, were he to make an appearance in church tomorrow. By adoring the sacrament, something Protestants cannot do, Catholics were once again drawing a bright line between themselves and the official enemy.

If secularism is to be the official enemy of contemporary Catholicism, devotions will have to be developed that draw a bright line between Catholicism and secularism. Of course, any kind of divine worship will draw such a line, since, from a secularist point of view (that is, from an atheistic or agnostic point of view), worshiping God makes no sense. Yet the more "supernaturalistic" the ritual is, the better. Some religions (e.g., Greek Orthodoxy, Catholicism, "high church" Anglicanism) have traditionally been highly ritualistic, hence highly supernaturalistic, while others (e.g., the Congregationalists, the Unitarians) have been low in ritual, hence almost naturalistic. It will be important, then, for Catholicism to maintain a high level of ritual in this, its antisecularist era.

But more will be needed than ritual in general. Just as Tridentine Catholicism stressed rituals that gave "offense" to Protestants by stressing particular ideas and values rejected by Protestants, so antisecularist Catholicism will have to develop rituals that give like offense to secularists and moral liberals. What these are I cannot say. They will have to be discovered with time and experiment and a certain amount of religious creative genius. But let me make one suggestion, simply by way of illustration. Since abortion is such a bone of contention between Catholicism and moral liberalism, the Church would do well to develop rituals having to do with abortion — or rather, with the rejection of abortion and the affirmation of life. Some ceremony might be developed that would involve expectant mothers and their unborn babies: a rite that would take place, let us say, two or three months into the pregnancy, sometime around the point in the pregnancy when abortions usually take place. The ceremony, which would involve prayers for the health and safety of both mother and baby, would have the effect of affirming the humanity of the unborn child, while implicitly declaring the mother's decision to reject the abortion option.

It would be a kind of sacrament of "choice." At the same moment that some women, persuaded — or seduced — by the tenets of moral liberalism, are choosing abortion for the entity they are carrying (the tenets of moral liberalism prohibit them from calling this entity a baby), Catholic women are choosing life for their unborn babies.[88]

Summing up, then. Catholicism, if it is to survive and flourish in the United States, will have to create a new social form for

[88] Let me repeat that this is only an illustration. Whether a ritual along these lines would actually work, I cannot say. Only experimentation will tell.

itself: a form that is neither church nor sect nor denomination nor quasi-ghetto. What this form will be I cannot suggest. Its invention will be, like all worthwhile invention, the work of time and imagination and experiment. But it will have to be found; otherwise American Catholicism will continue its downhill slide until it becomes a small and socially insignificant religion.

One thing we can be sure of, however: that this new form of Catholicism will have to have an "official enemy." The enemy is not hard to find, and only an unfortunate combination of the denominational mentality plus poor leadership has prevented American Catholicism from clearly defining this enemy in the past. Now it must draw bright lines — many bright lines — of differentiation between itself and secularism.

Conclusion

"Holy Troy Shall Fall"

I have now reached the end of my argument. I have contended that the once-flourishing Catholic Church in the United States was undermined by an unlucky convergence of three factors in the 1960s: Vatican II, the end of the old Catholic quasi-ghetto, and the rise to cultural hegemony of secularism and moral liberalism. These factors combined to produce a dangerously tolerant and open-minded mentality among Catholics (the "denominational mentality") at precisely the moment when the old mainline Protestant dominance of American culture was being replaced by a new secularist dominance. Catholics — except for a small minority — came to be infected by secularism and moral liberalism, and their *de facto* religion became no longer Catholicism, but generic Christianity or Christianity-in-general.

But Christianity of this sort, nondogmatic or liberal Christianity, as it may be called, always leads to religious decline, as the history of liberalism in American Protestantism has shown. Hence, we may anticipate that American Catholicism, which has been in decline since the 1960s, will continue to decline in the future. Increasingly the Catholic Church, at one time large and powerful, will become a small and insignificant factor in American life.

I have been reluctant to end with that thoroughly pessimistic conclusion: reluctant both as a Catholic and as an American. As a

The Decline and Fall of the Catholic Church in America

Catholic, I am distressed to see that the Church, which was in many ways a magnificent thing in the days of my youth, is in such poor condition today and in probably poorer condition tomorrow. As an American, I fear that the triumph of secularism and moral liberalism will eventually undermine the republic, by encouraging a kind of moral anarchy and by draining life of its higher or "transcendental" meaning; and I believe that a revived Catholicism is needed to check the advance of secularism and moral liberalism. I rejoice that conservative Protestantism is flourishing at the moment, but conservative Protestantism alone cannot do the job — partly because its numbers are not sufficient, and partly because it is intellectually deficient, being more a religion of the heart than of the head. It needs an alliance with a revived Catholicism if the forces of Christianity are to halt the advance of the secularist juggernaut.

I said that what the Church needs in order to revive is an "official enemy." Such an enemy is available: secularism or moral liberalism. But can a Church that is itself tainted with moral secularism and moral liberalism effectively draw the line against such an enemy? And will a Church that has had inadequate leadership for the past thirty or forty years find the leadership it needs to wage such a battle?

Even great things pass away

The ancient historian Polybius (second century B.C.) tells the story of the destruction of Carthage following the Third Punic War. The razing of the city — the fulfillment of the oft-repeated wish of Cato the Censor ("Carthage, it seems to me, must be destroyed," Cato would say at the end of every speech he delivered in the Senate) — was presided over by Publius Scipio Africanus the Younger, the Roman general who had defeated Carthage in this final war between the two great powers. As Scipio watched the city of his enemy being destroyed, he wept, sadly reflecting, Polybius tells us, on how a similar destruction would someday befall his own beloved city, Rome. All earthly things are mortal, including great cities and great empires, and although Rome at the present moment stood on a mountaintop of power and glory, it, too, would eventually meet its demise. Such was the way of the world.

> At the sight of the city utterly perishing amidst the flames [Polybius tells us], Scipio burst into tears, and stood long reflecting on the inevitable change which awaits cities, nations, and dynasties, one and all, as it does every one of us men. This, he thought, had befallen Ilium, once a powerful city, and the once mighty empires of the Assyrians, Medes, Persians, and that of Macedonia lately so splendid. And unintentionally or purposely he quoted — the words perhaps escaping him unconsciously —

> "The day shall be when holy Troy shall fall
> And Priam, lord of spears, and Priam's folk."

It requires a fine sense of proportion, a great capacity to take long views, and an acute sense of the fragility of earthly things for the representative of a triumphant institution to realize, at the very moment when his institution is most triumphant, that this triumph will eventually turn to ashes and dust. Picture Cardinal Cushing of Boston at the John Kennedy Inauguration in January 1961.[89] The Catholic Church in the United States was flourishing like a green bay tree, at the peak of its power and glory; and now, to add glory on top of glory, a Catholic had actually been elected president of the United States. Was it a sad moment for Cushing? Did he, Scipio-like, weep when reflecting that this enormously successful American Catholic Church was doomed to go into decline, that someday it would end in ashes and dust? Perhaps he did.

---

[89] Cushing delivered one of the prayers at the Inaugural.

More probably he did not. For the possibility of decline, let alone the likelihood of decline, was something almost beyond the imagination of American Catholics in those glory days.

Christ's promise is no reason for complacency

When Catholics reflect on the long-term future of their Church, they have often taken comfort from the Gospel words of Jesus: "Upon this rock I will build my Church, and the gates of Hell shall not prevail against it."[90] Catholics have taken this to be a promise from God that the Church will endure until the end of human time, that its many enemies will never be able to crush it utterly.

But the common Catholic conviction of the immortality of the Church rests on something more than this particular scriptural text. It rests on the belief that the Catholic Church is indeed the true Church of God. And if God has taken the trouble to introduce a true Church into the world, an introduction accompanied by the suffering, death, and Resurrection of his Son, it stands to reason that this Church will be no passing affair, that it is something God will keep alive in the world for as long as the world lasts. The belief that the Catholic Church is endowed with a God-warranted immortality is beneficial in some ways. It encourages confidence in good times and sustains hope in bad times. For most of us, it is easier to strive for victory when we have an assurance ahead of time that we belong to a winning team. But the conviction also has its downside, for it can tempt Catholics to rest on their oars, to assume that their Church has a kind of magical protection against death and that their own efforts are hardly necessary. Adrift on a sea of trouble, they say to themselves, "This, too, shall pass," and consequently they leave undone what might have been done to shorten the time of trouble.

[90] Matt. 16:18.

Now, a superficial glance at the history of the Church tends to justify this attitude, for the Church has found itself in apparently mortal danger on a number of occasions, and yet these dangers have passed; the Church has endured. Think of the Reformation, think of the French Revolution, think of Communism. These were all powerful and openly declared enemies of the Church; but look — the Church has survived all these attacks.

But a look at history that is something better than superficial tells us that these survivals were not achieved by Catholics who did nothing but wait until the bad times blew over. Rather, they were achieved by Catholics — especially popes, bishops, and members of male and female religious societies — who possessed extraordinary energy and clear-sightedness. Think, for example, of the Council of Trent; of the Jesuits of the sixteenth and seventeenth centuries; of the religious revival in France following the fall of Napoleon; of the sturdiness of Polish Catholicism under Communist government. Unless Catholic leaders of similar energy and clear-sightedness emerge in the United States, the downhill slide of American Catholicism is not likely to be reversed.

At all events, even if the famous "Upon this rock" passage, upon which Catholics have routinely relied as a justification for confidence in the Church's long-term future, is indeed a divine promise that the Church will survive until the end of time, it nonetheless says nothing about the survival of the Church in the *United States*. For all this passage has to tell us, the Church may survive elsewhere in the world — in Africa, for instance, or in Asia or Latin America — while perishing in America. American Catholics, therefore, have no right to be overly comforted by this scripture.

A surge of vitality provides false signs of hope

After describing many aspects of decline in the American Church in his very fine book *American Catholic*, Charles Morris strikes this very optimistic note:

On the bright side, however, the large numbers of very active core Catholics, whose commitment is *chosen* rather than merely inherited or imposed, have created an extraordinarily vibrant and participatory grassroots parish life, just as post–Vatican II liberals dreamed might happen. Whether smaller numbers of highly engaged Catholics are to be preferred to the larger, more passive turnouts of the 1950s is, of course, a source of endless argument. But smaller numbers in this case is a purely relative concept, for by any reasonable measure, highly committed Catholics still add up to the largest single American religious body by a good margin.[91]

True enough, there are many signs of vitality in the Church in the United States. But the question is this: Is it a truly *Catholic* vitality? Or is it a vitality more proper to generic Christianity? Religions undergoing a process of dissolution due to the abandonment of traditional doctrine often experience, in the short term, a great burst of energy, especially ethical energy. It is something like, in the world of physics, the conversion of matter into energy. It is as if a great amount of energy had been pent up in the traditional dogmatism of the religion, and as soon as this dogmatic structure is destroyed, this pent-up energy is released into the world. But soon the explosion is finished, this ethical energy is spent, and little or nothing is left. The liberalized religion in question no longer has its traditional dogmas, and now it no longer has the great energy it exhibited for a while.

The Unitarianism of Massachusetts in the first half of the nineteenth century is a striking case in point. The state's Congregational churches had been operating under the dogmatic yoke of Calvinism for the better part of two centuries: a strict Calvinism in much of the state, a somewhat "softer" Calvinism in other parts

---

[91] *American Catholic* (New York: Vintage Books, 1998), 320.

of the state that were already veering in the direction of liberalism (and it was this "softer" Calvinism that would eventually be transmuted into Unitarianism). In the first quarter of the nineteenth century, the Unitarian movement destroyed much of the dogmatic structure of Calvinism — repudiating such doctrines as the Trinity, the divinity of Christ, Predestination, and Original Sin — and the new religion entered into an era of tremendous ethical and intellectual creativity. It produced Ralph Waldo Emerson and his Transcendentalist circle; it produced Longfellow and Hawthorne; it produced the utopian community of Brook Farm at West Roxbury; and it produced a multitude of social reformers who worked and agitated for the betterment of slaves, women, the poor, children who needed a free public education, the blind, criminals, drunkards, the insane, and so forth.[92]

By the end of the nineteenth century, however, the great creative impulse given off by Unitarianism had pretty much petered out, and the religion (if it can any longer be called a religion, as distinguished from a kind of ethical culture society) was well on its way to becoming what it is today: a small and relatively insignificant Sunday-morning meeting place for decent people who, while making earnest efforts to be open-minded and progressive, have little or no religious faith.

As I say, this burst of vitality, especially ethical vitality, is not at all unusual in religions that are throwing overboard many of their traditional dogmas. It should not be surprising, then, that American Catholicism, as it downshifted from traditional high-dogma

[92] Incidentally, it made a couple of important contributions to American Catholicism. A Unitarian minister and early Transcendentalist was Orestes Brownson, who, converting to Rome in the early 1840s, became America's leading Catholic nineteenth-century intellectual. Isaac Hecker, another convert to Catholicism who became a priest and eventually the founder of the Paulist Fathers, had been a member of the Brook Farm community.

Catholicism to low-dogma generic Christianity, would demonstrate considerable vitality, a great release of ethical and other energies. But this phenomenon may turn out to have little staying power. In a generation or two, most of the ethical energy may well have been spent, leaving the religion with little doctrine to fall back on. (Further, this shortage of doctrine makes it harder to pass the religion on to children; their moral education no longer anchored in theological beliefs.) Only time will tell.

The Church in America must
cease to compromise — or cease to exist

The call for Catholicism to get in step with the modern world is, I concede, a call that resonates with vast numbers of American Catholics. But a "modernized" Catholicism is a contradiction in terms. For Catholicism, whether we like it or not, is an ancient religion, and it is so not just incidentally, but essentially. The first premise of Catholicism is that something exceedingly strange and wonderful took place at the eastern end of the Roman Empire about two thousand years ago. A God-man appeared in the world, and he suffered and died for our sins, and he rose from the dead, and he left behind him a revelation and a Church. This is a story that makes no sense from a "modern" point of view. And more was to follow. During the next few centuries, in a civilization that was growing old and losing much of its confidence (a "failure of nerve," as Gilbert Murray once called it), in an intellectual climate permeated with neo-Platonism and a moral climate tilting toward asceticism, the Christian revelation was theologically elaborated, culminating in the trinitarian and incarnational creed of Nicea (A.D. 325) and in the mind and personality of St. Augustine (354-430). Nothing could be more unmodern than Augustine and the Nicean Creed.

Yet that is the religion which, for better or worse, Catholics are stuck with. It may well be that Catholics can be modern when it comes to going to movies and using computers and doing science and arranging business deals and dropping "smart bombs" when making war. But they cannot be modern when it comes to having a religion. He who would modernize Catholicism — making it more or less compatible with the empiricism, skepticism, individualism, and optimistic hedonism of the present age — would destroy it. Catholicism is a religion of late Western antiquity, or it is nothing. The Catholic religion presumes that a window on ultimate truth opened for a few centuries in late antiquity, revealing metaphysical and moral principles that have a permanent validity for the human race. Therefore, no matter how "advanced" our modern and post-modern civilization may become, when it comes to religion, we must constantly return to these ancient insights.

It is unlikely that many American Catholics, swimming as they do in a sea of cultural modernity, will be willing or able to sustain this ancient religious mentality. And thus, I am, on the whole, pessimistic about the chances for a revival of American Catholicism. But some will be able to do it, even in the midst of very modern twenty-first-century America (just as, for example, John Henry Newman was able to do it in the midst of very modern nineteenth-century England). These will be the "saving remnant" of American Catholicism. But whether they will be numerous enough and intense enough and judicious enough — and all three are needed: numbers, religious intensity, and prudential good judgment — to produce a mass revival of their religion, remains to be seen.

Appendixes

Statistical Evidence of
American Catholic Decline

The following statistics (along with many others) can be found in a book by Ken Jones, *Index of Leading Catholic Indicators: The Church Since Vatican II* (St. Louis: Oriens Publishing Company, 2003).

Jones seems to believe that Vatican II is wholly responsible for the decline of the Church in the United States, a view I disagree with, since I hold that Vatican II is at most *partly* responsible — only one of three major factors. Jones also seems to believe that Vatican II was a mistake, that the Church would have done better to omit the council and continue with the religious style that prevailed through the reign of Pope Pius XII. Again I disagree, since it seems to me that Vatican II was a historical necessity — a very painful necessity, it is true, something like major surgery; but a necessity nonetheless. Despite these disagreements, I find Jones's book to be a small treasure-house of statistics showing how sharp and dramatic has been the decline of the Church in America since 1965, the closing year of Vatican II.

• Between 1965 and 2002, the number of priests in the United States dropped from 59,000 to 46,000, a drop of 22 percent (p. 14).

• In 1965, the number of ordinations of new priests outnumbered the number of priests lost through death and departures by

725. In 1998, it was quite reversed, as deaths and departures out-numbered ordinations by 810 (p. 17).

• In 1965, 3 percent of all parishes were without a resident priest; in 2002, this figure had climbed to 15 percent (pp. 18-19).

• In 1965, there were 7.87 diocesan priests for every 10,000 Catholics; in 2002, there were 4.6, a decline of 41 percent (p. 20).

• Moreover, the average age of priests is going up and up. In 1999, there were more diocesan priests in the 80-to-84 age group than in the 30-to-34 age group (pp. 24-25).

• In 1965 there were 49,000 seminarians; in 2002, that number had dropped to 4,700 — despite the fact that the total number of Catholics in the United States had grown by nearly 20 million in that period (pp. 11, 27).

• In 1965, there were 180,000 religious sisters in the United States; by 2002, that number had dropped to 75,500 — with half of them being past age 70 (p. 37).

• In 1965, the number of parochial grade-school students was 4.5 million; by 2002, it had declined to 1.9 million (p. 53).

• In 1968, 338 annulments were granted; by 1983, this number had climbed to 66,417 — a 197-fold increase (p. 71).

• Estimates on average weekly Mass attendance vary wildly, depending on who is doing the estimating. But what everyone agrees on is that there has been a substantial drop in attendance between the mid-1960s and today (pp. 72-76).

• In the year 2000, the percentages of lay religion teachers in Catholic elementary schools who agreed with the Church's offi-cial teaching on the following topics: contraception, 10 percent; abortion, 26 percent; infallibility of the pope, 27 percent; an exclusively male priesthood, 33 percent; the Real Presence, 63 percent; life after death, 74 percent; the Resurrection, 87 percent; the divinity of Christ, 91 percent; and the existence of God, 98 percent (p. 79).

Appendix 2

A Critique of the Personal Liberty Principle

I am reluctant to leave the Personal Liberty Principle (PLP) without at least a brief evaluation, for it is, to my mind, a singularly stupid principle. The fact that so many Americans, especially young Americans, have embraced this stupidity is an important — and alarming — indicator of the state of our national intellect and character. What is more, the dominance of the PLP makes it very difficult for Catholicism to flourish, or even to survive, in the United States today. The PLP is the antithesis of Catholic morality. How can Catholics be full participants in the cultural life of the United States without being tainted by this principle? And how can they be tainted by it and remain genuine Catholics?

We may say that the PLP is made up of two inseparable subprinciples, related to one another as two sides of the same coin. There is the *autonomy principle*, which holds that we may do what we like, so long as we do not harm others. And there is the *tolerance principle*, which holds that we must tolerate the conduct of others, so long as this conduct does not harm people (other than the actor himself). My critique may be divided into four parts:

The PLP is simplistic
The PLP is easy to understand and to remember and to apply. Now, this would be a merit if morality were a simple thing. But

since morality is not a simple thing, the extreme simplicity of the PLP is not a merit; it is a shortcoming. And it is an especially vicious shortcoming in that it urges us to treat complex moral questions in simplistic ways.

The PLP rejects a rich heritage of moral thought

The tradition of moral thought in the Western world is especially rich, and most of the monuments of that thought have survived to this day; we can examine them any time we want. Think of the Old Testament, especially the Psalms and the writings of the great prophets; of Homer; of the Greek philosophers, especially Plato, Aristotle, and the Stoics; of Cicero and Virgil; of the Roman jurists; of the New Testament; of the Fathers and Doctors of the Church; of the Renaissance Christian humanists; of the Enlightenment anti-Christian humanists; of the nineteenth-century democrats and socialists; of the twentieth-century pragmatists; of the authors of papal encyclicals. It is an immense intellectual and moral legacy.

But it is a legacy that has to be claimed, that has to be appropriated. And if we decide to appropriate it, we have to do a lot of work on it, since not all elements of it are entirely compatible with all other elements. A great work of synthesis is needed: the kind of work that Thomas Aquinas did in the thirteenth century in his famous work on the principles of moral thought, "Treatise on Law."[93]

But this is hard work, hard thinking. How much easier to adopt a simple approach by embracing the PLP and throwing this inheritance out the window.

[93] This so-called treatise is part of Aquinas's magnum opus, the *Summa Theologica*. It comprises questions 90 through 105 of Part I-II of the *Summa*.

The PLP is at odds with itself

But the trouble with the PLP is not merely that it is simplistic and that it rejects a moral heritage of thirty centuries. This is a condemnation passed on it by outsiders, by those who (like me) are unsympathetic to the PLP ideal. Champions of the PLP can, of course, dismiss this condemnation. They can argue that the PLP is better than the ancient heritage of moral thought, that we will be better off when we get free of it, just as astronomers were better off when they unloaded their old Aristotelian-Ptolemaic baggage and embraced the Copernican Revolution.

But closer inspection reveals that the PLP is condemned by the PLP itself; or to put it another way, the PLP as intended is condemned by the PLP as fact.

What do I mean by this? Look at a crucial distinction that Mill makes in *On Liberty*: his distinction between "self-regarding" conduct and "other-regarding" conduct. By "self-regarding conduct," he means conduct that impacts the actor alone; it has no impact on others. By "other-regarding conduct," he means conduct that impacts on others. According to his principle of liberty, it is only other-regarding conduct that society has any business controlling, and this control may be exercised only when the other-regarding conduct hurts others. But this is a pointless distinction. For how can I engage in conduct that does not have some impact on others, whether for good or for bad?

For instance, how can I hurt myself without indirectly hurting others? If I take to drinking in excess, this will hurt me certainly, but will it not also hurt my spouse, my children, my boss, my co-workers, my neighbors, and others? The fact is that we humans are radically social beings; our lives are embedded in and interwoven with the lives of others. It is something like Isaac Newton's theory of universal gravitation, according to which every particle of matter in the universe, no matter how tiny or how remote, is affected by every other particle of matter. Likewise every member of society is affected, however indirectly, by every other member of society. As John Donne said, "No man is an island. Every man is a part of the continent, a piece of the whole."

These words of Donne may remind one of the radical alteration in the meaning of liberalism that took place within a generation. This view — that everybody is interconnected with everybody else, that no man is an island — was the standard liberal view of the mid to late 1930s. It is reflected in the title of Hemingway's novel of the Spanish Civil War of the '30s, *For Whom the Bell Tolls* — a novel whose hero, Robert Jordan (Gary Cooper in the movie), was a liberal, and the title of which was borrowed from John Donne, from the same passage from which the quote above was taken.

By the late 1960s and early '70s, liberalism had changed its stripes; or rather, a new mentality had usurped the name "liberalism." Instead of the old view, that whatever affects one person affects all others, the new liberalism held that there is a zone of absolute privacy that surrounds each individual, and that what happens inside this zone affects the individual only and is of no concern to the rest of the world.

Interestingly, many of these same moral liberals are also ardent environmentalists. They believe that in an ecosystem, everything is connected with everything else, and that if you damage one element in an ecosystem, you may well do grave damage to the entire system. And thus their great concern for preserving the natural habitats of this bird or that fish. This is a rational and admirable concern. But I am puzzled: How can people who have so firm a grasp on the biological interconnectedness of every member of an ecosystem fail to see that a similar moral interconnectedness exists in society?

Take sex as an example. One of the great principles of moral liberalism is that whatever happens in a bedroom between two consenting adults is nobody's business but their own. The idea seems to be that sex has no impact on anybody but the two involved parties; hence, there is nothing more private, nothing the public has less right to interfere with. If society can interfere, whether through law or through public opinion, with my sexual freedom, will any of my liberties be safe? If it can restrict sexual conduct, it can restrict anything. In other words, sexual intercourse has become the paradigm for individual liberty.[94]

But sexual intercourse between two consenting individuals, so far from being a matter in which society has no legitimate interest, is one of the most important of public interests. Sex has a tremendous impact on society, sometimes for good, sometimes for bad. It contributes to happy marriages; it produces healthy, happy, and well-brought-up children; but it also produces children born out of wedlock to poor and uneducated mothers, children at grave risk of growing up to be seriously troubled adults; it leads to the degradation of women through pornography and prostitution; and it results in sexually transmitted diseases, including AIDS. Few things, then, are more in the interests of society at large than promoting "good sex" (by which I mean sex having good consequences) and discouraging "bad sex." It is astonishing that any rational person could say that private sex is something the public has no right to concern itself with. Yet this astonishing thing is just what the PLP has led otherwise intelligent people to say.

Or take the issue of same-sex marriage, something that has been effectively legalized in Vermont (under the name "civil union")

[94] Beginning in the seventeenth century in the Anglo-American world, religious liberty was the paradigm. If my religious conscience could be controlled by society, which of my liberties would be safe? But moral liberals could not be content with this religious-liberty paradigm, for they were largely non-religious or antireligious. How could their argument for liberty depend on something that was of little or no importance to them? So the religious-liberty paradigm had to be replaced by the sexual-liberty paradigm.

and will more than likely be legalized in other states in the very near future. I have noticed that proponents of same-sex marriage often make their case by posing this PLP-style challenge to opponents: "How does it hurt *you* if two persons who love one another and happen to be of the same sex are allowed to marry?" Of course it will not hurt me in any direct and tangible way. My bank balance will remain the same as it was before they married, and so will my health, and so will my relationships with my family and friends. But it will alter the fabric of society by changing the definition of marriage, one of society's fundamental institutions. Perhaps the alteration will be for the better, or perhaps it will be for the worse; but it is nonsensical to imagine that it will make no difference at all.

And if this redefinition of marriage is for the worse (as I fear it will be), then it will certainly hurt me; for I am a member of American society (I am not an "island"), and whatever hurts American society hurts me. In a similar way, I was hurt when, in the late 1960s and early '70s, most states enacted laws permitting "no-fault divorce." It did not affect my life in a direct and tangible way — it did not lead me to get divorced; and so a champion of the PLP might say, "See, it did not hurt you that people are now able to get divorced more easily than in the old days."

But it did hurt me. It hurt me by making divorce more common, by helping to remove the stigma that used to be attached to divorce, by leaving millions of children in a state of poverty and fatherlessness, et cetera. You can say it did not hurt me only if you imagine that the well-being or ill-being of American society does not impinge on my interests. Champions of the PLP who think they have clinched an argument by asking the question, about gay marriage or no-fault divorce or anything else, "How does this hurt you?" have an exceedingly narrow notion of how people can get hurt. If you are not hurt in a direct and tangible way, if your leg is not broken and your pocket not picked, then, as they see it, you are not hurt. They might just as well have asked in Germany in the early 1920s, "How does it hurt you that a small group of people wearing swastika armbands gather from time to time in Munich to listen to a loud-mouthed little man rant about Jews and Communists?"[95]

Perhaps you see why I call the PLP a stupid principle. Those embracing it contradict themselves. On the one hand, they wish to maximize personal liberty — not just sexual liberty, but many other kinds as well. On the other, their PLP would, if taken seriously, justify society in greatly curtailing personal liberty; for to justify the curtailment of this or that personal freedom, all that would be needed would be to make a good *prima facie* case that the freedom in question leads, whether directly or indirectly, to more bad social consequences than good ones. Moral conservatives and anti-libertarians can use the "harm to others" proviso just as readily as can moral liberals and libertarians; and they can use it just as sincerely. It turns out that when moral liberals invoke the PLP and its "harm to others" proviso, they are quite uninterested in making a careful examination of the indirect and long-term harmful effects of this or that freedom.

And I suspect that if moral liberals were to examine the indirect and long-term consequences of certain kinds of freedom (especially sexual freedom), and conclude that the evidence indicated

[95] I do not mean to suggest that society should place a police officer in everyone's bedroom or that we should revive the sexual code of seventeenth-century Massachusetts. There are good reasons for society's toleration of a considerable amount of sexual freedom, including the freedom to behave foolishly and even wickedly. But I think we have gone overboard with our sexual tolerance, and it is time to retrench a bit; nonetheless, I also think that a wide zone of sexual tolerance is socially desirable. But this tolerance will have to find some other justification than the PLP and its pointless distinction between self-regarding and other-regarding conduct.

these freedoms to be socially dangerous, not many would withdraw their support for these freedoms. For the PLP is a rationalization as much as it is a reason. Liberals' real design is to demolish Christian morality and replace it with another and opposite kind of morality. As long as the PLP serves that purpose, they will use it. Once the PLP is refuted by a factual examination of consequences, they will drop it and find a new theory — perhaps one that says that individual autonomy is absolute, regardless of consequences. For the point of the exercise is not to find a sound moral theory; it is to get rid of Christian morality and introduce its opposite.

The PLP is easily abused

Moral rules are not merely speculative things; they are practical things; they are guides for conduct. Hence, if they fail to function as effective guides, they are not of much use. And this is the fourth problem with the PLP: it is not an effective guide for conduct. Or to be more precise, it is an effective guide if we are looking for a rule of permissiveness, one that says, "Go ahead, do anything you like." But if we are looking for a rule that restrains us, saying, "Thou shalt not do X, Y, or Z," it is useless. And what good is a morality that is all permissiveness and no restraint?

The more articulate champions of the PLP have a list of behaviors in mind that the PLP will justify, for these behaviors, in their view, do not hurt others. And they also have in mind a list of behaviors that the PLP will not justify, for these latter behaviors do hurt others. On the approved list are premarital sex, unmarried cohabitation, abortion, homosexuality, same-sex unions, the moderate use of recreational drugs, and physician-assisted suicide.[96] On the disapproved list are such things as murder, bank

---

[96] Abortion is difficult to justify by the PLP, since it appears to inflict grave harm — namely, death — on the fetus or unborn baby. Moral liberals have two strategies for dealing with this difficulty. The far more popular of the two is to deny that the

robbery, embezzlement, fraud, and beating up your girlfriend — not to mention any acts arising from motives of racism, sexism, or "homophobia."

But these two lists reflect, not so much the logical consequences of the PLP as the social values (or perhaps the prejudices) of the subculture to which these articulate champions belong or at least aspire. It is an upper-middle-class subculture. The people who belong to it are affluent and well educated; they hold good jobs; they live in fine houses in fine neighborhoods, and they drive fine automobiles; they have higher-than-average levels of social and political influence in their communities; they have discriminating tastes in coffee, wine, and interior decoration; and they are more or less secularist in their metaphysics and morals. They see nothing wrong with abortion or homosexuality, but they are horrified by wife-beating, stock fraud, and racism.

But the embezzler can use the PLP to justify his crimes just as surely as others can use it to justify abortion or homosexuality. The typical embezzler takes money that is not his own without thinking he is a criminal; he is simply "borrowing" the money because of a financial difficulty he has stumbled into; he fully intends to put it back when the stock market gets better or when he hits it big in Vegas.[97] Provided he puts the money back before anyone notices it is missing, how has he hurt anyone? And if he has hurt nobody, is his conduct not morally permissible according to the PLP?

---

fetus is a human being, a denial that is more usually accomplished by means of assertion and ridicule than by means of rational proof. The other, less popular strategy is to concede the obvious — namely, that the fetus is indeed a human life — and then argue that the rights of the pregnant woman trump the rights of the unborn baby.

[97] See the discussion of embezzlers and embezzling in Sutherland and Cressey, *Criminology*, ninth edition (Philadelphia: Lippincott, 1974), 253-255.

Or take the big-business executive who deceives the public about the value of his company, thereby inflating the value of his company's stock and thus greatly increasing his own personal wealth. Can he not justify this in terms of the PLP? "Yes, I am making myself wealthy," he can say, "but at the same time, I am keeping thousands of our workers employed and millions of our shareholders prosperous. And if certain of our business ventures turn out as expected — or at least as hoped for — no one will be the wiser, and no one will get hurt. We will all turn out to be winners."

Or take the rapist. "Oh, I know rape is wrong," he will say, "but this really wasn't rape. She was asking for it. Otherwise why was she in a place like this, dressed in the way she was, flirting with the guys? There is absolutely no doubt she encouraged me. Later she asked me to stop; but I don't think she meant it, and in the last analysis, I'm convinced she rather enjoyed the experience. I expect to see her again. Maybe we'll go to dinner and the movies. After all, I'm a gentleman."

Or take the person who submits a false or exaggerated insurance claim, or who cheats on his income taxes. "You can do whatever you want, as long as you don't hurt others; that's the rule. Well, how am I hurting other people by cheating on my taxes or my insurance claims? The insurance company is so rich and the government so vast that neither one will even notice the few dollars I have cheated them out of. No one is being hurt, or, at all events, the hurt is so trivial that the 'victim' won't even notice it; therefore, my cheating is morally permissible. Of course, I wouldn't cheat my next-door neighbor out of anything. That would hurt him; that would be wrong."

But how about the man who, from time to time, beats up his girlfriend? Surely this cannot be justified by the PLP — or can it? Well, let us hear what he has to say in his defense: "Yes, I inflict physical pain on her from time to time, but I do it for her own good, to teach her to be a better person. Like the way you spank a child."

But this will never do (we tell him), for an adult woman is not a child. "All right, then," he replies, "let's change the analogy. I damage her body by hitting her, but this is rather like the way the surgeon damages the body of his patient by cutting him. Yet the cutting is justified, because the patient is physically improved by the operation. Likewise my girlfriend is morally improved by the beating I give her."

We tell him again: This comparison will never do, for the patient consents to the surgery, whereas your girlfriend does not consent to the beating. "There you are mistaken," he replies. "She does consent; at least she does after the fact. We usually talk the incident over a day or two after it takes place, and she agrees with me that she deserved what she got and that the beating will help her, she hopes, to be a better girlfriend in the future."

The trouble with the PLP as a guide for conduct, as we can see from the above examples, is twofold. First, the principle is so general and abstract that specific rules of very opposite character can be derived from it (e.g., one man concludes from it that he must not cheat on his taxes, the next man that it is perfectly okay to cheat). To this criticism somebody may object: "What about the Golden Rule of Christianity, that we should do unto others as we would have them do unto us? Isn't that equally general or abstract?"

Yes, it is; but Christianity has never understood this rule to be the *sole* principle of morality, a stand-alone principle, leaving it up to the individual to deduce more specific rules from it. Instead, Christianity has, at the same time, provided many specific rules of morality (e.g., do not murder, do not steal, do not commit adultery) and has held that these specific rules, and not their opposites, derive from the general and abstract Golden Rule, thereby ruling out attempts to justify murder, theft, adultery, and so forth by means of the Golden Rule. And can there be any doubt that the Golden Rule, if left to stand on its own, would be used to justify sins otherwise condemned by Christianity? It would not take a great deal of ingenuity, and it would require only a small amount of self-deception, for an interested party to construct a "Golden Rule" justification for murder, theft, or adultery.

The Christian Golden Rule is a kind of inductive generalization based on a survey of the more specific rules of morality — a generalization that allows us to understand the spirit that informs these specific rules, and enables us, in keeping with that spirit, to derive still further specific rules. The PLP is altogether different. It is, of course, possible that it *began* as an inductive generalization from certain commonly accepted specific rules of conduct. But that is not the way it functions today in America. It is now a stand-alone principle. It is assumed that I, equipped with the PLP, can deduce from it more specific rules of conduct or figure out how I should act in this or that particular situation. As we have seen, however, this permits people to derive very opposite specific rules from the PLP. It permits me to do whatever I want, provided I am sufficiently clever (and I do not have to be terribly clever to do this) to construct an argument that appears to show that my conduct is compatible with the PLP.

Second and equally important, it allows a person to be a judge in his own case. For who else is to make the judgment? Not a pope or bishop. Not a moral philosopher from the local college. Not a clinical psychologist. Not Ann Landers. No, it is the person who, in a financial jam, has to decide for himself whether "borrowing" a few hundred dollars from his employer is right or wrong. And, of course, the world has always known that a person cannot be a fair judge in his own case.

As noted above, an ethical principle (which is what the PLP purports to be) is not a speculative thing; it is a practical thing. It is a guide to conduct. But it is clear that the PLP is no reliable guide to conduct. Rather, it permits me to rationalize any conduct I wish to engage in. If I am a decent person, I will engage in decent conduct and then explain that the PLP would not permit me to do otherwise. If, on the other hand, I am a cad or a scoundrel, I will engage in indecent conduct and then explain that the PLP permits me to do this — and, of course, I will deny, on the strength of this permission, that my conduct was indecent.

I have tried to justify my assertion that the PLP is a stupid — and, I may now add, dangerous — moral principle. But it is a principle that is immensely popular in American culture today. Yet it is in the midst of this culture that Catholics of the post-ghetto era have been living for the past thirty or forty years, and it is in its midst that they will have to continue living for the indefinite future. But how can they live in a PLP environment and not be affected by it? More important, how can kids come of age in a PLP environment and not be affected by it? But a Catholic with a PLP mentality is a contradiction in terms.

David Carlin

David Carlin is a lifelong resident of Rhode Island, where he served as a Democratic state senator from 1981 to 1992. He has been a professor of sociology and philosophy at the Community College of Rhode Island for twenty years, over which time he has written hundreds of essays on political, social, cultural, and religious issues for such publications as *New Oxford Review*, *First Things*, *America*, and the *New York Times*.

Carlin and his wife, Maureen, have three adult children and one grandchild, and currently live in Newport, Rhode Island.

An Invitation

Reader, the book that you hold in your hands was published by Sophia Institute Press.

Sophia Institute seeks to restore man's knowledge of eternal truth, including man's knowledge of his own nature, his relation to other persons, and his relation to God.

Our press fulfills this mission by offering translations, reprints, and new publications. We offer scholarly as well as popular publications; there are works of fiction along with books that draw from all the arts and sciences of our civilization. These books afford readers a rich source of the enduring wisdom of mankind.

Sophia Institute Press also serves as the publisher for the Thomas More College of Liberal Arts and Holy Spirit College. Both colleges are dedicated to providing university-level education in the Western tradition under the guiding light of Catholic teaching.

If you know a young person who might be interested in the ideas found in this book, share it. If you know a young person seeking a college that takes seriously the adventure of learning and the quest for truth, bring our institutions to his attention.

www.SophiaInstitute.com
www.ThomasMoreCollege.edu
www.HolySpiritCollege.org

SOPHIA INSTITUTE PRESS

THE PUBLISHING DIVISION OF